SQL
Crash Course

*Learn essential skills in querying,
security, and database management*

Thomas Liddle

bpb

www.bpbonline.com

First Edition 2025

Copyright © BPB Publications, India

ISBN: 978-93-65893-885

To View Complete
BPB Publications Catalogue
Scan the QR Code:

www.bpbonline.com

Dedicated to

My wife Monica and daughters Jennifer, Sophia, and Penelope
for supporting me in this adventure
I love you

About the Author

Thomas Liddle is an esteemed database expert with decades of experience in the field. Based in Smyrna, Delaware, Thomas has a rich background in managing and optimizing enterprise and open-source database management systems across various industries, including finance, technology, and banking.

Thomas began his career as a database administrator, honing his data modeling, warehousing, and performance tuning skills. His meticulous approach to database management, ensuring the security and integrity of critical data systems for numerous organizations, has instilled confidence in his clients and colleagues. Over the years, he has transitioned into roles that allowed him to lead and mentor teams, spearheading initiatives that streamlined operations and improved database performance.

As a team lead and senior database administrator, Thomas directed multiple large-scale database server consolidation projects. He was pivotal in database migration strategies. His ability to standardize database operations with best practices and automation tools has been widely recognized, earning him accolades and management recognition.

Thomas's commitment to continuous learning and innovation is unwavering. He holds multiple certifications, including AWS Certifications, Microsoft Certifications, and several CompTIA certifications. This dedication to staying at the forefront of the industry makes him a leading authority in database management and cloud technologies.

About the Reviewers

- Passionate about technology innovation, transformational leadership, and guiding the next generation of talent, **Pravin Pandey** is a globally recognized solution architect leader, mentor, and thought leader with extensive professional experience and advanced certifications. Currently working in the high-end luxury retail sector, Pravin specializes in managing architecture design globally, ensuring operational excellence and the seamless integration of cutting-edge technologies tailored to the unique demands of the industry.

  An active member of IEEE and ACM, Pravin is also a mentor who shares his expertise to inspire and develop future leaders in datacenter transformation, modernization, and data analytics. His mentorship reflects his commitment to fostering innovation and helping individuals excel in their professional journeys.

  Pravin's work in multi-cloud environments spans industries such as finance, retail, healthcare, technology, and manufacturing, where he has delivered tailored solutions resulting in significant cost savings, enhanced scalability, and optimized performance. He specializes in modernizing legacy systems, integrating AI-driven insights, and enabling data-driven decision-making, empowering organizations to achieve sustained growth and operational agility.

  Known for his ability to merge technical expertise with business strategy, Pravin is a trusted advisor in managing complex systems and delivering future-ready architecture designs. His role as a mentor, coupled with his global impact, solidifies his reputation as a leader who not only drives transformational IT solutions but also inspires others to innovate, grow, and succeed in their careers.

- **Ramesh Mohana Murugan** is a seasoned technology expert and senior IEEE member with more than 17 years of experience in the IT industry. He has collaborated with top-tier companies such as Meta Platforms, AWS, Amazon, and major financial institutions, spearheading innovation and excellence in data engineering/analytics and machine learning. Throughout his career, Ramesh has designed and implemented state-of-the-art data solutions that drive key products like Instagram Feed Recommendations, Meta Shops Ads, AWS Worldwide Revenue, and Alexa Shopping, processing billions of data points and reaching a global user base to accelerate business growth.

  Additionally, Ramesh is an active reader and reviewer of technical content in his field. He has contributed to the advancement of technology by reviewing journals and books.

Acknowledgement

I would like to express my sincere gratitude to all those who contributed to the completion of this book.

First and foremost, I extend my heartfelt appreciation to my family and friends for their unwavering support and encouragement throughout this journey (a.k.a my bucket list item). Their love and encouragement have been a constant source of motivation.

I am immensely grateful to BPB Publications for their guidance and expertise in bringing this book to fruition. Their support and assistance were invaluable in navigating the complexities of the publishing process.

I would also like to acknowledge the reviewers, technical experts, and editors who provided valuable feedback and contributed to the refinement of this manuscript. Their insights and suggestions have significantly enhanced the quality of the book.

Last but not least, I want to express gratitude to the readers who have shown interest in my book. Your support and encouragement are deeply appreciated.

Thank you to everyone who has played a part in making this book a reality.

Preface

SQL Crash Course is a complete learning guide for mastering **Structured Query Language** (**SQL**). Whether you are entering the data field for the first time or looking to level up your existing skills, this book will be your companion and reference as you grow in your understanding of relational databases and data manipulation.

I wrote this book after years of teaching, mentoring, managing database environments across the technology and finance industries, and managing and operating enterprise systems.

I have seen how a solid grasp of SQL opens doors—it empowers analysts to uncover insights, developers to build data-driven applications, and administrators to manage data with clarity and precision. In writing this book, I aim to bridge the gap between theory and practice, helping you build real-world skills that apply across industries and roles.

This book is divided into carefully structured sections that build your SQL knowledge progressively. Each chapter includes clear explanations, working examples, and practical applications designed to help you retain and apply what you learn. Here is a brief overview of what you can expect in each chapter:

Chapter 1: Introduction to SQL - Introduces the core of SQL—what it is, why it matters, and how it fits into the world of data. You will learn about SQL syntax, the structure of relational databases, and how to set up your SQL environment.

Chapter 2: Understanding Databases - Explores the structure of databases in more detail. You will explore tables, rows, columns, constraints, and normalization—everything you need to understand how data is organized.

Chapter 3: Basic SQL Queries - Walks you through writing basic SQL queries using clauses, operators, and functions. You will also get a strong foundation in filtering, sorting, and combining data.

Chapter 4: String Generation and Manipulation - Focuses on string generation and manipulation, teaching you how to work with text data effectively.

Chapter 5: Advanced Data Retrieval - Introduces advanced data retrieval techniques, including grouping, aggregation, and subqueries, giving you greater control over extracting insights.

Chapter 6: Modifying Data - Teaches how to insert, update, and delete data while managing NULL values responsibly.

Chapter 7: Working with SET Operators - Covers set operators like UNION, INTERSECT, and EXCEPT to combine result sets efficiently.

Chapter 8: Managing Database Objects - Explores creating and managing database objects, including tables, indexes, views, stored procedures, functions, triggers, and cursors.

Chapter 9: SQL Performance Optimization - Guides you through optimizing queries with indexing, execution plans, and performance tuning.

Chapter 10: Data Generation and Conversions - Deals with data generation and conversions across string, numeric, and temporal data.

Chapter 11: Advanced SQL Techniques - Explores advanced SQL features like window functions, common table expressions, recursive queries, and transaction management.

Chapter 12: Working with Different SQL Databases - Prepares you to work across different SQL platforms, highlighting the differences between MySQL, SQL Server, PostgreSQL, and SQLite. You will also learn how to connect and adapt your queries to various engines.

Chapter 13: Security Considerations in SQL - Focuses on database security and compliance. You will learn best practices for access control, encryption, auditing, backups, and ensuring data protection in regulated environments.

Chapter 14: Practical SQL Projects - Contains hands-on projects that simulate real-world scenarios. From building a CRM to analyzing rental data in the Sakila sample database, these step-by-step guides bring your learning to life.

Chapter 15: SQL Best Practices and Tips - Covers best practices for writing clean code, troubleshooting queries, tuning performance, and keeping up with industry trends.

Each chapter concludes with exercises to reinforce your understanding and points to remember as you work with SQL in the field. By the end of this book, you will be equipped to work confidently with SQL in a professional setting, whether you are analyzing data, developing applications, or managing enterprise databases.

SQL Crash Course will empower you with the knowledge and confidence you need to take your next steps in the world of data.

Code Bundle and Coloured Images

Please follow the link to download the
Code Bundle and the *Coloured Images* of the book:

https://rebrand.ly/275046

The code bundle for the book is also hosted on GitHub at
https://github.com/bpbpublications/SQL-Crash-Course.
In case there's an update to the code, it will be updated on the existing GitHub repository.

We have code bundles from our rich catalogue of books and videos available at **https://github.com/bpbpublications**. Check them out!

Errata

We take immense pride in our work at BPB Publications and follow best practices to ensure the accuracy of our content to provide with an indulging reading experience to our subscribers. Our readers are our mirrors, and we use their inputs to reflect and improve upon human errors, if any, that may have occurred during the publishing processes involved. To let us maintain the quality and help us reach out to any readers who might be having difficulties due to any unforeseen errors, please write to us at :

errata@bpbonline.com

Your support, suggestions and feedbacks are highly appreciated by the BPB Publications' Family.

Did you know that BPB offers eBook versions of every book published, with PDF and ePub files available? You can upgrade to the eBook version at www.bpbonline. com and as a print book customer, you are entitled to a discount on the eBook copy. Get in touch with us at :

business@bpbonline.com for more details.

At **www.bpbonline.com**, you can also read a collection of free technical articles, sign up for a range of free newsletters, and receive exclusive discounts and offers on BPB books and eBooks.

Piracy

If you come across any illegal copies of our works in any form on the internet, we would be grateful if you would provide us with the location address or website name. Please contact us at **business@bpbonline.com** with a link to the material.

If you are interested in becoming an author

If there is a topic that you have expertise in, and you are interested in either writing or contributing to a book, please visit **www.bpbonline.com**. We have worked with thousands of developers and tech professionals, just like you, to help them share their insights with the global tech community. You can make a general application, apply for a specific hot topic that we are recruiting an author for, or submit your own idea.

Reviews

Please leave a review. Once you have read and used this book, why not leave a review on the site that you purchased it from? Potential readers can then see and use your unbiased opinion to make purchase decisions. We at BPB can understand what you think about our products, and our authors can see your feedback on their book. Thank you!

For more information about BPB, please visit **www.bpbonline.com**.

Join our Discord space

Join our Discord workspace for latest updates, offers, tech happenings around the world, new releases, and sessions with the authors:

https://discord.bpbonline.com

Table of Contents

1. Introduction to SQL...1
    Introduction 1
    Structure 2
    Objectives 2
    Understanding SQL 2
    Importance of SQL in data management...3
    History and evolution of SQL 4
    Overview of relational databases..6
    Setting up your SQL environment..8
        Using Git to download the source code and database 8
        Downloading and installing SQLite 3..8
    Verifying your installation..9
    Tools and software for SQL development...9
        SQL with integrated development environments 9
        Database management tools 10
        Data visualization and business intelligence tools 11
        Version control and collaboration tools..11
    Your first SQL query...12
    SQL syntax and conventions 13
    Conclusion..15
    Exercises...16
        Query the staff table 16
            Querying a single row with two columns....................................16

2. Understanding Databases 17
    Introduction 17
    Structure 17
    Objectives 18
    Basic structure of a database..18
        Tables..18
        Columns 20

Index..20

Views...20

Types of databases 21

Exploring key concepts of a database 23

Entity relationship diagram 24

Tables...25

Rows 25

Columns 26

Indexes..27

Understanding the working of indexes 27

Types of indexes...28

When to use indexes 29

Understanding constraints...31

Normalization and denormalization...32

Normalization 32

First normal form 33

Second normal form...33

Third normal form 34

Denormalization..35

Conclusion..36

Exercises...37

Create a table 37

Create constraints 37

Perform normalization 37

3. Basic SQL Queries 39

Introduction 39

Structure 39

Objectives 40

Introduction to SQL syntax...40

Retrieving data in SQL 41

SQL clauses 41

Filtering data with WHERE 42

Sorting data with ORDER BY 42

Aggregating data with GROUP BY 43

Filtering grouped data with HAVING 43

Restricting results with LIMIT 44

Combining SQL clauses for complex queries 44

SQL operators 45

Comparison operators 45

Logical operators 46

Special operators 46

SQL joins 47

Understanding joins in SQL 48

Retrieving matching records with INNER JOIN 48

Retrieving records with LEFT JOIN 48

Retrieving records from right table with RIGHT JOIN 49

Retrieving records from both tables with FULL JOIN 49

Combining every row from both tables with CROSS JOIN 50

SQL functions 50

Aggregate functions 50

String functions 51

Date and time functions 52

Numeric functions 52

Using multiple functions in a query 53

Conclusion 53

Exercises 54

Retrieve data from tables 54

Using WHERE 54

Using ORDER BY and GROUP BY 55

Using LIMIT 55

Using table joins 56

4. String Generation and Manipulation 57

Introduction 57

Structure 57

Objectives 58

Introduction to string data types 58

CHAR data type *58*

VARCHAR data type *59*

Considerations with string data types *60*

Basic string functions *61*

CONCAT function *61*

SUBSTRING function *62*

LENGTH function *63*

TRIM function *63*

UPPER and LOWER functions *64*

REPLACE function *65*

INSTR function *66*

LPAD and RPAD functions *67*

CONCAT_WS function *68*

Extracting and modifying strings *68*

SUBSTRING function *68*

LEFT and RIGHT functions *69*

CHARINDEX function *69*

REPLACE function *70*

TRIM function *70*

Pattern matching with LIKE *70*

Formatting and splitting strings *73*

Conclusion *76*

Exercises *77*

Altering the customer table *77*

Populating the customer table *78*

Extracting information and displaying data from the customer table *78*

Displaying the first name and last name in uppercase *79*

5. Advanced Data Retrieval *81*

Introduction *81*

Structure *81*

Objectives *82*

Using aliases to rename columns and tables *82*

Using aliases for columns *82*

Using aliases for tables 83

Aliases in self-joins 83

Best practices for using aliases 84

Eliminating duplicate rows with DISTINCT... 85

Using DISTINCT with a single column... 85

Using DISTINCT with multiple columns 85

Performance considerations for DISTINCT 86

Combining DISTINCT with aggregate functions 86

DISTINCT with JOIN operations 87

Limitations of DISTINCT... 87

Practical use cases for DISTINCT 88

Grouping data with GROUP BY 88

Aggregate functions.. 90

COUNT aggregate function 91

SUM aggregate function.. 91

AVG aggregate function 91

MIN and MAX aggregate functions 92

COUNT DISTINCT aggregate function.. 92

Aggregate functions and GROUP BY 92

Subqueries and nested queries... 93

Handling NULL values in queries.. 96

Understanding the nature of NULL 96

Using IS NULL and IS NOT NULL... 96

Using NULL with comparison operators... 97

Using COALESCE to handle NULL values.. 97

NULL in aggregate functions 98

NULL in joins 98

Conclusion... 99

Exercises.. 100

Grouping data from tables... 100

Exploring the film table with aggregated functions............................. 101

Bringing data together with nesting and subqueries............................ 101

Average payment amount by customer.. 103

Determining which customers have no rentals..................................... 103

6. Modifying Data 105

   Introduction 105

   Structure 105

   Objectives 106

   Inserting data with INSERT INTO 106

      Transaction control with INSERT INTO.. 108

   Updating data with UPDATE 109

   Deleting data with DELETE... 112

   Handling NULL values in data modification 115

      Inserting NULL values 115

      Updating values to NULL 116

      Handling NULL values in conditional updates.. 116

      Deleting records with NULL values 117

      Best practices for managing NULL values 117

   Conclusion... 118

   Exercises... 118

      Inserting data 118

      Updating data... 119

      Deleting data 120

      NULL handling... 120

7. Working with SET Operators 121

   Introduction 121

   Structure 121

   Objectives 122

   Introduction to SET operators 122

      Using UNION and UNION ALL 124

   Using INTERSECT 127

   Using EXCEPT 130

   In-depth usage of SET operators... 133

      Combining multiple SET operators 134

      Using parentheses for complex operations.. 134

      Order and precedence of SET operators 135

      Practical applications of in-depth SET operations 136

SET operators with ORDER BY clause..*137*

Combining SET operators with subqueries...*139*

Conclusion...140

Exercises...140

Using UNION *140*

UNION ALL..*141*

INTERSECT *141*

EXCEPT...*142*

8. **Managing Database Objects** 143

Introduction 143

Structure 143

Objectives 144

Creating and modifying tables..144

Improving queries with indexes 148

Simplifying complex queries with views...151

Stored procedures and functions 155

Automating database tasks with triggers 159

Conclusion..163

Exercises...164

Managing tables...*164*

Managing indexes *164*

Using views...*165*

Using functions..*165*

Using triggers *166*

9. **SQL Performance Optimization**..167

Introduction 167

Structure 167

Objectives 168

Understanding execution plans 168

Accessing query execution plans..*168*

Key elements of an execution plan *168*

Analyzing common performance issues..*169*

Using indexes to improve execution plans...170

Interpreting key metrics in the plan..170

Optimizing query plans 170

Indexing strategies 171

Basic indexing concepts...171

Choosing the right columns to index 171

Composite indexes 171

Covering indexes...172

Index maintenance and monitoring 172

Balancing indexing trade-offs 173

Using indexes in joins 173

Dynamic indexing strategies 173

Optimizing joins 174

Understanding join types and their impact 174

Indexing join columns..174

Reducing the number of rows processed 175

Optimizing multi-table joins 175

Avoiding Cartesian products 175

Using EXPLAIN to analyze join performance 176

Using temporary tables for complex joins..176

Using modern join techniques 176

Optimizing subqueries 177

Understanding the role of subqueries 177

Replacing subqueries with joins...177

Using correlated subqueries efficiently 178

Using CTEs for complex subqueries 178

Avoiding SELECT * in subqueries 179

Minimizing nested subqueries 179

Indexing columns used in subqueries 180

Using EXPLAIN to analyze subquery performance....................................180

Avoiding common pitfalls 180

Overuse of SELECT *...181

Neglecting indexes 181

Improper use of joins 182

Ignoring query execution plans 182

Relying on nested subqueries 182

Overuse of temporary tables 183

Using wildcards in LIKE clauses 183

Failing to optimize aggregate functions 184

Conclusion 184

Exercises 185

Understanding query execution plans 185

Indexing strategies 186

Optimizing joins 186

Optimizing subqueries 187

Avoiding common performance pitfalls 188

10. **Data Generation and Conversions** 189

Introduction 189

Structure 189

Objectives 190

Generation and manipulation of string data 190

Generating strings dynamically 190

Extracting substrings 191

Transforming string case 191

Trimming and padding strings 191

Replacing and searching within strings 192

Using regular expressions for advanced manipulation 192

Combining string functions for advanced use cases 193

Arithmetic functions and handling numeric data 193

Performing basic arithmetic operations 193

Using aggregate functions for summary calculations 194

Handling precision and decimal points 195

Handling division and NULL values 195

Advanced numeric functions 196

Formatting numeric data 196

Combining numeric functions for advanced use cases 197

Best practices for numeric data handling 197

Generation and manipulation of temporal data 197

    Generating temporal data 197

    Extracting components from temporal data 198

    Manipulating temporal data 199

    Calculating date and time differences 199

    Formatting temporal data 200

    Working with time zones 200

    Using temporal data in conditional logic 201

    Combining temporal functions for advanced queries 201

Converting between data types and pitfalls 201

    Implicit and explicit data type conversions 202

    Common data type conversions 202

    Pitfalls of data type conversions 203

    Dealing with NULL values 203

    Best practices for data type conversions 203

    Combining data type conversions with other functions 204

Conclusion 204

    Exercises 205

    Generation and manipulation of string data 205

    Arithmetic functions and handling with numeric data 206

    Generation and manipulation of temporal data 206

    Converting between data types and pitfalls 207

11. Advanced SQL Techniques 209

Introduction 209

Structure 209

Objectives 210

Windows functions 210

    Understanding window functions 210

    Partitioning with window functions 210

    Using ranking functions 211

    Calculating running totals and averages 211

    Lag and lead functions 212

    Combining window functions 212

Best practices for using window functions 212

Common table expressions 213

Defining and using CTEs 213

Benefits of CTEs 213

Recursive CTEs 214

CTEs for complex calculations 214

Chaining multiple CTEs 215

Limitations and considerations 216

CTEs in reporting 216

Recursive queries 217

Understanding recursive queries 217

Practical use cases for recursive queries 218

Controlling recursion depth 218

Working with cyclic data 219

Performance considerations 220

Advanced applications 220

Transaction and concurrency control 221

Understanding transactions 221

ACID properties of transactions 221

Concurrency issues and their solutions 222

Locking mechanisms 223

Deadlocks and their resolution 223

Optimistic versus pessimistic concurrency control 223

Savepoints and partial rollbacks 224

Best practices for transaction and concurrency control 224

Conclusion 225

Points to remember 225

12. **Working with Different SQL Databases** 227

Introduction 227

Structure 227

Objectives 228

Overview of SQL database systems 228

Relational database management systems 228

MySQL.. 228

PostgreSQL... 229

Microsoft SQL Server 229

SQLite 229

Oracle database.. 230

Choosing the right SQL database system.. 230

Database-specific features and differences.. 230

Speed and simplicity in MySQL.. 230

Advanced features and standards compliance in PostgreSQL 231

Lightweight and self-contained in SQLite 231

Microsoft SQL Server enterprise integration 232

Scalability and reliability in Oracle database.. 232

Key differences between SQL databases 232

Choosing the right database 233

Choosing the right database for your project.. 233

Assessing project requirements... 233

Use case scenarios 234

Evaluating performance and scalability... 234

Considering database management and maintenance 235

Security and compliance 235

Evaluating ecosystem and integration... 235

Testing and prototyping.. 236

Future-proofing your database choice 236

Connecting to SQL databases 236

Understanding connection basics 236

Connecting to MySQL.. 237

Connecting to PostgreSQL 238

Connecting to Microsoft SQL Server 239

Best practices for secure connections 240

Troubleshooting connection issues.. 240

Conclusion.. 241

Points to remember 241

13. Security Considerations in SQL 243

    Introduction 243

    Structure 243

    Objectives 244

        Introduction to database security 244

        Importance of database security 244

        Core principles of database security 245

        Common threats to SQL databases 245

        Building a strong security foundation 245

        Regulatory compliance and security 246

        Integrating security into the development lifecycle 246

        Role of monitoring and auditing 246

        Developing a security mindset 247

    Access control and permissions 247

        Authentication and verifying user identity 247

        Authorization and defining user roles 247

        Implementing the principle of least privilege 248

        Auditing access and permissions 249

        Dynamic access control 249

        Challenges and best practices 249

        Integrating access control with application logic 250

    Data encryption 250

        Understanding encryption basics 250

        Encrypting data at rest 250

        Encrypting data in transit 251

        Key management 252

        Compliance and regulatory requirements 252

        Encryption overheads and performance 253

        Best practices for data encryption 253

    Preventing SQL injection attacks 253

        Understanding SQL injection 253

        Parameterized queries 254

        Stored procedures 254

        Input validation 255

Escaping special characters 255

Least privilege principle 255

Using web application firewalls 255

Logging and monitoring 256

Testing for vulnerabilities 256

Educating developers 256

Combining measures for maximum security 257

Auditing and monitoring 257

Understanding database auditing 257

Types of auditing 258

Monitoring database activities 258

Using built-in database features 258

Third-party and open-source tools 259

Storing and managing audit logs 259

Compliance and reporting 260

Proactive monitoring strategies 260

Backup and recovery 260

Understanding backup types 260

Creating a backup strategy 262

Automating backups 262

Testing backup integrity 263

Understanding recovery models 263

  Microsoft SQL Server 263

  MySQL 264

  PostgreSQL 264

  Oracle database 265

  SQLite 265

  Summary of recovery models by database engine 266

  Point-in-time recovery 267

Handling ransomware and disasters 267

Versioning and archiving 267

Best practices for backup and recovery 267

Compliance and data protection 268

Understanding compliance requirements 268

Implementing data protection policies 269

Encryption for data protection 269

Auditing and monitoring for compliance 269

Incident response and breach management... 270

Data anonymization and pseudonymization 270

Training and awareness 270

Regular assessments and audits.. 271

Maintaining an incident-free environment 271

Conclusion... 271

Points to remember 272

14. Practical SQL Projects 273

Introduction 273

Objectives 274

Project one, building a simple CRM database 274

Use case and scenario 274

Step 1: Set up SQLite 3 275

Step 2: Create the database structure.. 275

Step 3: Insert sample data 275

Step 4: Query customer data.. 276

Step 5: Update and manage data.. 276

Step 6: Analyze and summarize data 277

Step 7: Secure the database.. 277

Project two, analyzing sales data 278

Use case and scenario 278

Step 1: Set up SQLite 3 and create the database 278

Step 2: Design the database schema 279

Step 3: Insert sample data 279

Step 4: Query basic sales data 280

Step 5: Analyze sales trends... 280

Step 6: Identify seasonal patterns... 281

Step 7: Optimize and secure the database 281

Step 8: Visualize data.. 282

Project three, creating a blog platform 282

Use case and scenario 282

Step 1: Set up SQLite 3 and create the database 283

Step 2: Design the database schema 283

Step 3: Insert sample data 284

Step 4: Query blog data 285

Step 5: Update blog content 285

Step 6: Delete blog content 285

Step 7: Analyze blog performance 286

Step 8: Optimize and secure the database 286

Project four, data visualization with SQL 287

Use case and scenario 287

Step 1: Set up SQLite 3 and the environment 287

Step 2: Design the database schema 287

Step 3: Populate the database 288

Step 4: Query data for visualization 288

Step 5: Export data for visualization 289

Step 6: Visualize data using Python and Matplotlib 289

Step 7: Interpret and present results 291

Project five, automating data reports 291

Use case and scenario 292

Step 1: Set up SQLite 3 and Python 292

Step 2: Design the database schema 292

Step 3: Populate the database 293

Step 4: Write SQL queries for reports 293

Step 5: Automate report generation using Python 294

Project six, creating a customer feedback system 295

Use case and scenario 295

Step 1: Set up SQLite 3 and the Sakila sample database 295

Step 2: Design the customer feedback table 296

Step 3: Populate the customer feedback table 296

Step 4: Query customer feedback 296

Step 5: Analyze trends in feedback 297

Step 6: Secure the feedback data 298

Step 7: Generate reports from feedback data 298

Project seven, creating a customer rating system 299

    Use case and scenario 299

    Step 1: Set up SQLite 3 and the Sakila sample database 299

    Step 2: Design the customer rating table 300

    Step 3: Populate the customer rating table 300

    Step 4: Query and analyze ratings 300

    Step 5: Generate summary reports 301

    Step 6: Optimize and secure the ratings data 302

    Step 7: Present and interpret results 302

Project eight, creating rental data reports 303

    Use case and scenario 303

    Step 1: Set up SQLite 3 and the Sakila sample database 303

    Step 2: Analyze rental revenue 304

    Step 3: Generate customer activity reports 304

    Step 4: Analyze monthly rental trends 305

    Step 5: Generate inventory performance reports 305

    Step 6: Create advanced reports 306

    Step 7: Present and interpret results 307

Conclusion 308

15. SQL Best Practices and Tips 309

Introduction 309

Structure 309

Objectives 310

Writing clean and efficient SQL code 310

    Use descriptive naming conventions 310

    Write modular and reusable code 310

    Follow indentation and formatting standards 311

    Optimize joins and filtering 312

    Minimize use of SELECT 312

    Leverage indexes wisely 312

    Avoid hardcoding values 313

    Document your code 313

    Use aggregate functions judiciously 314

Test and refactor regularly 314

Debugging and troubleshooting SQL queries 314

Understanding common SQL query issues 314

Techniques for debugging SQL queries 315

Troubleshooting logical errors 316

    Optimizing query performance 317

    Best practices for debugging SQL queries 317

Performance tuning 318

Analyzing query execution plans 318

Indexing strategies 319

Optimizing join operations 319

Efficient use of aggregate functions 320

Minimizing data scanning 320

Caching results 321

Optimizing storage and resources 321

Monitoring and refining queries 322

Keeping up with SQL trends and updates 322

Conclusion 323

Points to remember 324

Index 325-335

CHAPTER 1
Introduction to SQL

Introduction

Welcome to the world of **Structured Query Language** (**SQL**), the backbone of modern data management. SQL is a powerful and universal language that enables users to store, retrieve, and manipulate data efficiently. Whether handling small-scale datasets or managing enterprise-level databases, SQL provides a structured approach to organizing and analyzing data. From powering websites and applications to driving data analytics and business intelligence, SQL plays a critical role in virtually every industry that relies on data.

This chapter will introduce the fundamentals of SQL and relational databases, exploring how they structure and store data. You will learn about SQL's significance in data management, its evolution over time, and the essential components that form the foundation of a database: tables, rows, and columns. Additionally, we will cover SQL syntax and conventions, ensuring you can write clear and compelling queries. You will also set up your SQL environment, including SQLite 3, so you can start working with databases immediately. By the end of this chapter, you will have a strong understanding of SQL's role in managing data and be ready to write your first query to retrieve information from a simple table.

Structure

This chapter covers the following topics:

- Understanding SQL
- Importance of SQL in data management
- History and evolution of SQL
- Overview of relational databases
- Setting up your SQL environment
- Tools and software for SQL development
- Your first SQL query
- SQL syntax and conventions

Objectives

By the end of this chapter, you will have thorough knowledge and skills to start working with SQL. You will also gain insights into the history and evolution of SQL, helping you understand its significance in modern data systems. Additionally, you will be introduced to the basic structure and concepts of relational databases, equipping you with the knowledge that you need to navigate them effectively.

Readers will also learn the fundamental syntax and conventions used in SQL queries, setting the stage for confidently writing and executing queries. This chapter will also guide you through setting up an SQL development environment on your system, familiarizing you with the tools and software needed to work with SQL. Finally, you will apply this knowledge by writing and executing your first SQL query to retrieve data from a simple table, marking the beginning of your hands-on experience with SQL.

Understanding SQL

SQL is a standardized programming language designed to manage and manipulate relational databases. It serves as the backbone of database systems, enabling users to interact with the data stored within them in a structured and efficient manner. Whether retrieving specific information, updating existing records, or even creating and deleting tables, SQL provides a comprehensive set of tools that make these tasks straightforward and accessible.

At its core, SQL is built on the principles of set theory and relational algebra, which are foundational mathematical concepts dealing with data sets and their relationships. This mathematical underpinning allows SQL to handle complex queries involving multiple tables and conditions efficiently. For example, SQL can retrieve data from several tables simultaneously, apply conditions to filter the results, sort the data according to specified criteria, and even perform calculations or aggregate functions on the data, all in a single query.

SQL is universally recognized and adopted across various database systems, including popular platforms like MySQL, PostgreSQL, Oracle, Microsoft SQL Server, and SQLite. Although each system might have slight variations or extensions to the SQL standard, the core functionality remains consistent. This makes SQL a highly portable and transferable skill, highlighting the adaptability and versatility of a developer or database administrator proficient in SQL. These roles can work across different database platforms with minimal adaptation, making it one of the most versatile and valuable skills in data management.

One of the critical strengths of SQL lies in its declarative nature. Unlike imperative programming languages, where the focus is on how to perform a task (step-by-step procedures), SQL allows users to focus on what they want to achieve. For example, when writing an SQL query, the user specifies the data they want to retrieve or manipulate, and the **database management system** (**DBMS**) determines the most efficient way to execute the query. This abstraction simplifies working with data, allowing users to focus on the business logic rather than the underlying data retrieval or manipulation mechanics.

SQL is not just about data retrieval (although this is one of its most common uses). It encompasses a wide range of functionalities that include defining database structures, controlling access to the data, and ensuring the integrity of the information stored. These functionalities include:

- **Data Definition Language (DDL):** Commands like `CREATE`, `ALTER`, and `DROP`, SQL provides the means to define and modify the structure of databases.

- **Data Control Language (DCL):** Commands like `GRANT` and `REVOKE` in SQL allow for managing permissions and access controls.

- **Data Manipulation Language (DML):** Commands like `INSERT`, `UPDATE`, `DELETE`, and `SELECT`.

Importance of SQL in data management

SQL is central to the modern data ecosystem, serving as the standard language for managing, retrieving, and manipulating data across various industries and applications. Its versatility and efficiency make it an essential tool for anyone working with data, from beginners to seasoned professionals. Here is why SQL is so important in data management:

- **Universal standard for databases**: SQL is the most widely used language for interacting with relational databases like MySQL, PostgreSQL, and SQLite. Its widespread adoption makes SQL skills highly transferable across different systems and industries.

- **Efficient data retrieval and manipulation**: SQL lets users quickly retrieve specific data from large datasets using simple commands like `SELECT`, `INSERT`, `UPDATE`, and `DELETE`. This makes managing and modifying data intuitive and fast, even in complex databases.

- **Supports decision-making**: SQL helps businesses uncover patterns, trends, and insights that drive data-informed decisions by enabling fast and accurate data analysis through queries and aggregations.

- **Data integrity and consistency**: SQL maintains data reliability using constraints like primary keys, foreign keys, and unique constraints, ensuring that the database structure remains consistent and accurate.

- **High-level security controls**: SQL allows administrators to control user access and define permissions at various levels, protecting sensitive information. While advanced commands like **GRANT** and **REVOKE** manage access, the emphasis remains on securing data and maintaining privacy.

SQL's powerful capabilities make it a cornerstone of modern data management. It empowers users to harness the full potential of their data while ensuring accuracy, security, and efficiency.

History and evolution of SQL

The history of SQL is deeply intertwined with the development of relational DBMSs and the evolution of data management practices. SQL originated in the early 1970s when data processing transitioned from hierarchical and network databases to more flexible and efficient relational models.

The conceptual foundation for SQL was laid by *Edgar F. Codd*, a British computer scientist working for IBM, who introduced the relational model for databases in a landmark paper published in 1970 titled *A Relational Model of Data for Large Shared Data Banks*. *Codd's* model proposed that data should be stored in tables, where each table is a set of rows (tuples) and columns (attributes), and that data relationships should be represented using keys. This was a radical departure from the existing database systems based on hierarchical or network models, where data was stored in complex tree-like or graph structures that were difficult to navigate and query.

Codd's relational model introduced the idea that a database should not only store data but also be able to retrieve and manipulate it using a declarative query language. This language would allow users to specify what data they wanted to retrieve rather than detailing how to retrieve it, thus separating the logical representation of data from its physical storage. IBM recognized the potential of *Codd's* ideas and began to develop a system based on the relational model.

In the early 1970s, *Donald D. Chamberlin* and *Raymond F. Boyce*, also at IBM, took *Codd's* theoretical work and began developing a practical query language for relational databases. Initially, they developed a language called **Structured English Query Language (SEQUEL),** which was intended to allow users to interact with the relational database system in a more user-friendly manner. SEQUEL was designed to be easy to use, even for people without a deep understanding of database theory, and it emphasized English-like syntax to make querying more intuitive.

SEQUEL was first implemented in a prototype relational database system called System R, developed by IBM's *San Jose* research laboratory in the mid-1970s. System R was a groundbreaking project that demonstrated the practical viability of the relational model and provided a working implementation of SEQUEL. However, due to trademark issues with SEQUEL, IBM shortened the name to SQL, which became the standard abbreviation.

System R and SQL garnered attention from the academic community and the emerging database industry. The success of System R inspired other companies to develop their relational database systems, incorporating SQL as the query language. This period saw the emergence of several influential DBMSs, including Oracle database, one of the first commercial implementations of SQL. It was released in 1979 by a company then known as *Relational Software, Inc.* (later *Oracle Corporation*).

In 1986, the **American National Standards Institute** (**ANSI**) recognized the growing importance of SQL by adopting it as a standard for relational DBMSs. The **International Organization for Standardization** (**ISO**) followed suit in 1987, establishing SQL as an international standard. These standards helped solidify SQL's position as the dominant query language for relational databases, ensuring consistency and compatibility across different database systems. The standardization of SQL also contributed to its widespread adoption in various industries, as businesses could now rely on a consistent and reliable language for their data management needs.

As the database industry evolved, so too did SQL. Over the years, SQL has undergone numerous revisions and extensions to accommodate new features and capabilities. For example, the SQL-92 standard introduced significant enhancements, including support for new data types, enhanced query capabilities, and improved transaction control. Subsequent standards, such as SQL:1999, SQL:2003, SQL:2008, and SQL:2011, continued to expand the language's functionality, adding support for object-relational features, recursive queries, XML integration, and temporal data, among other advancements.

In parallel with these developments, the rise of data warehousing and business intelligence in the 1990s and 2000s further emphasized the importance of SQL. SQL's ability to handle complex queries, aggregate large datasets, and generate insightful reports made it the go-to language for data analysts and decision-makers. The introduction of **online analytical processing** (**OLAP**) tools, which leveraged SQL for multidimensional data analysis, further cemented its role in the burgeoning field of data analytics.

Despite the rise of NoSQL databases and other non-relational data models in the 21st century, SQL has maintained its relevance and continues to evolve. Many modern database systems, including those designed for big data and distributed computing, support SQL or SQL-like query languages, recognizing their value in querying and managing large, complex datasets. SQL's enduring success can be attributed to its adaptability, robustness, and the fact that it has become a universal language for data interaction, understood and used by millions of developers, analysts, and database administrators worldwide.

The evolution of SQL is a testament to its foundational principles and the vision of its creators, who sought to simplify and standardize the way we interact with data. As data grows in importance across all sectors of society, SQL remains at the forefront, providing the tools needed to unlock the full potential of the information age.

Overview of relational databases

In this section, we are going to briefly review the constructs of what makes a relational database. As we move into later chapters, we will expand on these topics more. For example, in *Chapter 2, Understanding Databases*, we will explore the topics a bit more.

Let us take a look at the major components briefly:

- **Tables:** A relational database's core is the table, which can be considered a two-dimensional grid. Each table is designed to store information about a specific entity, such as customers, orders, and shipments. The rows in a table represent individual records, while the columns represent the attributes or properties of those records. For example, a **customers** table might have columns for **customer_id**, **customer_name**, and so on, with each row representing a different customer.

- **Primary keys:** One of the defining characteristics of relational databases is the use of **primary keys** (**PK**) to ensure data integrity and uniqueness. A PK is a unique identifier for each record in a table, guaranteeing that no two rows are identical. For instance, in the **customers** table, the **customer_id** might serve as the primary key, ensuring each customer has a unique identifier that distinguishes them from other customers, as represented in *Figure 1.1*. This uniqueness is crucial for maintaining the accuracy and reliability of the data stored in the database.

- **Foreign keys:** In addition to primary keys, relational databases use **foreign keys** (**FK**) to establish relationships between tables. An FK is a column or set of columns in one table that refers to the primary key in another table. This relationship allows for linking related data across multiple tables, enabling the construction of complex queries that draw information from different parts of the database. For example, an **orders** table might include a foreign key column referencing the **customer_id** in the **customers** table, allowing the database to associate each order with the corresponding customer, as represented in *Figure 1.1*:

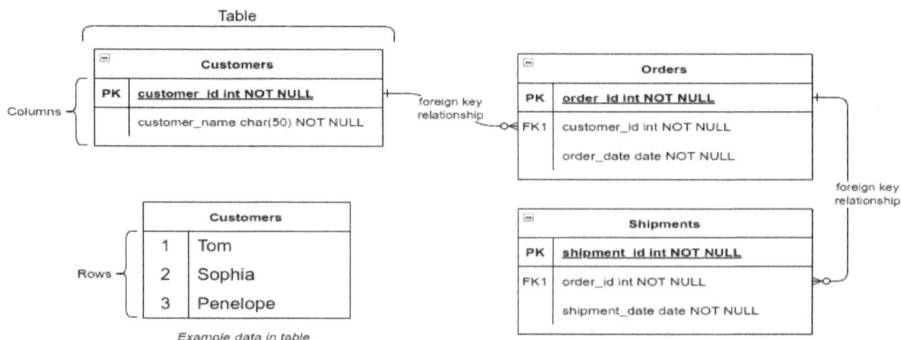

Figure 1.1: Sample relational database model

The relational model's ability to create and manage relationships between tables is one of its most powerful features, facilitating the organization and retrieval of related data without redundancy. This is achieved through the normalization process, which involves designing database tables to minimize data duplication while maintaining data integrity. Normalization typically involves breaking down large, complex tables into smaller, more manageable ones and establishing relationships using primary and foreign keys. This approach conserves storage space and reduces the risk of data inconsistencies, such as having multiple versions of the same information in different places.

Relational databases are also known for their robustness and reliability, particularly in handling transactions. A transaction is a sequence of one or more SQL operations executed as a single unit of work. Relational databases adhere to **atomicity, consistency, isolation, and durability** (ACID) properties to ensure that transactions are processed reliably. Atomicity guarantees that all operations within a transaction are completed successfully; if any operation fails, the entire transaction is rolled back, leaving the database in its original state. Consistency ensures that a transaction transforms the database from one valid state to another, maintaining the integrity of the data. Isolation ensures that transactions are executed independently, preventing dirty reads or lost updates. Durability guarantees that once a transaction is committed, its effects are permanently recorded in the database, even in a system failure.

Relational databases have become widely adopted because of their scalability and flexibility. They can handle small amounts of data, such as a small business's local inventory system, and massive datasets, such as those managed by global corporations with millions of customers. Relational databases can be deployed on a single server or distributed across multiple servers in a network, allowing them to scale horizontally and vertically to meet the needs of growing organizations.

The relational database model's ability to enforce data integrity, manage complex relationships, and ensure reliable transaction processing has made it the standard for DBMS for several decades. Leading RDMSs, such as Oracle, Microsoft SQL Server, MySQL, and PostgreSQL, have become essential tools for businesses and institutions worldwide. These systems offer a range of features, from advanced security mechanisms to support for large-scale distributed computing, making them suitable for virtually any application.

The evolution of relational databases continues as they adapt to meet the demands of cloud computing, big data analytics, and real-time processing. Cloud-based relational databases offer scalability and flexibility, enabling organizations to manage their data more efficiently and cost-effectively. Additionally, advancements in database technology, such as in-memory processing and parallel query execution, enhance the performance of relational databases, allowing them to handle increasingly complex workloads easily.

Relational databases have become the cornerstone of data management, providing a structured and reliable way to store, organize, and retrieve data. Their ability to maintain data integrity, support complex relationships, and ensure robust transaction processing has made them indispensable in various applications, from business operations and financial systems to web applications and data analytics. As technology continues to evolve, relational databases will likely remain a vital component of the data management landscape, adapting to new challenges and opportunities in the years to come.

Setting up your SQL environment

In this section, we will set up a development environment so that we can run database queries used throughout this book. We will work with the *Sakila* sample database, designed for MySQL but converted to SQLite 3, to provide easy transport for this book.

The Sakila sample database is a well-known test database designed for MySQL. It is a fictional database created by MySQL to showcase its features and provide a sample schema and data set for learning and testing purposes.

The Sakila database models a DVD rental store and contains information about customers, payments, inventory, films, actors, etc. It includes various tables with relationships that allow you to explore SQL queries, database design, and other tasks.

We will use this database throughout the book as a test database to learn the key concepts of SQL and relational databases.

Using Git to download the source code and database

To download and install Git for Linux and Windows, follow these steps:

1. **For Linux**, Git is installed on most distributions. Run the following code to ensure Git is installed:

   ```
   sudo apt install git -y
   ```

   For Windows, Git will have to be installed manually. Download **Git for Windows** from **https://git-scm.com/downloads/win** and install Git directly from the installer.

2. Open a command prompt, type in the following command, and hit *Enter*:

   ```
   mkdir ~/workspace
   cd ~/workspace
   ```

3. Using the **git** command, we will clone this book's repository to access the Sample Database. Type the following command and hit *Enter*:

   ```
   git clone https://github.com/bpbpublications/SQL-Crash-Course.
   cd workspace/sql-crash-course-book
   ```

Downloading and installing SQLite 3

To download and install SQLite 3, follow these steps:

1. **For Windows**, download the tools ZIP file under the **Precompiled Binaries for Windows** (Command-line tools for Windows x64) section from **https://www.**

sqlite.org/download.html and place the contents of the zip file in a folder called `C:\Windows`.

2. **For Linux (Ubuntu)**, type in the following command to install:

```
sudo apt update -y && sudo apt install sqlite3 -y
```

Verifying your installation

To verify the installation of SQLite 3 and that the repository was downloaded successfully, follow these steps:

1. In the command prompt, type in the following command and hit Enter to enter the SQLite 3 shell command:

```
sqlite3 sqlite-sakila.db
```

Tools and software for SQL development

SQL development is critical to working with databases, and having the right tools and software can significantly enhance productivity and efficiency. Whether you are a beginner just getting started or an experienced developer, the tools you choose can affect how effectively you can write, manage, and optimize SQL queries. This section will cover some of the most widely used tools and software in SQL development, providing an overview of their features and how they can be leveraged to streamline database tasks.

SQL with integrated development environments

One of the most essential tools for SQL development is the **integrated development environment (IDE)**. An IDE provides a comprehensive environment for writing, testing, and debugging SQL queries. These platforms often include features, like syntax highlighting, code completion, and query execution, which simplify the development process and reduce the likelihood of errors.

SQL Server Management Studio (SSMS) is a free, popular IDE developed by Microsoft for managing SQL Server databases.

It provides a user-friendly interface for writing SQL queries, managing database objects, and executing stored procedures. SSMS also includes performance tuning and security management tools, making it a robust choice for SQL Server environments.

SSMS features an Object Explorer, which allows users to browse database objects like tables, views, and stored procedures. Additionally, the Query Editor supports T-SQL with features like code snippets, error detection, and query execution plans, helping developers optimize their code.

MySQL Workbench is a free, open-source IDE designed specifically for MySQL databases. It provides a visual database design tool, a Query Editor, and a comprehensive administration interface. MySQL Workbench supports multiple database connections, making it ideal for managing different MySQL servers simultaneously.

The tool includes features like visual query building, reverse engineering, and forward engineering, allowing users to design and model databases visually. The Query Editor in MySQL Workbench provides syntax highlighting and execution capabilities, making writing and testing SQL queries easier.

Oracle SQL Developer is a free IDE from Oracle that supports Oracle database environments. It offers a wide range of tools for database development, including SQL worksheets for writing and executing queries, data modeling, and database administration features.

Oracle SQL Developer supports PL/SQL development, allowing users to write and debug complex PL/SQL code. The tool integrates seamlessly with Oracle database, offering advanced features like data import or export, reporting, and schema comparison.

Database management tools

In addition to IDEs, database management tools are essential for administering, monitoring, and maintaining databases. These tools provide functionality beyond query writing, such as data migration, backup and recovery, and performance monitoring.

phpMyAdmin is a web-based tool for managing MySQL and MariaDB databases. It provides a graphical interface that simplifies database management tasks, such as creating tables, inserting data, and running SQL queries. phpMyAdmin is particularly popular in web development environments because it can be accessed through a browser, making it convenient for managing databases on remote servers. The tool also includes features for exporting and importing data, managing user privileges, and monitoring server status.

pgAdmin is a powerful, open-source management tool for PostgreSQL databases. It offers a graphical interface for database administration, allowing users to create, modify, and delete database objects, run SQL queries, and manage database users and roles. pgAdmin includes a Query Tool for writing and executing SQL queries with features like syntax highlighting, autocompletion, and result set management. Additionally, pgAdmin provides database backup, restoration, and maintenance tools, making it an essential tool for PostgreSQL administrators.

Navicat is a commercial database management tool that supports multiple database systems, including MySQL, PostgreSQL, Oracle, and SQL Server. It offers rich features, including data modeling, data synchronization, and query building.

Navicat's user-friendly interface allows users to perform complex database tasks efficiently. The tool also includes advanced features like SSH tunnelling for secure connections, data transfer between databases, and scheduled backups, making it a versatile choice for database management across different platforms.

Data visualization and business intelligence tools

SQL development involves writing queries, managing databases, and extracting insights from data. Data visualization and **business intelligence** (**BI**) tools are crucial in transforming raw data into meaningful visual representations that aid decision-making. Here are some BI tools:

- **Tableau** is a leading BI tool that allows users to connect to various data sources, including SQL databases, and create interactive visualizations. Tableau's drag-and-drop interface makes it easy to build dashboards and reports without extensive SQL knowledge. This tool integrates seamlessly with SQL databases, enabling users to write custom SQL queries to extract specific data for visualization. The tool also supports live data connections, ensuring that visualizations are always up to date with the latest data.

- **Power BI** is a business analytics service by Microsoft that provides interactive visualizations and business intelligence capabilities. It can connect to SQL databases and other data sources to create reports and dashboards that can be shared across an organization. This tool supports DirectQuery, which allows users to run SQL queries directly against the database, providing real-time data analysis. The tool's integration with SQL Server and Azure SQL Database makes it a powerful choice for organizations using Microsoft's data platform.

- **DBeaver** is an open-source database management and SQL client tool that supports many databases, including MySQL, PostgreSQL, SQLite, Oracle, and SQL Server. It offers a comprehensive SQL editor with syntax highlighting, autocompletion, and the ability to execute queries across multiple databases. DBeaver also includes data visualization features that allow users to generate charts and graphs directly from query results. This makes it a versatile tool for both SQL development and data analysis.

Version control and collaboration tools

In collaborative development environments, version control and collaboration tools are essential for managing changes to SQL scripts and database schemas. These tools help teams work together more efficiently and ensure that changes are tracked and documented. Let us explore them in detail:

- **Git** is a widely used version control system that allows developers to track changes to SQL scripts and database schemas over time. Teams can collaborate on SQL development, merge changes, and resolve conflicts by using Git. It integrates with various IDEs and CI/CD pipelines, making it easy to incorporate version control into the SQL development process. Git repositories can be hosted on platforms like GitHub, GitLab, or Bitbucket, enabling distributed teams to work together seamlessly.

- **Liquibase** is an open-source tool for database schema change management. It tracks, manages, and applies database changes, making maintaining consistency across different environments easier. Liquibase integrates with version control systems like Git and supports multiple databases, including MySQL, PostgreSQL, Oracle, and SQL Server. It also provides rollback capabilities, allowing developers to revert database changes if necessary.

- **Flyway** is another open-source database migration tool that allows developers to manage and apply changes to database schemas. Flyway supports multiple databases and integrates with CI/CD pipelines to automate the deployment of database changes. This tool's straightforward approach to database migrations makes it a popular choice for developers who maintain version-controlled database schemas across different environments.

These tools and software are integral to SQL development, providing the necessary capabilities to write, manage, and optimize SQL code and collaborate effectively in team environments. Choosing the right combination of tools based on your specific needs and database environment can enhance your productivity and the quality of your SQL development work.

Your first SQL query

Earlier in this chapter, we set up your environment, and you ran a query to verify that the database opened. This was a great verification; however, let us run a few more queries to get you comfortable in the environment:

- **Opening the command prompt for SQLite 3**
    - Open a command prompt and type in the following command:
      ```
      cd ~/workspace/sql-crash-course-book
      sqlite3 sqlite-sakila.db
      ```
- **Retrieve all the films in the database**
    - At the sqlite3 prompt, type in the following command and hit *Enter*:
      ```
      .mode box
      SELECT * FROM film;
      ```
    - This will give you a list of all the films in the database. The **SELECT** tells what action you are taking on the database. The asterisk (*****) indicates you want all records, and the **FROM films** outlines what table to select the data from.
- **Retrieve all the customers in the database**
    - At the sqlite3 prompt, type in the following command and hit *Enter*:
      ```
      SELECT * FROM customer;
      ```
    - This will give you a full list of all customers in the database.

SQL syntax and conventions

At the core of SQL syntax is the structure of a typical SQL statement, which is composed of various clauses, each performing a specific function. The most common SQL statement is the **SELECT** statement, used to retrieve data from a database. The basic structure of a **SELECT** statement includes the **SELECT** clause, followed by the **FROM** clause, and often accompanied by optional clauses like **WHERE, GROUP BY**, **HAVING**, and **ORDER BY**.

A simple **SELECT** statement might look like this:

```
SELECT first_name, last_name
FROM actor;
```

In this example, **first_name** and **last_name** represent the columns from which data will be retrieved, and the **actor** is the name of the table containing the data. This basic structure can be expanded with additional clauses to filter, group, and sort the data as needed.

SQL is case-insensitive, meaning keywords such as **SELECT**, **FROM**, and **WHERE** can be written in either uppercase or lowercase. However, by convention, SQL keywords are typically written in uppercase to distinguish them from the names of tables and columns, which are usually written in lowercase or camelCase. For example:

```
SELECT first_name, last_name
FROM customer
WHERE active = 0;
```

Here, **SELECT**, **FROM**, and **WHERE** are in uppercase, while **first_name**, **last_name**, **customer**, and **active** are in lowercase. Adhering to this convention improves the readability of SQL code, making it easier for others to understand and maintain.

SQL also supports using comments, which are essential for documenting code and explaining complex queries. SQL comments can be written in two ways: single-line and multi-line. Single-line comments start with two hyphens (**--**) and extend to the end of the line, while multi-line comments are enclosed between **/*** and ***/**. For example:

```
-- This is a single-line comment
SELECT first_name, last_name /* This is a multi-line comment */
FROM customer
WHERE active = 0;
```

Comments are ignored by the SQL interpreter and do not affect the query's execution. Including comments in SQL code is considered good practice, as they provide context and clarification, especially in complex queries involving multiple tables and conditions.

SQL uses a specific set of data types to define the data that can be stored in each table column. Common SQL data types include **INT** for integers, **VARCHAR** for variable-length strings, **DATE** for dates, and **DECIMAL** for precise numeric values with fixed decimal points. Understanding these data types is crucial for defining table structures and ensuring data integrity. For example, when creating a table, you might specify data types as follows:

```
CREATE TABLE employees (
    employee_id INT PRIMARY KEY,
    first_name VARCHAR(50),
    last_name VARCHAR(50),
    hire_date DATE,
    department VARCHAR(50),
    salary DECIMAL(10, 2)
);
INSERT INTO employees (employee_id, first_name, last_name, hire_date,
department, salary)
VALUES (1, 'John', 'Doe', '2022-01-15', 'Engineering', 75000.00);
INSERT INTO employees (employee_id, first_name, last_name, hire_date,
department, salary)
VALUES (2, 'Jane', 'Smith', '2021-11-22', 'Marketing', 65000.00);
INSERT INTO employees (employee_id, first_name, last_name, hire_date,
department, salary)
VALUES (3, 'Michael', 'Johnson', '2023-03-05', 'Sales', 55000.00);
INSERT INTO employees (employee_id, first_name, last_name, hire_date,
department, salary)
VALUES (4, 'Emily', 'Davis', '2020-07-18', 'IT', 60000.00);
INSERT INTO employees (employee_id, first_name, last_name, hire_date,
department, salary)
VALUES (5, 'David', 'Miller', '2019-02-25', 'IT', 70000.00);
INSERT INTO employees (employee_id, first_name, last_name, hire_date,
department, salary)
VALUES (6, 'Sarah', 'Wilson', '2023-06-10', 'Customer Support', 48000.00);
INSERT INTO employees (employee_id, first_name, last_name, hire_date,
department, salary)
VALUES (7, 'Christopher', 'Brown', '2021-09-30', 'Product Development',
80000.00);
INSERT INTO employees (employee_id, first_name, last_name, hire_date,
department, salary)
VALUES (8, 'Jessica', 'Garcia', '2022-04-19', 'Engineering', 77000.00);
INSERT INTO employees (employee_id, first_name, last_name, hire_date,
department, salary)
VALUES (9, 'Matthew', 'Martinez', '2020-12-12', 'Legal', 90000.00);
INSERT INTO employees (employee_id, first_name, last_name, hire_date,
department, salary)
```

```
VALUES (10, 'Amanda', 'Rodriguez', '2023-07-07', 'Engineering', 65000.00);
```

In this example, **employee_id** is defined as an integer (**INT**), **first_name** and **last_name** as variable-length string of a range of 50 characters (**VARCHAR (50)**), **hire_date** as a date, and **salary** as a decimal value with up to 10 digits, including two decimal places.

SQL also employs operators and expressions to perform calculations, comparisons, and logical operations within queries. Common SQL operators include arithmetic operators like **+**, **-**, *****, and **/**, comparison operators like **=**, **<**, **>**, **<=**, **>=**, and **<>** (not equal), and logical operators like **AND**, **OR**, and **NOT**. These operators allow for the creation of complex conditions within queries. For example:

```
SELECT first_name, last_name, salary

FROM employees

WHERE salary > 50000 AND department = 'IT';
```

In *Chapter 3, Basic SQL Queries*, we will explore the **SELECT** clause, operators, and data types in depth.

Conclusion

In this chapter, we introduced the foundational concepts of SQL and relational databases, offering a comprehensive overview that sets the stage for a deeper understanding of data management. We explored what SQL is and why it plays a crucial role in working with databases. SQL's ability to efficiently retrieve, manipulate, and store data makes it indispensable for anyone involved in data-driven tasks.

As you read the chapter, the importance of SQL in data management becomes even more apparent. The discussion of how SQL helps maintain data integrity, enforce security measures, and facilitate complex data analysis truly highlights the language's versatility. Understanding SQL's impact on managing large volumes of data and ensuring consistent relationships between data entities is crucial, especially when dealing with real-world applications that require precision and reliability.

The historical context provided is not just a footnote but a crucial part of understanding SQL. Learning about its evolution from the 1970s to becoming the standard for relational DBMSs today gives you a deeper appreciation of its relevance and adaptability. It is fascinating to see how SQL has withstood the test of time, evolving alongside the changing demands of data management.

We conclude with an essential overview of relational databases, which is crucial for understanding how data is structured and accessed. By breaking down the concepts of tables, rows, and columns and explaining how these elements interact, the chapter lays a solid foundation for working with databases.

In the next chapter we will learn about the basic structure of a database, including key concepts, constraints, types of databases, normalization, and denormalization.

Exercises

In this exercise, we will query more tables in the Sakila database, like **customer** and **payment**.

Query the staff table

Here, we will query another table in the Sakila database called **staff**. This table is a complete list of staff members. We will query all the rows in the database, a single row with all columns, and finally, a single row with only two columns:

- **Querying all rows:** Here, we will query all the rows on the **staff** table:

```
sqlite> .mode box
sqlite> SELECT * FROM staff;
```

  There are two commands here. The first statement, **.mode box**, sets how SQLite 3 will display the data. In this case, it will put all the data in a box format. This is only for formatting reasons and must only be run once. The second statement will select all rows from the **staff** table.

- **Querying a single row**: Here, we will query a single row in the staff table:

```
sqlite> SELECT * FROM staff WHERE last_name = 'Stephens';
```

  In this statement, we are using the **WHERE** clause to select a staff member with the last name of **Stephens**.

Querying a single row with two columns

In this exercise, we will query the **staff** table for *John Stephens*, and we will only display the **store_id** and the **active** column:

```
sqlite> SELECT last_name, active FROM staff WHERE last_name = 'Stephens';
```

Join our Discord space

Join our Discord workspace for latest updates, offers, tech happenings around the world, new releases, and sessions with the authors:

https://discord.bpbonline.com

CHAPTER 2
Understanding Databases

Introduction

This chapter explores the foundational concepts of databases, focusing on their structure and functionality. You will learn about the components of a database, such as tables, rows, and columns, and the relationships between them. We will also explore key concepts like constraints, normalization, and denormalization, which are crucial for maintaining data integrity and efficiency in relational databases.

Structure

This chapter covers the following topics:

- Basic structure of a database
- Types of databases
- Exploring key concepts of a database
- Understanding constraints
- Normalization and denormalization

Objectives

By the end of this chapter, you will have a thorough understanding of a relational database's basic structure and components, be able to differentiate between various types of databases, and recognize their key characteristics. You will also learn how tables, rows, and columns function within a database and how these relate. Additionally, you will explore the importance of constraints, such as primary and foreign keys, and how they ensure data integrity. Finally, you will gain insights into normalization and denormalization, enabling you to design efficient databases that minimize redundancy while ensuring optimal performance.

Basic structure of a database

In this section, we will look at the basic structure of databases. A database is an organized collection of data that allows users to store, retrieve, and manage information efficiently. It provides a structured way to handle large volumes of data, ensuring consistency, security, and quick access. Databases are widely used in applications ranging from websites and business systems to scientific research and financial records.

Tables

A table is the core structure of a relational database, designed to store and organize data in a structured manner. It consists of multiple rows and columns, where each row represents an individual record, and each column defines a specific attribute of the data. Tables allow for efficient data retrieval, modification, and organization, making them an essential component of database management. Each table is designed for specific purposes, such as storing customer details, tracking orders, or managing inventory. Relationships between tables ensure that data remains connected and consistent across the database.

Each table consists of the following key components:

- **Columns (Fields)**: Define the attributes of the data. Each column has a specific name and data type, such as **INTEGER**, **VARCHAR**, or **DATE**. Columns determine what kind of information can be stored in a table.
  - **Example**: A customer table may have columns such as customer_id, name, and email.

- **Rows (Records)**: Represent individual data entries in a table. Each row contains values corresponding to the defined columns and stores a unique instance of the data.
  - **Example**: A row in the **customers** table could be (1, 'John Doe', 'johndoe@email.com').

Tables form the foundation of any relational database, allowing structured storage and efficient data retrieval. By organizing data into well-structured tables, databases ensure consistency, accuracy, and scalability.

In *Figure 2.1,* you can see a visual representation of columns and rows in a table:

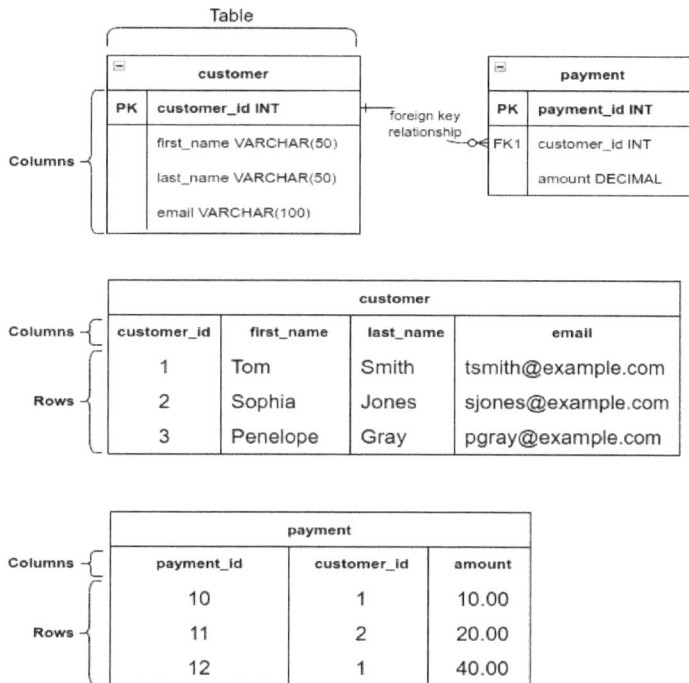

Figure 2.1: *Diagram of tables, columns, and rows*

There are several types of relationships between tables, including one-to-one, one-to-many, and many-to-many relationships, which are defined as follows:

- **One-to-one relationship:**
  - Each record in Table A corresponds to precisely one record in Table B, and vice versa.
  - Less common but useful for splitting data for security or organizational purposes.

- **One-to-many relationship:**
  - Each record in Table A can be associated with multiple records in Table B.
  - Each record in Table B can be associated with only one record in Table A.
  - The most common type of relationship in relational databases.

- **Many-to-many relationship:**
  - Each record in Table A can be associated with multiple records in Table B.
  - Each record in Table B can also be associated with multiple records in Table A.
  - Requires a junction table (also called a bridge table or associative entity) to break down the relationship into two one-to-many relationships.

Columns

Now, let us take a closer look at columns in a table. Each column in a table has a specific data type that defines the kind of data it can store. The choice of data type is crucial because it determines how data is stored, retrieved, and manipulated within the database. Common data types include **INT** for integers, **VARCHAR** for variable-length strings, **DATE** for storing date values, and **DECIMAL** for precise numeric calculations.

Selecting the appropriate data type ensures that operations, such as mathematical computations or date comparisons, can be performed efficiently. For example, a column defined with the **DATE** data type allows the database to calculate the difference between two dates or sort records chronologically.

In addition to data types, columns may have constraints that enforce rules on the data they store. The primary key constraint ensures that each row in a table has a unique identifier, which is essential for retrieving specific records quickly and efficiently. This concept is discussed in more detail in the *Understanding constraints* section of this chapter. Other typical constraints include UNIQUE and NOT NULL, where the UNIQUE constraint prevents duplicate values in a column, and the NOT NULL constraint ensures that a column cannot contain missing values, meaning data must always be entered. Another important constraint is the foreign key, which establishes relationships between tables by linking a column in one table to the primary key of another. These constraints help maintain data integrity, consistency, and reliability in relational databases.

Index

Indexes are another critical aspect of the basic structure of databases. Let us learn a little more about them.

An index is a database object that improves the speed of data retrieval operations by providing quick access to rows in a table. Indexes are created on columns frequently used in search conditions, such as primary keys or columns used in **WHERE** clauses.

While indexes significantly speed up query performance, they also require additional storage. They can slow down write operations, such as inserts and updates, because the index must be updated whenever the data in the indexed column changes.

Therefore, it is essential to use indexes judiciously, balancing the need for fast data retrieval with the overhead they introduce.

Views

Views are virtual tables in a database that simplify complex queries and abstract the underlying table structure. They can also provide a level of security by exposing only the required data to a user, not all the data in a table.

A **SELECT** query defines a view that retrieves data from one or more tables.

The view itself does not store data; instead, it dynamically generates data based on the query each time it is accessed.

Views are useful for encapsulating complex joins, aggregations, or calculations, allowing users to interact with the data through a more straightforward, intuitive interface. For example, you might create a view that combines data from several tables to provide a comprehensive report on sales performance without exposing the underlying complexity to the end user.

Types of databases

Different databases are designed to handle several types of data, workloads, and use cases, making understanding the distinctions between them a prerequisite. The most common types of databases include relational, NoSQL, object-oriented, graph, and in-memory databases, as shown in *Figure 2.2*. Each type offers unique features and benefits that suit specific applications.

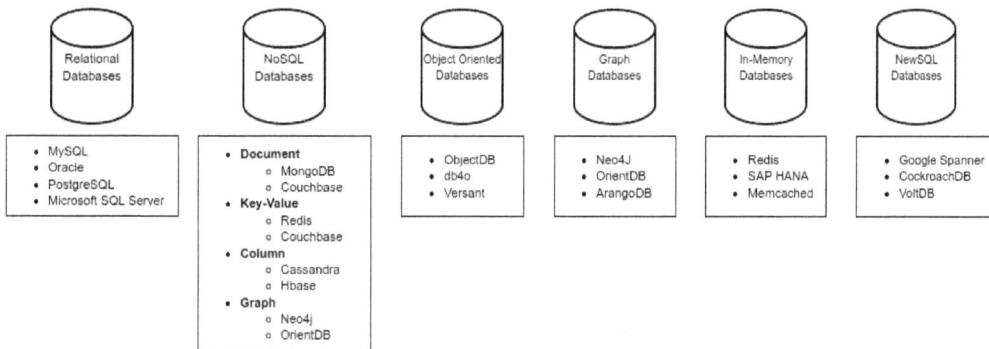

Figure 2.2: Different types of databases

Now, let us look at different types of databases:

- **Relational databases:** As we learned in *Chapter 1, Introduction to SQL,* relational database is a widely used model used to organize data into tables or relations, where each table represents a specific entity, such as *customer, rental,* or *payment,* in our Sakila database example. The tables are composed of rows and columns, each representing a unique record and each representing an attribute of that record.

  Relational databases use SQL to define and manipulate data, making them highly versatile and capable of handling complex queries and transactions. The relational model's key feature is its ability to establish relationships between tables using primary and foreign keys, enabling the connection of related data across different tables. This allows for efficient data management without redundancy and ensures data integrity.

Examples of relational databases include MySQL, PostgreSQL, Oracle database, and Microsoft SQL Server. These databases are ideal for applications that require high data accuracy, consistency, and support for complex transactions, such as financial systems, **enterprise resource planning (ERP)** systems, and **customer relationship management (CRM)** systems.

- **NoSQL databases:** NoSQL databases, also known as non-relational databases, emerged in response to the limitations of relational databases when dealing with large-scale, unstructured, or semi-structured data. Unlike relational databases, NoSQL databases do not use tables to store data. Instead, they use a variety of data models, including document, key-value, column-family, and graph models.

- **Document databases:** Document databases store data in JSON, BSON, or XML format, where each document represents a single record. These documents are flexible, allowing different records to have varying structures, making them ideal for handling unstructured or semi-structured data. Examples of document databases include MongoDB and Couchbase. They are commonly used in content management systems, real-time analytics, and applications where the data schema can change frequently.

- **Key-value databases:** Key-value databases store data as a collection of key-value pairs, where each key is unique, and the associated value can be a simple data type or a complex object. This model is highly scalable and efficient for lookups, making it ideal for caching and session management. Examples of key-value databases include Redis and Couchbase. They are often used in applications requiring fast data retrieval, such as online gaming, e-commerce, and real-time bidding systems.

- **Column-family databases:** Column-family databases, inspired by Google's Bigtable, store data in columns rather than rows, allowing for efficient storage and retrieval of sparse data. Each column family contains rows with a unique key and multiple columns, and different rows can have different columns. Examples of column-family databases include Apache Cassandra and HBase. They are well-suited for handling large-scale, distributed data and are often used in big data applications, time-series data, and recommendation engines.

- **Graph databases**: Graph databases store data in nodes and edges, where nodes represent entities and edges represent relationships between entities. This model is particularly effective for representing and querying complex relationships, such as in social networks, fraud detection, and recommendation systems. Examples of graph databases include Neo4j and OrientDB. They are used in applications that require the traversal of relationships, such as social networking platforms, fraud detection systems, and knowledge graphs. NoSQL databases are highly scalable and can handle large volumes of data with varying structures, making them a popular choice for modern web applications, big data analytics, and real-time data processing. However, they often sacrifice some features of relational databases, such as strong consistency and **atomicity, consistency, isolation, and durability**

(**ACID**) transactions, in favor of performance and flexibility.

- **Object-oriented database management system (OODBMS)**: These are designed to store data as objects, like how data is represented in object-oriented programming languages like Java, C++, and Python. In an object-oriented database, each object encapsulates both data and behavior, allowing for the storage of complex data types, such as multimedia, CAD drawings, and scientific data. OODBMS are well-suited for applications that require the representation of complex relationships and the manipulation of complex data structures. They integrate seamlessly with object-oriented programming languages, making it easier for developers to work with the database without converting objects into relational tables. Examples of OODBMS include ObjectDB, db4o, and Versant. These databases are commonly used in scientific research, engineering design, and multimedia applications, where the data model closely aligns with the object-oriented programming paradigm.

- **In-memory databases (IMDB)**: IMDB stores data in a computer's RAM rather than on disk, providing high-speed data access and processing times. This type of database is designed to handle high-performance applications that require real-time data processing, such as financial trading platforms, telecommunications networks, and gaming engines. Since data is stored in memory, in-memory databases can perform read and write operations at lightning speed, making them ideal for applications where response time is critical.

  However, this also means that data stored in an IMDB is volatile and may be lost if the system crashes or is powered down. Many IMDBs offer features like persistent storage, data replication, and backup options to mitigate this risk. Examples include Redis, SAP HANA, and Memcached. These databases, such as real-time analytics, caching, and high-frequency trading, are used when high-speed data access is crucial.

- **NewSQL databases:** NewSQL databases aim to combine the scalability of NoSQL databases with the strong consistency and transactional integrity of traditional relational databases. These databases are designed to handle the massive scale of modern applications while providing the familiar SQL interface and ACID compliance. NewSQL databases use distributed architectures and advanced algorithms to achieve high performance and scalability without sacrificing the reliable features of relational databases. They are often used in scenarios where the scalability of NoSQL is needed, but firm consistency and complex queries are also required. Examples of NewSQL databases include Google Spanner, CockroachDB, and VoltDB. These databases are increasingly adopted in finance, e-commerce, and telecommunications industries, where scalability and consistency are critical.

Exploring key concepts of a database

Earlier in the chapter, we discussed tables, rows, and columns, which form the backbone of relational databases, providing the structure necessary to organize, store, and retrieve data efficiently. Understanding these key concepts in detail is essential for anyone working with SQL or managing a database. Each element is distinct in how data is modeled and accessed, making it fundamental to the relational model.

Entity relationship diagram

An **entity relationship diagram** (ERD) is a graphical representation used to visualize the structure of a database. It illustrates the relationships between different entities within the database, where an entity represents a real-world object or concept, such as a customer, store, or payment. Entities are depicted as rectangles, and each entity can have attributes, which are characteristics or properties that describe it. For example, our customer entity has attributes like **customer_id**, **first_name** and **last_name**. ERDs provide a clear and organized way to plan and communicate the database's structure, making understanding how data is connected and interacted easier.

Using ERDs, database designers can effectively model complex systems and identify potential issues before implementation. ERDs serve as a blueprint for the database, guiding the development process and ensuring that all necessary entities and relationships are considered. They are a fundamental tool in the database development design phase, helping translate real-world scenarios into a structured data model that can be implemented in a relational database system.

In *Figure 2.3*, the ERD for our Sakila database, which we will use throughout this book, is given. It is important to review it. In the real-world, database administrators, data engineers, and data architects rely on ERDs to understand a database structure.

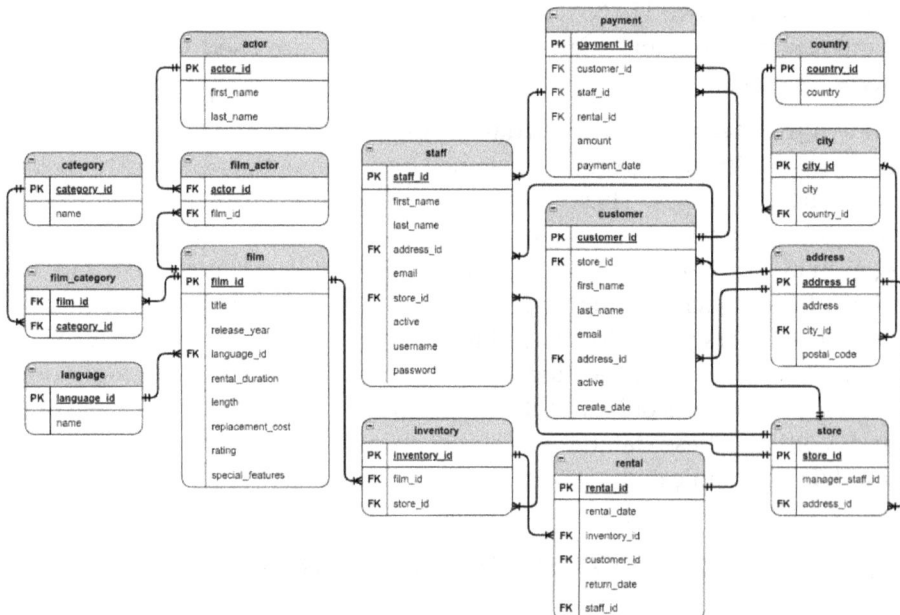

Figure 2.3: Sakila database entity relationship diagram

Tables

Earlier in the chapter, we discussed that tables are the foundational building blocks of a relational database. They organize data into a grid format, like a spreadsheet, where data is stored in rows and columns. For example, in *Figure 2.4*, the table storing customer information is named customer, while the table tracking payments is named payment.

Tables are designed to store data in a structured way, with each table focusing on a single entity type. This approach simplifies data management and allows for efficient querying and manipulation of data. When designing a table, it is essential to identify the attributes that define the entity and create corresponding columns for each attribute. Each column in the table holds a specific type of data, such as text, numbers, or dates, and each row represents a single instance of the entity, shown as follows:

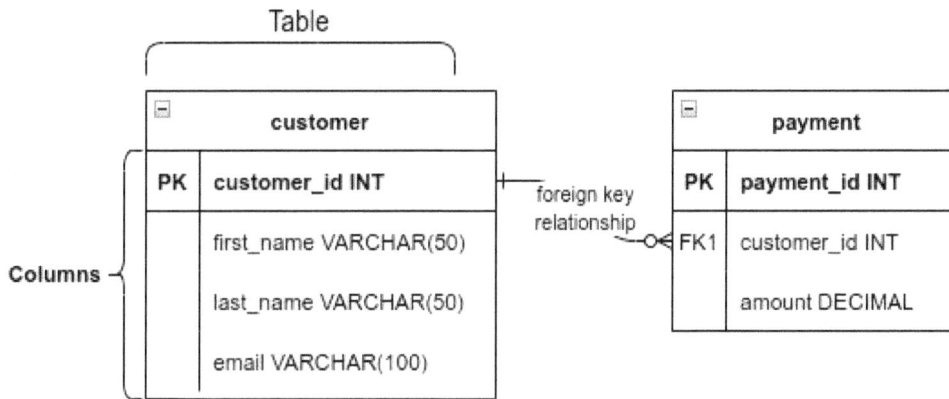

Figure 2.4: Example of tables and columns in a database

Rows

Rows, also known as records or tuples, are the individual entries in a table. Each row represents a unique instance of the entity the table describes. For example, in our `customer` table, shown in *Figure 2.4*, each row represents a different customer, with columns providing details such as the customer's name, address, and contact information.

As we learned earlier in the chapter, rows are distinguished from one another by a unique identifier called the primary key. The primary key ensures that each row can be uniquely identified and retrieved, preventing duplicate entries. In the `customer` table, the primary key is called `customer_id`, which assigns a unique number to each customer. This unique identifier is crucial for maintaining the database's integrity and establishing relationships between different tables.

Rows are central to relational databases because they allow the database to manage large volumes of data while maintaining structure and order. When querying a database, you typically retrieve or manipulate data at the row level, selecting rows that meet certain criteria or updating specific rows based on their unique identifiers. The ability to precisely target individual rows through queries is one of the strengths of the relational model.

Columns

Columns, also known as fields or attributes, define the specific data that each row in a table will contain. Each column corresponds to an attribute of the entity that the table represents. For example, as shown in *Figure 2.5*, in our **customer** table, columns include **first_name**, **last_name**, and **email**. These columns define the data structure and ensure that each row contains consistent information.

Columns are defined by their data type, which specifies the data that can be stored in the column. Common data types include **INT** for integers, **VARCHAR** for variable-length strings, **DATE** for dates, and **DECIMAL** for precise numeric values. The choice of data type is essential because it affects how the data is stored, retrieved, and manipulated. For example, defining a column as **DATE** allows the database to perform date-specific operations, such as calculating the number of days between two dates or sorting records by date.

Columns can also have constraints applied to them, which we will discuss in more detail later in the chapter, which enforce rules on the data they store. Typical constraints include NOT NULL, which ensures that a column cannot have a NULL value, and UNIQUE, which ensures that all values are distinct. These constraints help maintain data integrity and prevent errors, such as duplicate entries or missing information.

Refer to the following figure:

	customer			
Columns →	customer_id	first_name	last_name	email
	1	Tom	Smith	tsmith@example.com
Rows →	2	Sophia	Jones	sjones@example.com
	3	Penelope	Gray	pgray@example.com

	payment		
Columns →	payment_id	customer_id	amount
	10	1	10.00
Rows →	11	2	20.00
	12	1	40.00

Figure 2.5: Example of rows and columns in a database

Indexes

Indexes are an integral part of database management, designed to improve the speed and efficiency of data retrieval operations. Just as a book's index allows you to quickly locate information without scanning every page, a database index enables the database engine to find and retrieve specific rows of data without scanning the entire table. Understanding how indexes work and how to implement them effectively is crucial for optimizing the performance of your SQL queries, particularly in large databases where the volume of data can significantly impact query execution times.

Understanding the working of indexes

At a basic level, an index in a database is a data structure, typically a B-tree or a hash, that stores a sorted copy of one or more columns from a table. This sorted structure allows the database engine to quickly locate rows matching a query's search criteria. The B-tree is highly capable of storing systems that write large blocks of data. The B-tree simplifies the binary search tree by allowing nodes with more than two children, as shown in *Figure 2.6*:

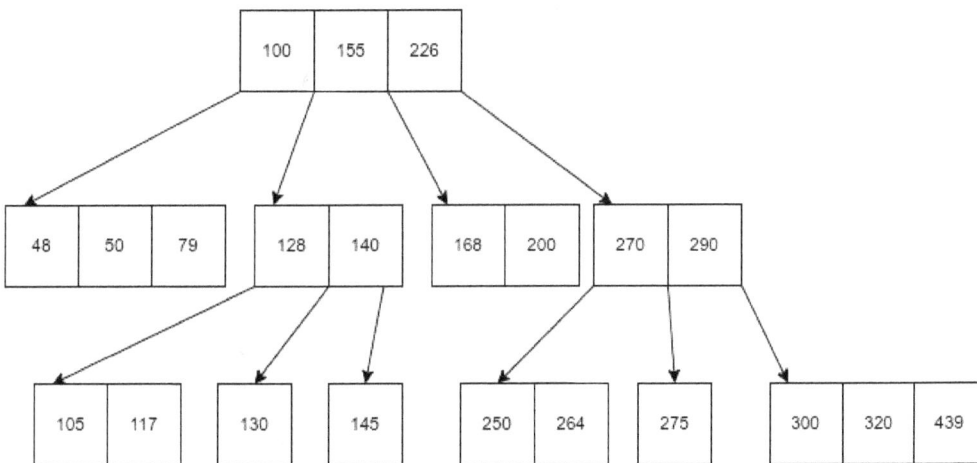

Figure 2.6: Example of a B-tree index

For example, in *Figure 2.7*, if you frequently query the **customer** table based on the **last_name** column, creating an index called **idx_customer_asc** on that column will allow the database to locate the relevant rows much faster than scanning the entire table:

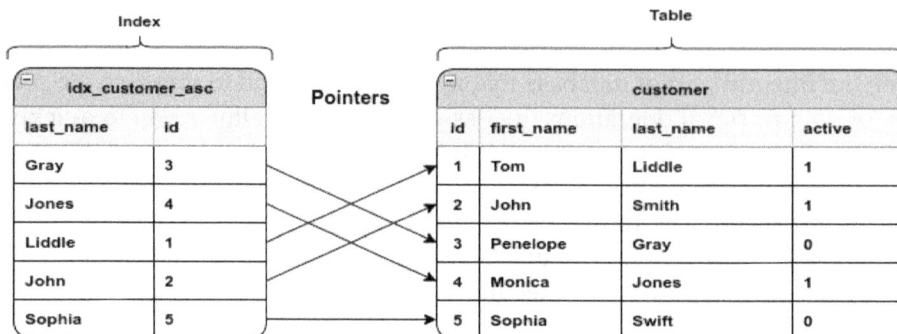

Figure 2.7: An ascending index on the customer table

When a query is executed, the database engine checks if there is an index that can be used to satisfy it. If an appropriate index exists, the engine can traverse it to quickly find the rows that meet the query criteria, dramatically reducing the amount of data that needs to be processed. Without an index, the engine would perform a full table scan, examining each row to determine if it matches the search condition, which can be time-consuming for large tables.

Types of indexes

There are several types of indexes, each suited to different use cases and query patterns:

- **Primary index**: This is automatically created when a table defines a primary key. The primary index ensures that the primary key column(s) is unique and provides fast access to rows based on the primary key. For instance, if we create a new table called **special_feature**, we need a primary key called **special_feature_id**. This will create a row with a unique identifier for each feature. You would specify that in the **CREATE TABLE** statement when creating the table. Refer to the following code:

```
CREATE TABLE special_feature(
special_feature_id INT NOT NULL PRIMARY KEY,
name VARCHAR(50)
);
```

- **Unique index**: Like the primary index, a unique index enforces uniqueness across the indexed columns. However, unlike the primary index, a table can have multiple unique indexes on different columns. Unique indexes are useful for columns that require unique values, such as email addresses or usernames. For instance, if we want to ensure that someone does not enter a duplicate special feature name in the **special_feature** table, we will execute the following code to create a unique index on the **name** column. Refer to the following code:

```
CREATE UNIQUE INDEX IDX_SPECIAL_FEATURE_NAME
ON special_feature (name);
```

- **Composite index**: A composite index is an index on multiple columns. It is beneficial when queries are often filtered or sorted by multiple columns. For example, an index on both **last_name** and **first_name** in the **customer** table can speed up queries that search by both names:

```
CREATE INDEX IDX_CUSTOMER_FIRST_LAST_NAME
ON customer (first_name, last_name);
```

- **Clustered index**: A clustered index determines the physical order of data in the table. Each table can have only one clustered index, usually on the primary key. The data rows in the table are stored in order based on the clustered index key. This index type is highly efficient for range queries. However, it can add overhead to data modification operations (like inserts, updates, and deletes) due to the need to maintain the order of the rows. For example, let us say the **customer_id** column in the **customer** table was out of order, 2,5,6,10,1. You can add a cluster index to order the data in the table to 1,2,5,6,10. Refer to the following code:

```
CREATE CLUSTERED INDEX IDX_CUSTOMER_CUSTOMER_ID
ON customer (customer_id ASC);
```

  Note: **The preceding code will not work on SQLite 3, but will work on other DBMS.**

- **Non-clustered index**: Unlike clustered indexes, non-clustered indexes do not affect the physical order of the data in the table. Instead, they create a separate structure that points to the rows in the table. You can have multiple non-clustered indexes on a table, each serving different query patterns. For instance, if you want to search by **last_name** in the **customer** table, you will create a non-clustered index on the **last_name** column:

```
CREATE INDEX IDX_CUSTOMER_LAST_NAME
on customer (last_name ASC);
```

- **Full-text index**: Full-text indexes are specialized indexes designed for searching text-based data efficiently. They are particularly useful for columns that store large amounts of textual information, such as descriptions and documents. Full-text indexes support advanced search capabilities like searching for words or phrases within text and are optimized for performance in these scenarios. This is one of those examples where the SQL syntax is different in each DBMS. Consult the DBMS you are working with on how to implement this index. This could require special extensions or add-ons installed on your DBMS to work properly.

When to use indexes

While indexes significantly improve query performance, they are not without trade-offs. Indexes consume additional storage space, and each index must be maintained as data in the table changes. This maintenance can add overhead to insert, update, and delete operations because the database must update the indexes accordingly.

Therefore, it is essential to use indexes judiciously. Indexes are most beneficial in the following scenarios:

- **Frequent queries:** Columns frequently used in search conditions (`WHERE` clauses), sorting (`ORDER BY` clauses), or join conditions should typically have indexes. This ensures that these operations are performed efficiently.

- **Large tables:** In large tables, the performance impact of not having an index can be significant because full table scans become increasingly costly as the table grows. Indexes help mitigate this by allowing the database to retrieve only the relevant rows.

- **Unique values:** Columns that store unique values (such as email addresses, employee IDs, or social security numbers) are good candidates for indexes, as they allow quick retrieval of individual records.

While indexes offer significant performance improvements for data retrieval, they have certain trade-offs that need careful consideration. One of the primary drawbacks is the increased storage requirements. Each index is an additional data structure that the database must maintain, consuming disk space. In environments with large tables and multiple indexes, the storage cost can become substantial, which may strain the database's resources, especially when managing large volumes of data.

Another key drawback is the performance overhead on data modification operations, such as inserts, updates, and deletes. Whenever data in an indexed column is modified, the corresponding index must be updated to reflect the change. This maintenance process can slow down these operations, particularly in tables with numerous indexes. For example, inserting a new row into a table with several indexes requires the database to update each index to account for the new data, potentially adding latency to what would otherwise be a quick operation.

Finally, indexes can sometimes introduce complexity in query optimization. While their primary purpose is to speed up queries, poorly designed or unnecessary indexes can result in suboptimal query plans. The database engine must decide which index to use for a given query, and in certain cases, it may select an index that does not offer the best performance. This can lead to slower query execution times and be particularly problematic if many indexes are on a table, as the engine may only sometimes choose the most efficient one. Proper monitoring and analysis of index usage are necessary to avoid these issues.

It is important to implement indexing selectively and strategically to maximize the benefits of indexes while minimizing their drawbacks. Focus on creating indexes for columns frequently used in queries, particularly those involved in search conditions, sorting, or join operations. Over-indexing should be avoided, as it can lead to unnecessary storage costs and performance overhead during data modifications. Regularly monitor query performance and analyze the use of existing indexes. Most modern database systems offer tools to help track index usage, making it easier to identify underutilized or unused indexes, which can be candidates for removal.

In addition to being selective, consider using composite indexes when queries often filter or sort by multiple columns. A well-designed composite index can be more efficient than separate indexes on individual columns. It is also essential to periodically review and rebuild indexes, particularly on tables that undergo frequent updates.

This helps maintain the efficiency of the indexes and ensures optimal query performance. By staying proactive in index management, you can significantly enhance query speeds while keeping the associated storage and maintenance costs in check.

Understanding constraints

Constraints in SQL are another key component. They are rules applied to table columns to enforce data integrity, accuracy, and reliability within a relational database. They are for maintaining the consistency of the data stored in a database, ensuring that the information adheres to predefined rules and structures. By understanding and correctly implementing constraints, you can prevent invalid data from being inserted into your tables, thus protecting the integrity of your database. Let us look at the types of constraints:

- **Primary key constraint:** One of the most fundamental types of constraints is the primary key constraint. A primary key uniquely identifies each record within a table, ensuring that no two rows have the same value in the primary key column(s). This constraint is crucial because it allows the database to retrieve, update, and delete records efficiently. It is often applied to a single column, such as an ID number, but it can also be composed of multiple columns, known as a composite key. For instance, in the table storing **staff** information, the **staff_id** column could be designated as the primary key, ensuring staff have a unique identifier.

- **Foreign key constraint:** Another important constraint is the **foreign key constraint**, which enforces a link between two tables. A foreign key in one table points to a primary key in another, creating a relationship between the two tables. This constraint is vital for maintaining referential integrity in the database. For example, our Sakila database has two tables: **staff** and **store**. The **staff_id** column in the **staff** table can be a foreign key referencing the **staff_id** column in the **store** table. This setup ensures that a staff member is associated with a valid store, preventing the insertion of a **staff_id** in the **store** table that does not exist in the **staff** table.

- **Unique constraint:** The unique constraint is another critical tool in SQL. This constraint ensures that all values in a column or a group of columns are distinct across the table. While, like the primary key, the unique constraint allows for NULL values unless explicitly prohibited by the NOT NULL constraint. Unique constraints are particularly useful when you need to ensure the uniqueness of values without designating them as primary keys. For example, an **email** column in a **staff** table might have a unique constraint applied to prevent two users from registering with the same email address.

- **Check constraint:** Check constraint allows you to define specific conditions that data must meet before being inserted into the table. This constraint is highly flexible, enabling the enforcement of a wide range of business rules at the database level. For instance, if you have a **rental_rate** column in the **film** table, you could apply a check constraint to ensure that the **rental_rate** value is always greater than zero. The check constraint might look like this:

```
CHECK (rental_rate > 0)
```

With this constraint in place, any attempt to insert or update a record with a non-positive salary would be rejected by the database.

- **Default constraint:** It is used to automatically assign a default value to a column if no value is specified during the insertion of a record. This constraint ensures that specific columns are always populated with valid data, even when the user does not provide input. For example, in our **staff** table, you could use a default constraint to automatically populate the column active with a 1 (active) or 0 (inactive) when a new staff member is created:

```
DEFAULT 1
```

- **Domain constraint:** In addition to these standard constraints, there are also **domain constraints**, defined by specifying the allowable values for a column. This constraint is not always explicitly named in SQL syntax but is applied through data types, enumerations, or custom domains. For example, the *active* column in the **staff** table might be limited to only accept values like 1 or 0. This constraint ensures that no invalid statuses are entered into the database.

Constraints are crucial in maintaining data integrity, accuracy, and reliability within a relational database. By enforcing rules at the database level, constraints help ensure that data is consistent and meaningful across all tables and relationships. Proper use of constraints also simplifies data management. It reduces the need for complex error-checking logic in application code, as many validation tasks are handled directly by the database system.

Normalization and denormalization

Normalization and denormalization are two critical processes in database design that directly impact a relational database's structure, performance, and integrity. These processes determine how data is organized across tables, influencing how efficiently data can be stored, retrieved, and maintained. Understanding the principles and trade-offs of normalization and denormalization is essential for creating effective database systems that meet specific business and application requirements.

Normalization

Normalization involves organizing data in a database to reduce redundancy and improve data integrity. The primary goal of normalization is to ensure that each piece of data is stored only once, eliminating unnecessary duplication and preventing potential anomalies that can arise during data manipulation. To achieve this, normalization involves dividing a database into multiple related tables and defining relationships between them using primary and foreign keys.

Normalization is typically guided by standard forms, each with rules and criteria. The most applied standard forms are the **first normal form (1NF)**, **second normal form (2NF)**, and **third normal form (3NF)**.

First normal form

A table is in 1NF if it only contains atomic (indivisible) values, with each column containing a single value per row. Additionally, each column must have a unique name, and the order in which data is stored does not matter. 1NF eliminates repeating groups and ensures that each attribute contains only one value per record. For example, consider the table that stores films.

Each column in the **film** table stores only single, atomic values for **film_id**, **title**, and **actor**. The **film_id** column serves as the primary key, uniquely identifying each film record. However, if you have multiple actors in a film, you can normalize this by storing a unique record for each actor and the film (**title**), as shown in *Figure 2.8*:

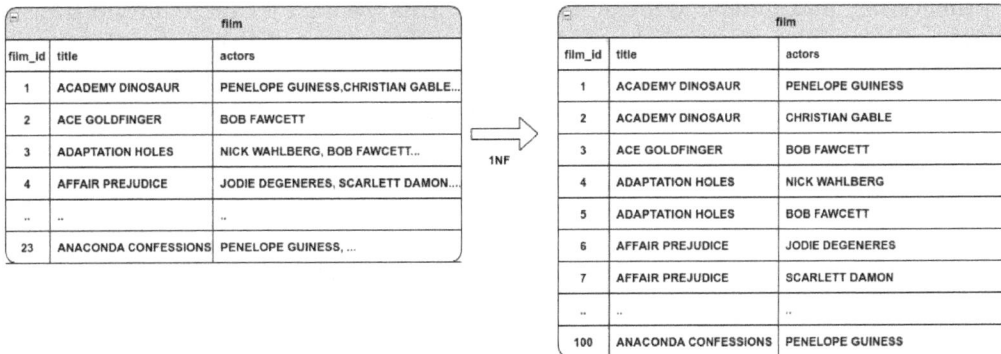

Figure 2.8: 1NF example of the film table

Second normal form

A table is in 2NF if it is already in 1NF, and all non-key attributes are entirely functionally dependent on the primary key. This means that each non-key column must depend on the entire primary key, not just a part of it. 2NF addresses issues related to partial dependency, where a column depends on only part of a composite primary key. For example, in *Figure 2.8*, we have duplicate records with **title** columns. Now let us look at the **film_actor** table, which has a many-to-many relationship between the **film** and **actor** tables. The composite primary key is **actor_id** and **film_id**:

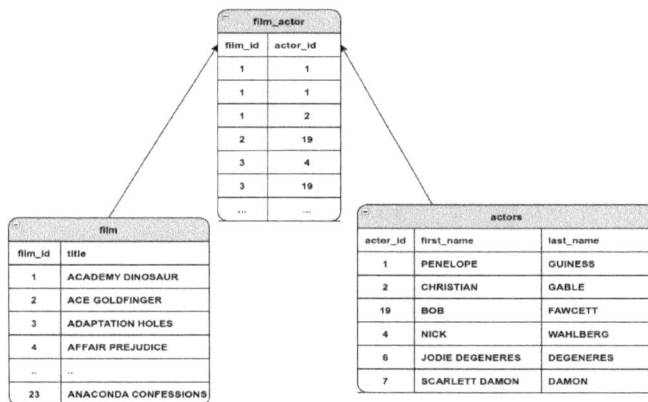

Figure 2.9: 2NF example of film_actor table

Third normal form

A table is in 3NF if it is in 2NF, and all non-key attributes are functionally dependent on the primary key and independent of each other. This means that there are no transitive dependencies where a non-key column depends on another non-key column. For example, as shown in *Figure 2.10*, if a table-like film contained a column **language_name** that depended on **language_id** rather than the primary key **film_id**, it would violate 3NF by introducing a transitive dependency. This means **language_name** would not rely on the primary key but on another non-key attribute, leading to redundancy and potential update anomalies.

To bring such a table into 3NF, the transitive dependency must be removed by storing the **language_name** in a separate **language** table that is linked to the **film** table through a foreign key. This ensures that all non-key attributes in the film table are directly dependent on the primary key, making the database schema more efficient and reducing redundancy. By adhering to 3NF, the database design becomes more robust, helping to maintain data integrity and simplify database maintenance. Refer to the following figure:

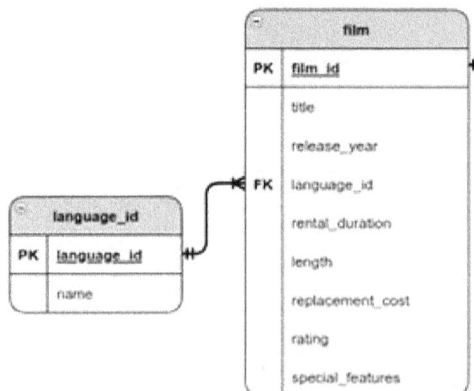

Figure 2.10: 3N example of the film and language table

Normalization improves data integrity by ensuring that each piece of data is stored in only one place, reducing the risk of inconsistencies when data is updated, deleted, or inserted. It also makes the database more flexible, allowing for more accessible updates and maintenance as the data model evolves.

Denormalization

Denormalization intentionally introduces redundancy into a database by merging tables or adding redundant data. While normalization is focused on reducing redundancy and improving data integrity, denormalization is often used to optimize database performance, particularly in scenarios where read operations significantly outweigh write operations.

In a normalized database, data retrieval can require multiple table joins, which can be time-consuming and resource-intensive, especially with large datasets or complex queries. Denormalization reduces the need for these joins by storing related data in the same table, thereby speeding up data retrieval at the cost of increased storage space and potential redundancy.

Denormalization can take various forms, depending on the application's specific performance requirements. Some standard techniques include merging tables, adding redundant columns, using summary tables, and storing derived data.

Let us look at them in detail:

- **Merging tables:** One of the most straightforward forms of denormalization involves merging two or more related tables into a single table. This reduces the number of joins required in queries and improves read performance. For example, instead of having separate `customer` and `rental` tables, you might create a single `customer_rentals` table that includes customer details and rental information.

  While merging tables can simplify data retrieval, it also introduces redundancy, as customer information is repeated for each order. If the redundant data is not consistently updated, this can lead to data anomalies.

- **Adding redundant columns:** Another common denormalization technique is adding redundant columns to a table to store frequently accessed data. For instance, you might have columns in the `payment` table that are for `order_amount`, `tax`, and `deliver_charge`. Instead of summing all those up in the program or software, you might have an amount column that does the summing of information for you.

  This approach improves query performance by eliminating the need to aggregate data at runtime, but it requires additional storage space and introduces the risk of data becoming out of sync if updates are not properly managed.

- **Using summary tables:** Summary tables, also known as materialized views, store precomputed results of complex queries, such as aggregates or counts. These tables speed up reporting and analytics by providing quick access to summarized data. For example, a summary table might store the total sales for each day, week, or month, allowing staff to retrieve sales figures quickly without querying the entire transaction table. However, maintaining these summary tables requires additional processing and storage through **extract, transform, and load** (ETL) programs

- **Storing derived data:** In some cases, derived data, data calculated or derived from other columns, may be stored directly in the table to improve query performance. For instance, instead of calculating a customer's total sales amount for the lifetime of the customer, you might store the calculated sales amount as a separate column called `lifetime_sales_amount` in the `customer` table. This approach saves computation time during queries but requires careful management to ensure that the derived data remains accurate as the underlying data changes.

Normalization and denormalization are complementary processes that address several aspects of database design. Normalization focuses on reducing redundancy and improving data integrity, making databases easier to maintain and update. On the other hand, denormalization prioritizes performance by reducing the need for complex joins and improving query speed, especially in scenarios where fast data retrieval is crucial. Understanding when and how to apply these processes is essential for creating a database that meets your application's functional and performance requirements.

Conclusion

In this chapter, we explored in detail the core concepts of relational database design, offering insights for anyone serious about managing data effectively. We explored how tables, rows, and columns unlock the basic building blocks of a database, showing you just how crucial it is to grasp these elements to work confidently with data. Understanding how these components fit together to store and organize information made designing databases seem logical and intuitive.

Using constraints highlights the importance of ensuring data integrity. The way constraints work together to maintain unique records and link related data across tables is the secret to handling reliable and powerful in handling complex queries. Additionally, we explored how these keys are technical necessities and vital tools that make a database function smoothly and effectively.

Normalization and denormalization highlight the delicate balance between keeping data clean and efficient through normalization and making strategic decisions to improve performance with denormalization. The section on normalization and denormalization also touched upon the trade-offs when considering an application's practical needs. Mastering these concepts is critical to designing databases that can handle accuracy and performance.

With this knowledge, you are well-prepared to move into more advanced topics, where these principles will continue to guide your approach to SQL and relational database management. The solid foundation built-in this chapter will support your efforts to design, query, and manage databases with confidence and precision.

In the next chapter, we will explore how to use the SQL syntax to retrieve rows of data from tables, views, and columns.

Exercises

In these exercises, we will enhance the Sakila database by adding new tables, constraints, and an index, and normalizing the data.

Create a table

In this exercise, we will create the **special_feature** table in the Sakila database:

Open a command prompt and type in the command to open the database:

sqlite3 sqlite-skila.db

At the **sqlite>** command prompt, type in the command to create the table called **special_feature** and add a primary key constraint on the table:

```
CREATE TABLE special_feature(
special_feature_id INT NOT NULL PRIMARY KEY,
name VARCHAR(50)
);
```

Create constraints

In this exercise, now that the **special_feature** table is created, we can create the 2NF table with the foreign key constraints from the **film** and **special_feature** table to a newly create **film_special_feature** table:

At the **sqlite>** command prompt, type the command to create the foreign key constraint for film and **film_special_feature** tables:

```
CREATE TABLE film_special_feature(
film_id INT,
special_feature_id INT,
FOREIGN KEY (film_id) REFERENCES film(film_id),
FOREIGN KEY (special_feature_id) REFERENCES special_feature(special_
feature_id)
);
```

Perform normalization

In this exercise, we will populate the **film_special_feature** table. However, before doing so, we need to insert data into the **special_feature** table (a topic we will explore further in *Chapter 6, Modifying Data*) to ensure that our foreign key constraints are upheld when populating the **film_special_feature** table:

1. At the **sqlite>** command prompt, type in the command to populate the **special_feature** table with data:

```
INSERT INTO special_feature (special_feature_id, name) VALUES (1,
'Trailers');
INSERT INTO special_feature (special_feature_id, name) VALUES (2,
'Deleted Scenes');
INSERT INTO special_feature (special_feature_id, name) VALUES (3,
'Behind the Scenes');
INSERT INTO special_feature (special_feature_id, name) VALUES (4,
'Commentaries');
```

2. At the **sqlite>** command prompt, type in the SQL command to populate the **film_special_feature** table with film as the special feature of Trailers:

```
INSERT INTO film_special_feature (film_id, special_feature_id)
  SELECT 1, film_id FROM film WHERE special_features LIKE '%Trailers%';
```

3. At the **sqlite>** command prompt, type in the SQL command to populate the **film_special_feature** table with film as the special feature of deleted scenes:

```
INSERT INTO film_special_feature (film_id, special_feature_id)
  SELECT 2, film_id FROM film WHERE special_features LIKE '%Deleted
Scenes%';
```

4. At the **sqlite>** command prompt, type in the SQL command to populate the **film_special_feature** table with film as the special feature of behind the scenes:

```
INSERT INTO film_special_feature (film_id, special_feature_id)
  SELECT 3, film_id FROM film WHERE special_features LIKE '%Behind the
Scenes%';
```

5. At the **sqlite>** command prompt, type in the SQL command to populate the **film_special_feature** table with film as the special feature of commentaries:

```
INSERT INTO film_special_feature (film_id, special_feature_id)
  SELECT 4, film_id FROM film WHERE special_features LIKE '%Commentar-
ies%';
```

Join our Discord space

Join our Discord workspace for latest updates, offers, tech happenings around the world, new releases, and sessions with the authors:

https://discord.bpbonline.com

CHAPTER 3
Basic SQL Queries

Introduction

In this chapter, you will explore the fundamental aspects of writing **Structured Query Language** (**SQL**) queries to interact with databases effectively. You will learn to retrieve data using the powerful **SELECT** statement, apply filters to narrow down results with the **WHERE** clause, join tables with **JOIN**, and sort your data using the **ORDER BY** clause. Additionally, you will understand how to limit query results and create calculated fields for dynamic data generation. By the end of this chapter, you will be equipped with essential querying skills that form the foundation for more advanced SQL operations in later chapters.

Structure

This chapter covers the following topics:

- Introduction to SQL syntax
- Retrieving data in SQL
- SQL clauses
- SQL operators
- SQL joins
- SQL functions

Objectives

By the end of this chapter, you will be able to write and execute basic SQL queries to retrieve data from a database with precision and control. You will understand how to use the **SELECT** statement to extract data, apply the **WHERE** clause to filter results, sort data using the **ORDER BY** clause, and join data between two tables. You will also learn to limit the number of results your queries return and create calculated fields to generate dynamic values. These essential skills will enable you to interact efficiently with databases and lay the groundwork for more advanced query techniques.

Introduction to SQL syntax

When you want to retrieve data from a database, you use SQL, a powerful yet straightforward language designed for interacting with relational databases. SQL statements resemble natural language, making them easy to understand while providing precise instructions for querying, updating, and managing data. Every query you run uses SQL behind the scenes, making it a universal data manipulation and retrieval tool.

SQL statements comprise keywords, identifiers, operators, and values arranged in a specific order. Statements typically begin with an SQL keyword such as **SELECT**, **INSERT**, **UPDATE**, **DELETE**, **CREATE**, **ALTER**, or **DROP**, followed by the necessary parameters to execute the desired action. All SQL statements end with a semicolon (;), which tells the database that the command is complete.

For example, to retrieve data from a database, you use the **SELECT** statement:

```
SELECT title, release_year
FROM film;
```

Let us understand this query in detail:

- **SELECT** specifies the columns to retrieve (**title** and **release_year**), while **FROM** identifies the table (**film**) where the data resides.
- SQL statements can also include clauses like **WHERE**, **ORDER BY**, **GROUP BY**, and **LIMIT** to refine queries and control the results.

Beyond data retrieval, SQL syntax supports data modification (**INSERT**, **UPDATE**, **DELETE**) and database management (**CREATE**, **ALTER**, **DROP**). For example, the **INSERT** statement adds new data to a table:

```
INSERT INTO actor (actor_id, first_name, last_name, last_update)
VALUES (1000, 'Chris', 'Banner', 07-4-2005);
```

This command inserts a new record into the actor table, assigning values to the specified columns.

Similar to the **UPDATE** statement modifies the existing records.

Understanding SQL syntax is the foundation for working with relational databases. Mastering these basic commands will allow you to retrieve, modify, and manage data efficiently, forming the basis for more advanced SQL techniques.

Retrieving data in SQL

SQL is the primary language for retrieving, managing, and manipulating data in relational databases. SQL enables users to interact with data structurally and efficiently, ensuring that information can be extracted based on specific needs. Whether working with small or large-scale datasets, SQL provides the tools to filter, sort, and organize data for meaningful analysis. The foundation of data retrieval in SQL lies in the **SELECT** statement, which allows users to extract specific data from one or more tables.

The **SELECT** statement is the most fundamental SQL command for retrieving data. It allows users to specify the columns they want to retrieve and define conditions to filter the results.

The basic syntax of a **SELECT** statement is as follows:

```
SELECT column1, column2, ...
FROM table_name;
```

For example, to retrieve the **title** and **release_year** of all films from the film table in the Sakila sample database, you would execute the following query:

```
SELECT title, release_year
FROM film;
```

Let us understand this query in detail:

- This query retrieves two specific columns, **title** and **release_year**, from the film table, returning all available records.
- If you need to retrieve all columns from a table, you can use the * wildcard:

  ```
  SELECT *
  FROM film;
  ```

However, using **SELECT** * should be done cautiously, especially when working with large tables, as it retrieves every column, which can lead to performance issues. Instead, specifying the required columns optimizes queries and improves efficiency.

SQL clauses

SQL clauses play a crucial role in structuring and refining queries to retrieve, filter, and manipulate data efficiently. Clauses define specific conditions or parameters that modify SQL statements, allowing users to extract relevant data from relational databases. While SQL statements like **SELECT**, **INSERT**, **UPDATE**, and **DELETE** form the foundation of data operations, clauses enhance their functionality by narrowing down results, sorting data, and grouping records.

Filtering data with WHERE

The WHERE clause filters records based on specific conditions, returning only the rows that meet the given criteria. It is commonly used with **SELECT**, **UPDATE**, and **DELETE** statements. The syntax is as follows:

```
SELECT column1, column2
FROM table_name
WHERE condition
```

For example, in the Sakila sample database, to retrieve all films released in 2006, the query is:

```
SELECT title, release_year
FROM film
WHERE release_year = 2006;
```

Multiple conditions can be applied using logical operators such as:

- **AND**: Requires both conditions to be true
- **OR**: Requires at least one condition to be true
- **NOT**: Excludes rows matching a condition

For example, to find all films released in 2006 that are not in the action category:

```
SELECT f.title, f.release_year, c.name AS category
FROM film f
JOIN film_category fc ON f.film_id = fc.film_id
JOIN category c ON fc.category_id = c.category_id
WHERE f.release_year = 2006
AND c.name != 'Action';
```

Sorting data with ORDER BY

The **ORDER BY** clause sorts query results in ascending (**ASC**) or descending (**DESC**) order. The default sort order is ascending. The syntax is as follows:

```
SELECT column1, column2
FROM table_name
ORDER BY column_name [ASC | DESC];
```

For example, to list films by rental rate in descending order:

```
SELECT title, rental_rate
FROM film
ORDER BY rental_rate DESC;
```

To sort by multiple columns, separate them with commas:

```
SELECT title, release_year, rental_rate
```

```
FROM film
ORDER BY release_year DESC, rental_rate ASC;
```

This query sorts films first by release year (newest first) and then, for films released in the same year, by rental rate in ascending order.

Aggregating data with GROUP BY

The **GROUP BY** clause groups records with the same values in specified columns, often used with aggregate functions like **COUNT**, **SUM**, **AVG**, **MIN**, and **MAX**. The syntax is as follows:

```
SELECT column1, aggregate_function(column2)
FROM table_name
GROUP BY column1;
```

For example, to count the number of rentals for each film in the Sakila sample database:

```
SELECT f.title, COUNT(r.rental_id) AS rental_count
FROM rental r
JOIN inventory i ON r.inventory_id = i.inventory_id
JOIN film f ON i.film_id = f.film_id
GROUP BY f.title
ORDER BY rental_count DESC;
```

This query groups rentals by film title, calculates the total number of times each film has been rented, and orders the results in descending order of rental count.

Filtering grouped data with HAVING

Unlike **WHERE**, which filters individual records, the **HAVING** clause filters grouped results. It is used with aggregate functions to refine query output. The syntax is as follows:

```
SELECT column1, aggregate_function(column2)
FROM table_name
GROUP BY column1
HAVING condition;
```

For example, to find films rented more than 50 times:

```
SELECT f.title, COUNT(r.rental_id) AS rental_count
FROM rental r
JOIN inventory i ON r.inventory_id = i.inventory_id
JOIN film f ON i.film_id = f.film_id
GROUP BY f.title
HAVING COUNT(r.rental_id) > 50
ORDER BY rental_count DESC;
```

If **WHERE** were used instead of **HAVING**, it would not work because aggregate functions (**COUNT**) operate on grouped results, not individual rows.

Restricting results with LIMIT

The **LIMIT** clause restricts the number of rows returned by a query, which is useful when working with large datasets. The syntax is as follows:

```
SELECT column1, column2
FROM table_name
LIMIT number_of_rows;
```

For example, to retrieve the top five most rented films:

```
SELECT f.title, COUNT(r.rental_id) AS rental_count
FROM rental r
JOIN inventory i ON r.inventory_id = i.inventory_id
JOIN film f ON i.film_id = f.film_id
GROUP BY f.title
ORDER BY rental_count DESC
LIMIT 5;
```

This query returns only the five most rented films, reducing query execution time when dealing with large databases.

Combining SQL clauses for complex queries

SQL clauses can be combined to create more advanced queries. For example, to find the top three most rented films from 2006, use the following code:

```
SELECT f.title, COUNT(r.rental_id) AS rental_count
FROM rental r
JOIN inventory i ON r.inventory_id = i.inventory_id
JOIN film f ON i.film_id = f.film_id
WHERE f.release_year = 2006
GROUP BY f.title
HAVING COUNT(r.rental_id) > 10
ORDER BY rental_count DESC
LIMIT 3;
```

This query retrieves the following:

- Films released in 2006 (**WHERE f.release_year = 2006**).
- Films rented more than 10 times (**HAVING COUNT(r.rental_id) > 10**).

- Films sorted by rental count in descending order (**ORDER BY rental_count DESC**).
- Only the top three results (**LIMIT 3**).

Using clauses together allows for precise and efficient data retrieval, enabling complex queries that provide valuable insights.

SQL operators

SQL operators are essential for SQL queries, allowing users to perform comparisons, arithmetic operations, and logical evaluations within statements. Operators refine queries by defining conditions in **WHERE** clauses, manipulating data in **SELECT** statements, and performing calculations in **UPDATE** or **INSERT** statements. SQL provides various categories of operators, including arithmetic, comparison, logical, and special operators, each serving a distinct function in data retrieval and manipulation.

Arithmetic operators perform mathematical operations on numeric data within a SQL query. These operators are commonly used in **SELECT** statements, calculations, and data transformations:

Operator	Description	Example
+	Addition	`SELECT rental_rate + 2 FROM film;`
-	Subtraction	`SELECT rental_rate - 1 FROM film;`
*	Multiplication	`SELECT rental_rate * 2 FROM film;`
/	Division	`SELECT rental_rate / 2 FROM film;`
%	Modulus (Remainder)	`SELECT rental_duration % 3 FROM film;`

Table 3.1: Operators

For example, to calculate a 10% discount on rental rates, use:

```
SELECT title, rental_rate, rental_rate * 0.90 AS discounted_price
FROM film;
```

This query applies a 10% reduction to **rental_rate** and returns the new price.

Comparison operators

Comparison operators allow users to filter and compare values within SQL queries, primarily in **WHERE** clauses:

Operator	Description	Example
=	Equal to	`SELECT * FROM film WHERE release_year = 2006;`
!= or <>	Not equal to	`SELECT * FROM customer WHERE first_name != 'John';`

Operator	Description	Example
>	Greater than	`SELECT * FROM payment WHERE amount > 5.00;`
<	Less than	`SELECT * FROM payment WHERE amount < 10.00;`
>=	Greater than or equal to	`SELECT * FROM payment WHERE amount >= 5.00;`
<=	Less than or equal to	`SELECT * FROM payment WHERE amount <= 10.00;`

Table 3.2: Comparison operators

For example, to retrieve all films released after 2005, use the following code:

```
SELECT title, release_year
FROM film
WHERE release_year > 2005;
```

Logical operators

Logical operators combine multiple conditions within a SQL query, helping refine the results:

Operator	Description	Example
AND	Both conditions must be true	`SELECT * FROM film WHERE rental_rate > 2 AND release_year > 2005;`
OR	At least one condition must be true	`SELECT * FROM customer WHERE first_name = 'John' OR first_name = 'Jane';`
NOT	Negates a condition	`SELECT * FROM rental WHERE NOT return_date IS NULL;`

Table 3.3: Logical operators

For example, to find all films released after 2005 that cost more than $3 to rent, use the following code:

```
SELECT title, rental_rate, release_year
FROM film
WHERE release_year > 2005 AND rental_rate > 3;
```

This query ensures that both conditions must be met.

Special operators

SQL includes several special operators that enable pattern matching, set membership checks, and range searches, which are outlined as follows:

- **IN operator:**

  The **IN** operator checks if a value exists within a predefined list.

  ```
  SELECT * FROM customer
  WHERE first_name IN ('John', 'Jane', 'Alice');
  ```

  This query retrieves all customers whose first name is **John, Jane,** or **Alice.**

- **BETWEEN operator:**

  The **BETWEEN** operator filters results within a specified range.

  ```
  SELECT title, rental_rate
  FROM film
  WHERE rental_rate BETWEEN 2 AND 5;
  ```

  This query selects films with an inclusive rental rate between $2 and $5.

- **LIKE operator:**

  The **LIKE** operator performs pattern matching using wildcards:

  - **%** matches any sequence of characters.
  - **_** matches a single character, for example:
  - ```
    SELECT title FROM film
        WHERE title LIKE 'A%';
    ```

  This query retrieves all films that start with A.

  To find films that contain *Adventure* anywhere in the title, use:

  ```
  SELECT title FROM film
  WHERE title LIKE '%Adventure%';
  ```

- **IS NULL operator:**

  The **IS NULL** operator checks for missing values:

  ```
  SELECT * FROM rental
  WHERE return_date IS NULL;
  ```

  This query retrieves rentals where films have not been returned.

SQL operators enhance the flexibility and precision of queries, allowing users to perform calculations, filter data, and apply logic to results.

SQL joins

SQL joins allow users to retrieve and combine data from multiple tables within a relational database. Since relational databases store data across multiple tables, joins are essential for efficiently querying related information. A join links two or more tables based on a related column, such as a primary key in one table and a foreign key in another. SQL provides several types of joins, each serving a distinct purpose for merging data effectively.
  ```

Understanding joins in SQL

Joins combine rows from two or more tables based on a matching condition. The basic syntax for a join is:

```
SELECT column1, column2
FROM table1
JOIN table2 ON table1.common_column = table2.common_column;
```

The **ON** clause specifies the condition for matching records between tables. Without a join, querying multiple tables would require running separate queries and manually combining results, making joins a more efficient solution.

Retrieving matching records with INNER JOIN

The **INNER JOIN** retrieves only the records with matching values in both tables. If there is no match, the row is excluded from the result. This is the most commonly used join type.

For example, to retrieve a list of customers and the films they have rented, you can use:

```
SELECT c.first_name, c.last_name, f.title
FROM rental r
JOIN customer c ON r.customer_id = c.customer_id
JOIN inventory i ON r.inventory_id = i.inventory_id
JOIN film f ON i.film_id = f.film_id;
```

This query retrieves customers who have rented films by linking four tables: rental, customer, inventory, and film, based on their relationships. Only customers who have rented films will appear in the result set.

Retrieving records with LEFT JOIN

The **LEFT JOIN** (or **LEFT OUTER JOIN**) retrieves all records from the left table and matches records from the right table. If no match exists, **NULL** values are returned for columns from the right table.

To retrieve a list of all customers, including those who have never rented a film, use the following code:

```
SELECT c.first_name, c.last_name, r.rental_id
FROM customer c
LEFT JOIN rental r ON c.customer_id = r.customer_id;
```

Let us understand this query in detail:

- The customer table is on the left.
- The rental table is on the right.

- Customers without rental records will have NULL values in the `rental_id` column.

Retrieving records from right table with RIGHT JOIN

The **RIGHT JOIN** (or **RIGHT OUTER JOIN**) works like a **LEFT JOIN**, but instead of keeping all records from the left table, it retains all records from the right table and matches values from the left table.

To retrieve a list of all rental transactions, including any customers who may not have details in the customer table, use:

```
SELECT c.first_name, c.last_name, r.rental_id
FROM rental r
RIGHT JOIN customer c ON r.customer_id = c.customer_id;
```

Since some customers might not have a corresponding rental record, their names will appear with NULL rental values. However, **RIGHT JOIN** is not natively supported in many databases like SQLite. Instead, you can achieve the same result by swapping table positions in a **LEFT JOIN**.

Retrieving records from both tables with FULL JOIN

The **FULL JOIN** (or **FULL OUTER JOIN**) retrieves all records from both tables, returning matching rows where possible and NULL values where no match exists. This join type is proper when combining datasets with missing values on either side.

To retrieve all customers and all rental transactions, even if a customer has never rented a film or a rental record exists without a linked customer, use:

```
SELECT c.first_name, c.last_name, r.rental_id
FROM customer c
FULL JOIN rental r ON c.customer_id = r.customer_id;
```

However, **FULL JOIN** is not supported in SQLite. Instead, you can mimic this behavior using a **UNION** of **LEFT JOIN** and **RIGHT JOIN**:

```
SELECT c.first_name, c.last_name, r.rental_id
FROM customer c
LEFT JOIN rental r ON c.customer_id = r.customer_id
UNION
SELECT c.first_name, c.last_name, r.rental_id
```

```
FROM customer c
RIGHT JOIN rental r ON c.customer_id = r.customer_id;
```

Combining every row from both tables with CROSS JOIN

The **CROSS JOIN** generates a Cartesian product, meaning every row from one table is paired with every row from another table. This join does not require a matching condition and results in a large dataset.

For example, to generate all possible store and film combinations:

```
SELECT s.store_id, f.title
FROM store s
CROSS JOIN film f;
```

If the store has three records and the film has 1,000 records, this query returns 3,000 rows (every store matched with every film). This type of join is rarely used unless specifically required.

SQL joins are fundamental to working with relational databases. They allow users to combine and analyze data from multiple tables efficiently. By understanding different types of joins, you can retrieve meaningful insights, enforce relationships, and optimize database queries for performance.

SQL functions

SQL functions are built-in operations that allow users to manipulate, transform, and analyze data efficiently. These functions simplify complex calculations, text manipulations, and data formatting, making queries more powerful and flexible. SQL functions are categorized into aggregate, string, date and time, and numeric functions, each serving a unique purpose in database management.

Aggregate functions

Aggregate functions perform calculations on multiple rows and return a single value. These functions are essential for summarizing data, such as counting records, calculating averages, or finding the maximum value in a dataset.

Refer to the following table:

Function	Description	Example
COUNT()	Returns the number of rows	SELECT COUNT(*) FROM rental;
SUM()	Returns the total sum of a numeric column	SELECT SUM(amount) FROM payment;

AVG()	Returns the average value of a numeric column	`SELECT AVG(rental_rate) FROM film;`
MAX()	Returns the highest value in a column	`SELECT MAX(amount) FROM payment;`
MIN()	Returns the lowest value in a column	`SELECT MIN(amount) FROM payment;`

Table 3.4: Aggregate functions

For example, to calculate the total revenue generated from film rentals in the Sakila sample database, use the following code:

```
SELECT SUM(amount) AS total_revenue
FROM payment;
```

This query retrieves the sum of all payments made by customers.

String functions

String functions manipulate and format text data in SQL. They allow operations such as converting cases, extracting substrings, and removing unnecessary spaces.

Refer to the following table:

Function	Description	Example
UPPER()	Converts text to uppercase	`SELECT UPPER(first_name) FROM customer;`
LOWER()	Converts text to lowercase	`SELECT LOWER(last_name) FROM customer;`
LENGTH()	Returns the length of a string	`SELECT LENGTH(email) FROM customer;`
SUBSTRING()	Extracts part of a string	`SELECT SUBSTRING(title, 1, 10) FROM film;`
TRIM()	Removes leading and trailing spaces	`SELECT TRIM(first_name) FROM customer;`

Table 3.5: String functions

For example, if you need to retrieve the first ten characters of each film title, use the following code:

```
SELECT title, SUBSTRING(title, 1, 10) AS short_title
FROM film;
```

This function is useful when displaying abbreviated titles in reports or UI applications.

Date and time functions

Date and time functions allow manipulation and formatting of date values in SQL. They are helpful for calculating time differences, formatting timestamps, and extracting specific date components.

Refer to the following table:

Function	Description	Example
CURRENT_DATE	Returns the current date	SELECT CURRENT_DATE;
CURRENT_TIME	Returns the current time	SELECT CURRENT_TIME;
DATE()	Extracts the date from a timestamp	SELECT DATE(rental_date) FROM rental;
YEAR()	Extracts the year from a date	SELECT YEAR(rental_date) FROM rental;
DATEDIFF()	Returns the difference between two dates	SELECT DATEDIFF(return_date, rental_date) FROM rental;

Table 3.6: Date and time functions

For example, to calculate the number of days a film was rented before being returned, use the following code:

```
SELECT rental_id, return_date, rental_date,
DATEDIFF(return_date, rental_date) AS days_rented
FROM rental;
```

This query calculates the rental duration for each transaction.

Numeric functions

Numeric functions perform mathematical operations on numerical values, including rounding, absolute values, and power calculations.

Refer to the following table:

Function	Description	Example
ROUND()	Rounds a number to a specific decimal place	SELECT ROUND(rental_rate, 1) FROM film;
CEIL()	Returns the next highest integer	SELECT CEIL(rental_rate) FROM film;
FLOOR()	Returns the next lowest integer	SELECT FLOOR(rental_rate) FROM film;
ABS()	Returns the absolute value	SELECT ABS(-10) AS absolute_value;
POWER()	Returns the result of a number raised to a power	SELECT POWER(2,3) AS result;

Table 3.7: Numeric functions

For example, if you want to round the rental rate of each film to the nearest whole number, use:

```
SELECT title, rental_rate, ROUND(rental_rate, 0) AS rounded_rate
FROM film;
```

This function ensures that rental rates are displayed as whole numbers.

Using multiple functions in a query

SQL functions can be combined within a query to perform complex data transformations. For example, to retrieve customer names in uppercase and the length of their email addresses, use:

```
SELECT UPPER(first_name) AS uppercase_name, LENGTH(email) AS email_length
FROM customer;
```

Similarly, to calculate the average rental duration in days, use:

```
SELECT AVG(DATEDIFF(return_date, rental_date)) AS avg_rental_duration
FROM rental;
```

SQL functions enhance database queries by providing efficient ways to manipulate, format, and analyze data. These functions are essential for performing calculations, transforming text, and managing date-related data within relational databases.

Conclusion

In this chapter, we explored the fundamental aspects of querying databases using SQL, focusing on the practical applications of the SELECT statement and its associated clauses. The SELECT statement, a cornerstone of SQL, enables you to specify and retrieve relevant columns from a dataset, forming the basis for all data queries. Mastering its syntax is crucial for effective interaction with relational databases.

We explored how the WHERE clause filters data by applying specific conditions, empowering you to narrow down results to the most relevant information. The ORDER BY clause adds functionality by sorting data in ascending or descending order, making it easier to analyze trends and present organized results. Additionally, the LIMIT clause allows you to control the number of rows returned, enhancing performance and efficiency, particularly in large datasets or high-traffic environments.

When used together, these clauses provide powerful data retrieval and manipulation tools. The skills gained in this chapter build a foundation for more advanced SQL operations, ensuring you can write efficient, precise queries tailored to your data management needs.

In the next chapter, we will discuss string data in SQL, focusing on how to work effectively with textual information. You will learn about the various string data types supported by SQL and explore functions for manipulating and formatting strings. The chapter will equip you with the skills to handle text-based data efficiently, from extracting specific characters to splitting strings and pattern matching.

Exercises

In these exercises, we will explore the Sakila database to understand the data in the database and database structure.

Retrieve data from tables

In this exercise, we will gain practical experience retrieving data from tables about customers in the database:

- **Querying all the customers**: At the **sqlite>** command prompt, type the command to assess all the customers in the **customer** table:

```
.mode box
SELECT first_name, last_name, email, active
FROM customer;
```

  There are two commands here. The first statement, the **.mode box**, sets how SQLite 3 will display that data. All the data will be put in a box format in this case. This is done for formatting reasons and must only be run once. The second statement will select all the customers' first names, last names, and active statuses from the **customer** table.

- **Querying all the payments**: At the **sqlite>** command prompt, type the command to assess all the payments made by customers in the payment table:

```
SELECT payment_id, customer_id, rental_id, amount
FROM payment;
```

  The **SELECT** statement will select the **payment_id**, **customer_id**, **rental_id**, and **amount** from the payment tables. This will help us understand which customer bought which rental, and for what amount.

Using WHERE

In this exercise, we will expand the **customer** and **payment** table to identify data in the tables, specifically using the **WHERE** clause and **AND** operator:

- **Querying for a specific customer**: At the **sqlite>** command prompt, type the command to search the **customer** table and find the **customer_id** for the customer with the name *Bill Gavin*:

```
SELECT customer_id, first_name, last_name, email, active
FROM customer
WHERE first_name = 'BILL' AND last_name = 'GAVIN';
```

  In this **SELECT** statement's output, we need to identify the **customer_id** for *Bill Gavin* because we will use that ID, 457, in the next statement.

- **Querying for payments made by a specific customer**: At the **sqlite>** command prompt, type the command to search the **payment** table and find all the payments made by *Bill Gavin*, with a **customer_id** of 457:

```
SELECT payment_id, customer_id, amount
FROM payment
WHERE customer_id = 457;
```

Using ORDER BY and GROUP BY

In this exercise, we will sort and group data in the **customer** and **payment** tables to understand how **ORDER BY** and **GROUP BY** can be used to aggregate data in a table:

- **Querying the number of customers**: At the **sqlite>** command prompt, type the command to determine how many customers are registered with the company and group them based on active (1) or inactive (0):

```
SELECT active, COUNT(customer_id)
FROM customer GROUP BY active
ORDER BY active;
```

- **Querying the total sales for specific customers**: At the **sqlite>** command prompt, type the command to determine how many sales a specific customer has made:

```
SELECT COUNT(payment_id) as 'number_of_sales'
FROM payment where customer_id = 457;
```

Using LIMIT

In this exercise, we will use **LIMIT** to reduce the number of rows returned from a query:

- **Querying for details on the first five customers**: At the **sqlite>** command prompt, type the command to review the data for the first five customers in the customer table:

```
SELECT customer_id, first_name, last_name, email
FROM customer
LIMIT 5;
```

- **Querying for details of the first five customers with inactive status**: At the **sqlite>** command prompt, type the command to review the data for customers that are active:

```
SELECT customer_id, first_name, last_name, email
FROM customer
WHERE active = 0
LIMIT 5;
```

Using table joins

In this exercise, we will join the customer and payment tables to get detailed information about specific customers and their sales:

- **Querying to list detailed payment history for a customer:** At the **sqlite>** command prompt, type the command to join the customer and payment tables to retrieve the detailed history of a specific customer, *Bill Gavin:*

```
SELECT customer.*, payment.* FROM customer
INNER JOIN payment
ON customer.customer_id = payment.customer_id
WHERE customer.customer_id = 457;
```

In this query, we used **INNER JOIN** to join the **customer** and **payment** tables to list all the sales that were made by the customer *Bill Gavin* or **customer_id** 457.

- **Querying the total sales for a specific customer**: At the **sqlite>** command prompt, type the command to join the **customer** and **payment** tables to get the total sales for customer *Bill Gavin:*

```
SELECT first_name, last_name, SUM(amount) as 'sales'
FROM customer
INNER JOIN payment
ON customer.customer_id = payment.customer_id
WHERE customer.customer_id = 457;
```

- **Query the sales for a specific rental**: At the **sqlite>** command prompt, type the command to join the rental, payment, and customer tables to retrieve sales for rentals made by *Bill Gavin:*

```
SELECT rental.rental_id,
(SELECT amount FROM payment WHERE rental_id = rental.rental_id)
as 'amount'
FROM rental
INNER JOIN customer ON rental.customer_id = customer.customer_id
    WHERE customer.customer_id = 457;
```

In this query, we use an **INNER JOIN** on the customer and rental tables and a subquery to query the payment table for the amount paid by *Bill Gavin* for the rental.

CHAPTER 4
String Generation and Manipulation

Introduction

In this chapter, you will explore the power of string manipulation and generation in **Structured Query Language** (**SQL**). Strings are a fundamental data type in databases, often used for storing textual information such as names, addresses, and descriptions. You will learn how to work with string data types, use basic string functions, and extract or modify strings to meet various data processing needs. Additionally, this chapter will guide you through advanced string operations, such as pattern matching with the **LIKE** operator and formatting or splitting strings for more complex data requirements. By the end of this chapter, you will be equipped with essential skills to handle string data effectively in your SQL queries.

Structure

This chapter covers the following topics:

- Introduction to string data types
- Basic string functions
- Extracting and modifying strings
- Pattern matching with LIKE
- Formatting and splitting strings

Objectives

By the end of this chapter, you will be able to work proficiently with string data types in SQL, including generating and manipulating strings to suit various data processing tasks. You will understand how to use basic string functions to extract, modify, and format strings within your queries. You will also learn how to employ the **LIKE** operator for pattern matching, enabling you to filter and retrieve data based on specific string patterns. Additionally, you will gain skills through which you will learn how to split strings and handle more complex textual data efficiently. These capabilities will enhance your ability to manage and analyze textual information in SQL databases effectively.

Introduction to string data types

String data types are fundamental in any database management system, allowing you to store and manipulate textual information. In SQL, strings are sequences of characters representing anything from simple words and phrases to more complex data like **JavaScript Object Notation (JSON)**, **Extensible Markup Language** (XML), or even serialized objects. Understanding how to work with string data types is essential for anyone who needs to manage, retrieve, and process text-based information in a database.

In most SQL databases, the primary string data types include **CHAR**, **VARCHAR**, and **TEXT**. Each serves specific purposes depending on the nature of the data and the application's requirements. Choosing the appropriate string data type is critical for optimizing storage, ensuring data integrity, and improving query performance. Let us explore in detail the types of data strings.

CHAR data type

The **CHAR** data type is used to store fixed-length strings. Here are some characteristics of **CHAR** data type:

- When you define a column with a **CHAR** data type, you specify a fixed-length for the string, such as **CHAR(10)**.

- Every value stored in this column will occupy precisely ten characters. If a string is shorter than the specified length, the database pads it with spaces to meet the fixed-length. For example, storing the string **'ABC'** in a **CHAR(10)** column will be stored as **'ABC'** (with seven trailing spaces).

- The **CHAR** data type is beneficial when storing data consistently of the same length, such as country codes, postal codes, or specific identifiers.

VARCHAR data type

However, the fixed-length nature of **CHAR** can lead to inefficient storage if the data varies significantly. The **variable character** (**VARCHAR**) data type is often a better choice in such cases. Here are some characteristics of the **VARCHAR** data type:

- **VARCHAR** is designed to store strings of varying lengths up to a specified maximum. For example, **VARCHAR(255)** can store any string with up to 255 characters.

- Unlike **CHAR**, **VARCHAR** does not pad shorter strings with spaces, which means it only uses as much storage as necessary for the length of the string.

- This makes **VARCHAR** more efficient in terms of storage space, especially when dealing with strings of unpredictable or varying lengths, such as email addresses, names, or product descriptions.

- When using **VARCHAR**, one important consideration is the maximum length you define for the column. Although **VARCHAR** is flexible, setting an appropriate length is important to ensure that the column can accommodate the data while avoiding unnecessary overhead. For instance, if you expect names in a database to be no longer than 50 characters, defining the column as **VARCHAR(50)** is a practical choice. However, overestimating the length, such as setting it to **VARCHAR(1000)** when not needed, could lead to wasted memory and potential performance issues.

TEXT data type

In addition to **CHAR** and **VARCHAR**, most SQL databases also support a **TEXT** data type, which is used for storing very large amounts of text. Here are some characteristics of **TEXT** data type:

- Unlike **VARCHAR**, which has a specified maximum length, **TEXT** can store much larger strings, often up to several gigabytes, depending on the database system. This makes **TEXT** ideal for storing long documents, articles, or any unstructured data that does not have a predictable length.

  Note: **However, it is important to note that TEXT columns can be less efficient in terms of performance than VARCHAR, mainly when used in searches or sorting operations, because of their larger data size.**

- The **TEXT** data type in SQL stores large amounts of character data. Unlike the **CHAR** and **VARCHAR** data types, which limit the maximum number of characters they can store, the **TEXT** type can hold more extensive text content, making it ideal for storing paragraphs, long descriptions, or even entire articles.

- One key consideration when using the **TEXT** data type is that it is stored outside of the table row, with a pointer to the location of the actual data. This can impact performance if you frequently query these fields or use them in indexes.

- When working with **TEXT** data, it is crucial to understand the limitations and variations in different SQL databases. For example, in MySQL, **TEXT** can store up to 65,535 bytes of data (roughly 64 KB).

- For even larger text storage, MySQL offers **MEDIUMTEXT** and **LONGTEXT**. In PostgreSQL, the **TEXT** data type can store strings of any length, limited only by the maximum size of the database row. This knowledge empowers you to make informed decisions when designing your database.

Here is a basic example of how to use the **TEXT** data type in a table definition:

```
CREATE TABLE articles (
    article_id INT PRIMARY KEY,
    title VARCHAR(255) NOT NULL,
    content TEXT
);
```

In this example, the content column uses the **TEXT** data type to store potentially large articles. You can insert data into this column just like any other string type:

```
INSERT INTO articles (article_id, title, content)
VALUES (1, 'Introduction to SQL', 'SQL is a standard language for managing and manipulating databases...');
```

- While **TEXT** is useful for storing large amounts of text, it is important to be cautious when using it for frequent search operations.

- Unlike **CHAR** and **VARCHAR**, **TEXT** columns are typically not suitable for indexing due to their size, which can lead to performance issues.

- If you need to perform frequent searches or sorts on textual data, consider using **VARCHAR** with a length limit or utilize full-text indexing where supported. This awareness can help you avoid potential performance issues in your database.

Considerations with string data types

When working with string data types, it is also important to consider the character set and collation used by the database. A character set defines the encoding used to store the string data, such as UTF-8 or **American Standard Code for Information Interchange** (**ASCII**), while collation determines how strings are compared and sorted. For example, a collation can specify whether the comparison is case-sensitive or case-insensitive. Choosing the correct character set and collation is crucial for ensuring the database can store and process text in the desired language and format. Most modern databases support a variety of character sets and collations, allowing you to tailor the storage and comparison of string data to your specific needs.

In addition to basic storage, SQL provides a range of functions and operators for working with string data types. These include functions for concatenation, substring extraction, pattern matching, and case conversion, among others. Understanding these functions is critical to effectively managing and manipulating string data within your queries. For example, the **CONCAT** function allows you to join two or more strings together, while the

SUBSTRING function enables you to extract a portion of a string based on specified starting and ending positions.

Another important aspect of working with string data types is handling special characters and escaping sequences. In SQL, certain characters, such as single quotes ('), can have special meanings and must be properly escaped to be included in a string literal. For example, to include a single quote within a string, you would use two single quotes ('') like this:

```
SELECT 'It''s a great game, Sophia';
```

This query returns the string *it's a great game, Sophia* correctly interpreting the embedded single quote. Being aware of these nuances is essential for writing accurate and secure SQL queries, especially when dealing with user input or dynamically generated strings.

Understanding the basics of string data types is a foundational skill for anyone working with SQL. By choosing the appropriate data type, considering storage efficiency, and utilizing SQL's string functions effectively, you can manage text data in a practical and efficient way. Whether storing simple names and addresses or dealing with complex documents and metadata, mastering string data types will enable you to build robust and scalable database applications.

Basic string functions

Working with strings is essential to database management, and SQL provides a robust set of functions to handle various string operations. Whether manipulating text data, extracting specific information, or formatting output, SQL's string functions allow you to perform these tasks efficiently. Understanding these essential string functions is crucial for anyone who needs to manage textual data within a database.

CONCAT function

The **CONCAT** function is one of SQL's most used string functions. It is used to combine two or more strings into a single string. This function is handy when you need to merge different pieces of text, such as combining a first name and last name into a full name. Refer to the following example:

```
SELECT CONCAT(first_name, ' ', last_name) AS full_name
FROM staff;
```

In this example, as shown in *Figure 4.1*, the **CONCAT** function combines the **first_name** and **last_name** columns with a space between them, producing a **full_name** for each employee. The **CONCAT** function can handle multiple arguments, allowing you to combine several strings in a single operation.

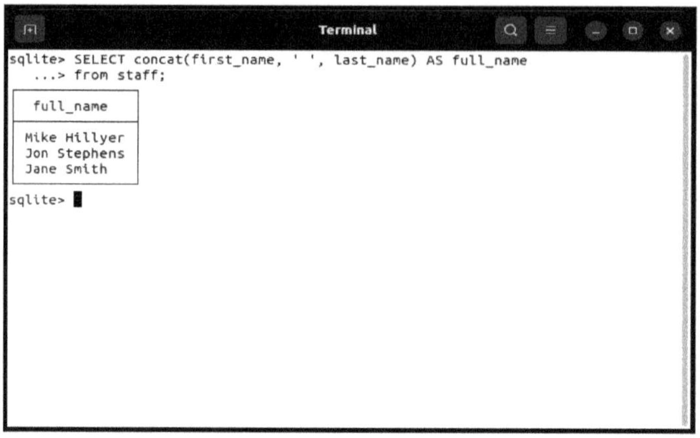

Figure 4.1: *Screenshot of CONCAT function*

SUBSTRING function

The **SUBSTRING** function extracts a portion of a string, starting from a specified position and continuing for a specified length. This function is proper when retrieving a specific string part, such as extracting an area code from a phone number or the domain from an email address. Refer to the following example:

SELECT SUBSTRING(email, 1, 5) AS first_five_email

FROM staff;

In this query shown in *Figure 4.2*, the **SUBSTRING** function extracts the first five characters from the email column, returning the **first_five_email**.

Let us break down the argument:

- The first argument specifies the string to be extracted
- The second is the starting position
- Third is the number of characters to extract

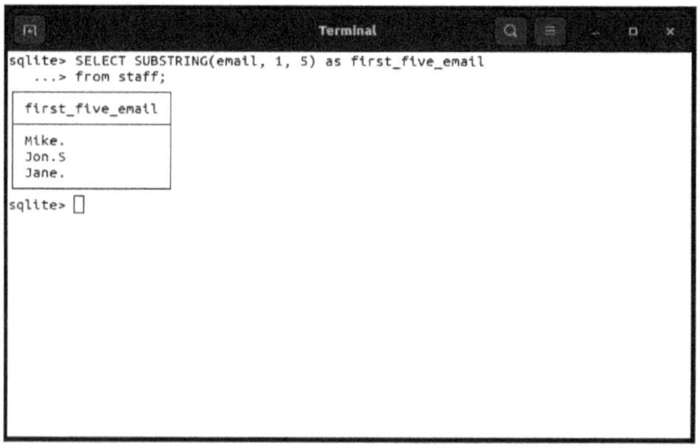

Figure 4.2: *Screenshot of SUBSTRING function*

LENGTH function

The **LENGTH** function returns the number of characters in a string, making it helpful in determining the size of text data. This function often enforces data validation rules, such as ensuring that a password meets minimum length requirements or that an input field does not exceed a specified length. Refer to the following example:

SELECT LENGTH(password) AS password_length

FROM staff;

As shown in *Figure 4.3*, the **LENGTH** function calculates the number of characters in each staff member's **password** column, providing the **password_length**. This information can identify passwords that are too short or too long, ensuring they meet security standards.

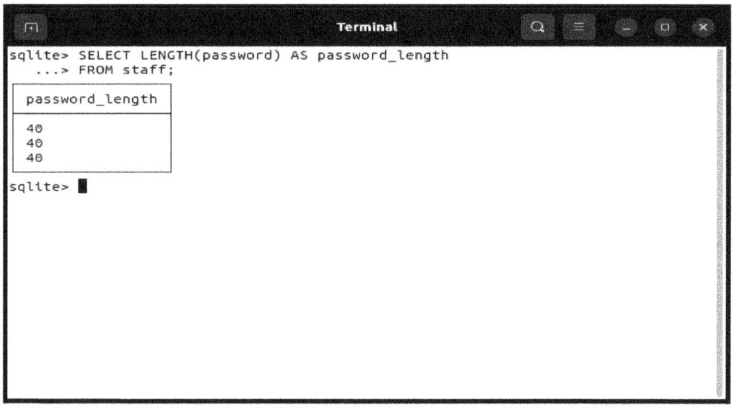

Figure 4.3: Screenshot of the LENGTH function

TRIM function

The **TRIM** function removes unwanted whitespace from the beginning and end of a string. This function is handy when dealing with user input, where extra spaces might be inadvertently included. By using **TRIM**, you can clean up text data, ensuring it is stored in a consistent format. Refer to the following example:

SELECT TRIM(first_name) AS trimmed_name

FROM staff;

In this example, as shown in *Figure 4.4*, the **TRIM** function removes leading and trailing spaces from the **first_name** column, resulting in **trimmed_name**:

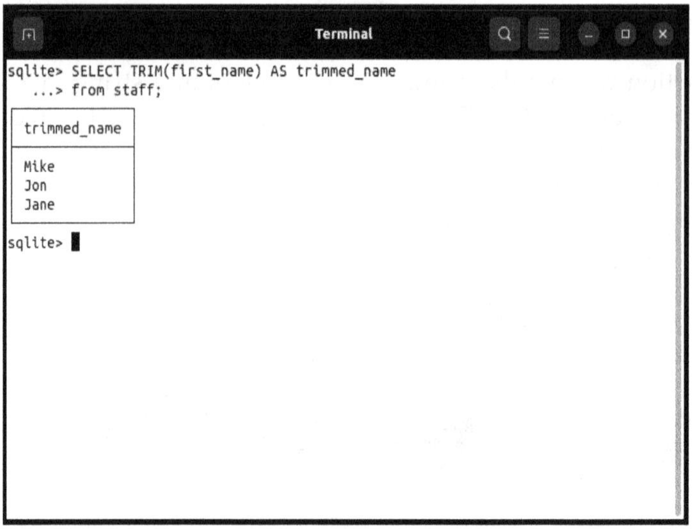

Figure 4.4: Screenshot of TRIM function

UPPER and LOWER functions

The **UPPER** and **LOWER** functions convert all characters in a string to uppercase or lowercase, respectively. These functions help standardize text data by converting all names to uppercase for consistent formatting or comparing strings case-insensitively. Refer to the following example:

```
SELECT UPPER(first_name) AS first_name_uppercase
FROM staff;
SELECT LOWER(first_name) AS first_name_lowercase
FROM staff;
```

Let us understand this function in detail:

- The **UPPER** function converts the **first_name** column to all uppercase letters in the first query, as shown in *Figure 4.5*.

- In contrast, the **LOWER** function converts the **first_name** column to all lowercase letters in the second query.

- These functions ensure that text data is treated consistently, regardless of how it was initially entered.

Refer to the following figure:

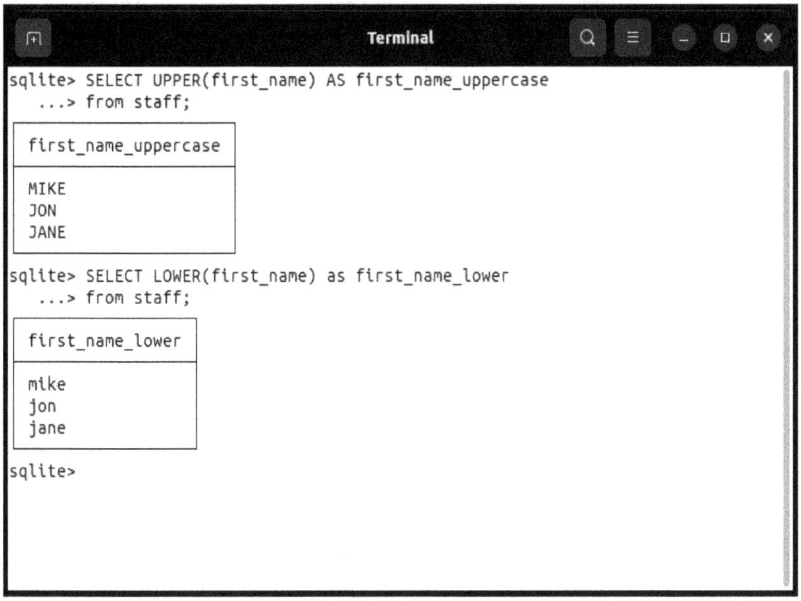

Figure 4.5: *Screenshot of UPPER and LOWER functions*

REPLACE function

The **REPLACE** function substitutes all occurrences of a specified substring within a string with a new substring. This function is handy for correcting data, such as replacing outdated terms or correcting common typos. Refer to the following example:

```
SELECT customer_id, REPLACE(active, '1', '0') AS active_status
FROM customer
WHERE customer_id = 1;
```

In this query, shown in *Figure 4.6*, the **REPLACE** function replaces all users in the active column from 1 to 0 (or active to inactive—this is not an **UPDATE**, just a **SELECT**), resulting in **all_status**.

Let us understand this function in detail:

- The first argument specifies the string to be searched
- The second argument specifies the substring to be replaced
- The third argument specifies the new substring to insert

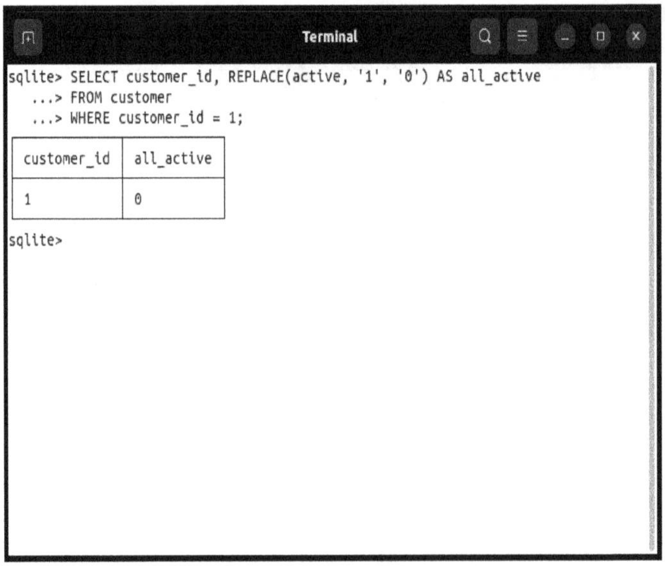

Figure 4.6: Screenshot of REPLACE function in SELECT statement

INSTR function

The **INSTR** function returns the position of the first occurrence of a specified substring within a string. This function helps locate specific characters or words within a text field, such as finding the position of the **@** symbol in an email address. Refer to the following example:

```
SELECT INSTR(email, '@') AS at_position
FROM staff;
```

Let us understand the preceding example:

- The **INSTR** function finds the position of the **@** symbol in the email column, returning at position.

- If the substring is not found, the function returns **0**. This function is beneficial when you need to validate or parse text data based on the presence of certain characters. Refer to the following figure:

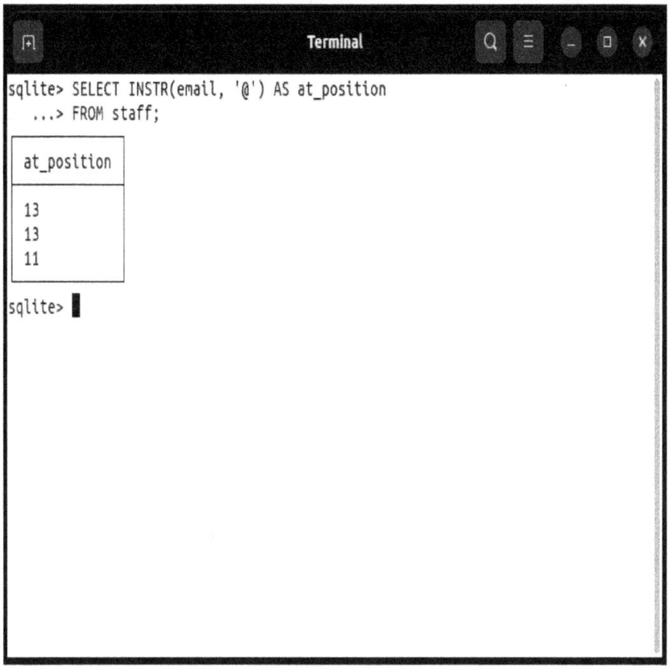

Figure 4.7*: Screenshot of INSTR function*

LPAD and RPAD functions

The **left pad** (**LPAD**) and **right pad** (**RPAD**) functions pad a string with a specified character to the left or right until the string reaches a certain length. These functions help format output, such as ensuring that all values in a column are the same length by adding leading or trailing spaces or zeros. Refer to the following example:

```
SELECT LPAD(rental_id, 10, '0') AS padded_rental_id
FROM rental;
SELECT RPAD(title, 20, '-') AS padded_title
FROM film;
```

Note: **LPAD and RPAD are common in other database systems. SQLite 3 does not support this function. It is important, however, to understand these functions with SQL.**

In this example:

- **In the first query:** The **LPAD** function pads the **rental_id** with leading zeros until it is ten characters long, resulting in **padded_rental_id**.

- **In the second query:** The **RPAD** function pads the title with trailing hyphens until it is twenty characters long, resulting in **padded_title**. These functions help ensure that text data is uniformly formatted, which can be important for reports, data exports, or user interfaces.

CONCAT_WS function

The **CONCAT_WS** function combines multiple strings into one, with a specified separator between each. This function is handy when creating a single string from multiple columns, with a consistent delimiter separating the values. Refer to the following example:

```
SELECT CONCAT_WS('/', username, password) AS username_password_combined
FROM staff;
```

Let us understand this query in detail:

- The **CONCAT_WS** function combines the email and password columns with a backslash as the separator, resulting in **username_password_combined**.

- Unlike the **CONCAT** function, **CONCAT_WS** allows you to specify a separator, making it more convenient when formatting strings that require consistent delimiters.

Extracting and modifying strings

In SQL, the ability to extract and modify strings is a crucial skill that allows you to manipulate text data within your database effectively. Whether you need to pull out specific information from a larger string, transform the text into a different format, or replace certain characters, SQL provides various functions designed to handle these tasks. Mastering these functions enables you to perform complex text processing directly within your queries, streamlining data management and analysis.

SUBSTRING function

SUBSTRING is one of the most commonly used functions for extracting portions of a string. The **SUBSTRING** function allows you to extract a specific segment of a string based on a starting position and a length. The basic syntax is straightforward. Refer to the following example:

```
SELECT first_name, SUBSTRING(last_name, 1, 1) AS last_name
FROM staff.02
```

Let us understand this query in detail:

- **SUBSTRING** starts at the first character of **last_name** and extracts only the first character, showing the first name and last initial of the staff member.

- This function is handy when dealing with data where different parts of the string represent distinct pieces of information, such as extracting area codes from phone numbers or domain names from email addresses.

LEFT and RIGHT functions

Another powerful function for string extraction is **LEFT** and its counterpart, **RIGHT**. These functions allow you to extract a specified number of characters from the beginning or end of a string. The **LEFT** function is useful when you need the initial characters of a string. Refer to the following example:

```
SELECT LEFT(last_name, 4) AS first_four_chars
FROM staff;
```

Let us understand this query in detail:

- Extracts the first four characters of **last_name**.

  Conversely, the **RIGHT** function works similarly but starts from the end of the string:

  ```
  SELECT RIGHT(last_name, 3) AS last_three_chars
  FROM staff;
  ```

Let us understand this query in detail:

- Returns the last three characters of **last_name**.

- These functions are convenient when you know the exact number of characters you need from the start or end of a string.

  Note: LEFT and RIGHT functions are common in other database systems. SQLite 3 does not support this function. It is important, however, to understand these functions with SQL.

CHARINDEX function

In other SQL dialects, the **CHARINDEX** function, sometimes known as **INSTR**, is another essential tool for working with strings. **CHARINDEX** returns the position of a specified substring within a string, allowing you to locate where a particular character or sequence of characters appears. This is especially useful when you need to dynamically determine the position of a substring before performing further operations:

```
SELECT CHARINDEX(' ', first_name) AS space_position
FROM staff;
```

Note: CHARINDEX function are common in other database systems. SQLite 3 does not support this function. It is important, however, to understand these functions with SQL.

Let us look at the preceding example in detail:

- **CHARINDEX** searches for the first occurrence of a space character in **first_name** and returns its position.

- Now, you can combine this position with **SUBSTRING** to dynamically extract the first or last name, depending on your needs.

REPLACE function

When modifying strings, SQL provides the `REPLACE` function, which allows you to substitute all occurrences of a specified substring within a string with a new substring. This is particularly useful for data cleansing tasks, such as correcting typos, standardizing formats, or removing unwanted characters. Refer to the following example:

```
SELECT REPLACE(phone_number, '-', '') AS cleaned_phone_number
FROM customer;
```

Let us understand this query in detail:

- `REPLACE` removes all hyphens from the **phone_number** column, resulting in a clean, uninterrupted string of digits.

- This versatile function can be applied to any situation where text needs to be standardized or cleaned up before further processing.

TRIM function

The `TRIM` function is another key tool for modifying strings, specifically for removing unwanted spaces from the beginning and end of a string. `TRIM` is particularly useful when dealing with user input, where extra spaces can be inadvertently included:

```
SELECT TRIM(last_name) AS trimmed_name
FROM staff;
```

Let us understand this query in detail:

- Removes any leading or trailing spaces from **last_name**, resulting in a clean, standardized string.

- Variations of `TRIM`, such as `LTRIM` and `RTRIM`, allow you to remove spaces specifically from a string's left or right side, providing additional flexibility in handling whitespace.

Pattern matching with LIKE

Pattern matching is a fundamental operation in SQL, and the `LIKE` operator is one of the most commonly used tools. The `LIKE` operator allows you to search for patterns within text fields, making it an essential feature for querying databases where you need to find data that matches a specific format or contains particular characters. By using `LIKE`, you can perform flexible and powerful searches beyond simple equality checks, enabling you to retrieve rows that meet complex criteria based on partial matches, wildcards, and patterns.

The basic syntax of the `LIKE` operator is as follows:

- Specifying a column, followed by the `LIKE` keyword, and then the pattern you want to match.

- Patterns can include literal characters and special wildcard characters that provide additional flexibility in your searches.
- The primary wildcard characters used with **LIKE** are the percent sign (%) and the underscore (_).

The percent sign (%) is a wildcard that matches zero or more characters in a string. For example, if you want to find all customers whose last name starts with Smith, you would use the following query:

```
SELECT * FROM customer
WHERE last_name LIKE 'Smith%';
```

Let us understand this query in detail:

- **LIKE 'Smith%'** tells SQL to search for any last name that begins with Smith and is followed by any additional characters.
- This could return results such as **Smithson**, **Smithers**, or simply **Smith**.
- The percent sign is particularly useful when you need to find data that shares a common prefix, suffix, or substring, but where the exact length and content of the text may vary.

Similarly, you can use the percent sign to find data that ends with a specific sequence of characters. For instance, if you want to find all email addresses that end with *gmail.com*, you would write the following code:

```
SELECT * FROM customer
WHERE email LIKE '%sakilacustomer.org';
```

Let us look at this example in detail:

- **LIKE '%sakilacustomer.org'** matches any email address that ends with **sakilacustomer.org**, regardless of what precedes it.
- This allows you to efficiently retrieve all rows that contain the desired domain, making it a valuable tool for filtering and organizing data.

The underscore (_) is another wildcard character used with **LIKE**, but it matches exactly one character. This is useful when finding data that matches a specific pattern with a fixed number of characters. For example, if you want to find all product codes that start with A and are followed by exactly three digits, you would use the following code:

```
SELECT * FROM film
WHERE title LIKE 'A___';
```

Let us understand this query in detail:

- **LIKE 'A___'** searches for film titles that start with *A* and have exactly three characters following it.

- The underscores act as placeholders for any single character, ensuring that only product codes with the desired format are returned.

- This approach is particularly useful when working with standardized codes, identifiers, or other data where the structure and length are important.

Combining the percent sign and underscore wildcards creates even more complex patterns. For instance, if you want to find all phone numbers that start with *555* and have exactly seven digits in total, you could use the following code:

```
SELECT * FROM customer
WHERE phone_number LIKE '555____';
```

Let us understand this query in detail:

- Searches for phone numbers that begin with *555* and have exactly four additional characters, ensuring that only valid numbers are retrieved.

- Mixing and matching wildcards allows you to tailor your searches to meet specific criteria, making **LIKE** an incredibly versatile tool for pattern matching.

It is also possible to use **LIKE** with other SQL clauses, such as **AND**, **OR**, and **NOT**, to create more complex queries. For example, if you want to find all customers whose last name starts with Smith but does not end with son, you could write the following code:

```
SELECT * FROM customer
WHERE last_name LIKE 'Smith%' AND last_name NOT LIKE '%son';
```

Let us understand this query in detail:

- Combines the **LIKE** and **NOT LIKE** operators to refine the search results, excluding any names that end with *son*.

- This flexibility allows you to craft precise queries that meet your requirements, whether filtering out unwanted data or zeroing in on specific patterns.

- One important consideration when using **LIKE** is that pattern matching can be case-sensitive or case-insensitive, depending on the database system and configuration.

- In some systems, **LIKE** is case-insensitive by default, meaning it treats Smith and smith as equivalent.

- In others, **LIKE** may be case-sensitive, requiring you to specify the exact case of the characters you are searching for.

Suppose you need to perform a case-insensitive search in a case-sensitive database. In that case, you can often use functions like **LOWER()** or **UPPER()** to normalize the text before applying the **LIKE** operator. Refer to the following example:

```
SELECT * FROM customer
WHERE LOWER(last_name) LIKE 'smith%';
```

Let us understand this query in detail:

- Converts all last names to lowercase before performing the pattern match, ensuring that names like **Smith**, **SMITH**, and **smith** are all included in the results.

- Understanding the case sensitivity of your database is essential for crafting effective **LIKE** queries and avoiding unexpected results.

Another consideration is performance. While **LIKE** is a powerful tool, it can be slower than exact match searches, especially when using wildcards like % at the beginning of a pattern. This is because the database must scan more data to find potential matches.

To optimize performance, you can limit the use of leading wildcards or consider using full-text search indexes if your database supports them. These indexes are designed to handle complex searches more efficiently, making them a good option for large datasets or frequent pattern matching queries.

Pattern matching with **LIKE** is an essential technique in SQL that enables you to perform flexible and efficient searches based on specific text patterns. By mastering the use of wildcards like the percent sign and underscore, you can craft powerful queries that retrieve exactly the data you need, even when the exact content of the text is unknown. Whether you are searching for partial matches, filtering data based on specific formats, or combining patterns to create complex search criteria, **LIKE** provides the tools to manage and analyze textual data within your database effectively.

Formatting and splitting strings

Working with strings is a common requirement in SQL, especially when dealing with data that needs to be formatted, parsed, or manipulated to meet specific needs. Formatting and splitting strings are essential techniques that allow you to control how text data is presented and how it can be broken down into meaningful components. Whether you are preparing data for display, extracting specific parts of a string, or restructuring data for further analysis, mastering these techniques is crucial for effective database management and query optimization.

Formatting strings in SQL typically involves:

- Using functions to modify the appearance of text data.

- These functions allow you to convert text to different cases, remove unwanted characters, or concatenate multiple strings into a single output.

- One of the most common string formatting operations is changing the case of text. SQL provides functions like **UPPER()** and **LOWER()** to convert strings to uppercase or lowercase, respectively.

For example, if you want to ensure that all email addresses are stored in lowercase to avoid case-sensitive issues, you would use the following code:

```
SELECT LOWER(email) AS formatted_email
FROM staff;
```

Let us understand this query in detail:

- Converts all email addresses in the staff table to lowercase, ensuring consistency across the dataset.

- Similarly, you can use the **UPPER()** function to convert text to uppercase, which is useful when standardizing data or ensuring that specific fields, such as codes or identifiers, are presented uniformly.

Another important aspect of formatting strings is concatenating multiple strings or columns into a single output. SQL provides the **CONCAT()** function, which allows you to combine two or more strings into one. For example, to create a full name by combining the **first_name** and **last_name** columns, you would use the following code:

```
SELECT CONCAT(first_name, ' ', last_name) AS full_name
FROM staff;
```

Let us understand this query in detail:

- **CONCAT()** merges the **first_name** and **last_name** columns with a space in between, producing a full name for each staff member.

- Concatenation is particularly useful when generating composite values from multiple fields, such as addresses, names, or custom identifiers.

Formatting can also involve removing unwanted characters or trimming whitespace from strings. SQL provides functions like **TRIM()**, **LTRIM()**, and **RTRIM()** to remove leading, trailing, or both leading and trailing spaces from a string. For example, if you have data that includes unnecessary spaces at the beginning or end of a string, you can clean it up using the following code:

```
SELECT TRIM(first_name) AS cleaned_name
FROM staff;
```

Let us understand this query in detail:

- Removes any extra spaces around the **first_name** field, ensuring the data is clean and ready for comparisons, searches, or display.

- Trimming is essential for maintaining data quality, especially when importing or processing data from external sources where inconsistent formatting may be an issue.

Splitting strings, however, involves breaking down a single string into multiple parts based on a specified delimiter. This operation is often necessary when dealing with data stored in a single field. However, it logically represents multiple pieces of information, such as a list of items, a comma-separated string, or a structured identifier. SQL provides various methods for splitting strings, depending on the database system and the complexity of the operation.

In many SQL databases, splitting strings can be achieved using functions like **SUBSTRING_ INDEX()** in MySQL or **STRING_SPLIT()** in SQL Server. For example, if you have a comma-separated list of tags in a tags column and you want to split them into individual tags, you can use the following code:

```
SELECT value AS tag
FROM STRING_SPLIT('SQL,Crash Course', ',');
```

In this query, **STRING_SPLIT()** takes a string with multiple values separated by commas and splits it into individual rows containing one tag. This approach is useful for transforming a list of values stored in a single field into a more normalized structure, making it easier to query, filter, and analyze the data.

In databases that do not have built-in functions for splitting strings, you can achieve similar results by combining functions like **SUBSTRING()** and **CHARINDEX()** to extract parts of a string based on a delimiter manually. For example, to extract the first part of a string before the first comma, you might use the following code:

```
SELECT SUBSTRING(special_features, 1, CHARINDEX(',', special_features) - 1)
AS special_features_tag
FROM film;
```

Let us understand this query in detail:

- Extracts the substring from the beginning of the **special_features** column to the first comma, effectively isolating the first tag in the list.

- While this method requires more effort and may be less efficient, it provides a flexible way to split strings when native functions are unavailable.

Another common scenario where splitting strings is useful is when dealing with structured identifiers, such as IP addresses, product codes, or hierarchical paths. For example, if you have a table that keeps track of the IP Address that a user comes from when renting a **Digital Versatile Disc** (**DVD**), and you want to extract the different components of an **Internet Protocol** (**IP**) address, you can split the string based on the periods that separate each octet, using the following code:

```
SELECT
    SUBSTRING_INDEX(ip_address, '.', 1) AS octet1,
    SUBSTRING_INDEX(SUBSTRING_INDEX(ip_address, '.', 2), '.', -1) AS
octet2,
    SUBSTRING_INDEX(SUBSTRING_INDEX(ip_address, '.', 3), '.', -1) AS
octet3,
    SUBSTRING_INDEX(ip_address, '.', -1) AS octet4
FROM customer_network_logs;
```

Let us understand this query in detail:

- Splits the IP address into its four components (octets), allowing you to analyze each part separately.

- This level of detail is often necessary when working with network data, product codes, or other structured identifiers where each string segment carries a specific meaning.

Combining formatting and splitting techniques can also be powerful, especially when preparing data for output or further processing. For example, if you need to reformat a phone number from a string containing only digits into a more readable format with dashes, you can use the following code:

```
SELECT
    CONCAT(
        SUBSTRING(phone_number, 1, 3), '-',
        SUBSTRING(phone_number, 4, 3), '-',
        SUBSTRING(phone_number, 7, 4)
    ) AS formatted_phone
FROM customer;
```

Let us understand this query in detail:

- **SUBSTRING()** extracts the different parts of the phone number, and **CONCAT()** combines them with dashes, producing a more user-friendly format like 123-456-7890.

- This type of formatting is essential for ensuring that data is human-readable and suitable for presentation or reporting.

Formatting and splitting strings are critical operations in SQL that enable you to effectively manipulate and present text data. By mastering these techniques, you can ensure that your data is clean, consistent, and ready for analysis or display, regardless of its original format. Whether preparing data for output, extracting specific components from a string, or transforming text into a more usable form, the ability to format and split strings gives you the flexibility and control needed to handle complex data scenarios in your SQL queries.

Conclusion

This chapter explored the foundational aspects of string manipulation and data retrieval in SQL. String data is one of the most prevalent forms of information in databases, making it vital for professionals to master storing, extracting, modifying, and limiting string data directly within their queries. These skills are critical for effectively managing and analyzing text-based data in relational databases.

We examined SQL string data types such as CHAR, VARCHAR, and TEXT. Each data type serves distinct purposes, from managing fixed-length strings to handling large and variable-length text entries. Selecting the correct string data type is vital to database design, as it directly influences storage efficiency and query performance. Ensuring the appropriate type aligns with the data needs optimizes your database's ability to store and retrieve text efficiently.

String extraction and modification were also covered, emphasizing their role in day-to-day database operations. Functions like SUBSTRING, LEFT, and RIGHT enable users to extract targeted portions of a string, such as isolating a first name or domain from a larger text field. Tools like CHARINDEX help locate specific sequences within strings, facilitating dynamic data manipulation. Additionally, functions like REPLACE allow for substituting text segments, while UPPER, LOWER, and TRIM ensure data standardization and cleanliness, which is critical for maintaining a reliable database.

Finally, we explored using the LIMIT clause to control the number of rows returned by queries, enabling efficient data handling in large datasets. When combined with ORDER BY, LIMIT creates precise queries, making working with subsets of relevant data easier. These tools empower you to manage string data precisely, making string manipulation a powerful asset in your SQL skillset.

In the next chapter, we will explore advanced data retrieval techniques that allow you to handle complex queries with precision and efficiency. You will learn how to join multiple tables to combine data, group information for insightful summaries, and utilize aggregate functions to perform calculations across datasets. Additionally, we will explore subqueries, enabling you to nest queries and extract highly specific data.

Exercises

In these exercises, we will explore the Sakila database to understand the data in the database and database structure.

Altering the customer table

In this exercise, we will alter the customer table to add two new columns, and add data to those columns by generating strings from the **first_name** and **last_name** columns:

- **Altering the customer table**: At the **sqlite>** command prompt, type the command to alter the customer table and add the columns **full_name** and **phone_number**:

```
ALTER TABLE customer
ADD full_name VARCHAR(100);
ALTER TABLE customer
ADD phone_number VARCHAR(12);
```

  In these two **ALTER TABLE** statements, we are modifying the customer table to add the columns for **full_name** and **phone_number**.

Populating the customer table

In this exercise, we will populate the customer table with data:

- First, we will populate the **full_name** column based on the **first_name** and **last_name** column.

- Second, we will populate the **phone_number** column with synthetic data (random numbers).

- **Populate the full_name column:** Here, we will use the **CONCAT** function to update the **full_name** column with the first and last name of the customer. At the **sqlite>** command prompt, type the command to combine **UPDATE** and subqueries to populate the column. Refer to the following example:

```
UPDATE customer
  SET full_name = (
  SELECT CONCAT(cust.first_name, ' ', cust.last_name)
  FROM customer cust
  WHERE customer.customer_id = cust.customer_id
  );
```

  With this command, we are updating the customer table's **full_name** column based on a subquery that concatenates the **first_name** and **last_name** columns.

- **Populate the phone_number column**: At the **sqlite>** command prompt, type the command to use the **SUBSTRING** function to get the first three and four numbers based on numeric values generated by the **RANDOM** function:

```
UPDATE customer
SET phone_number = '555' || SUBSTRING(RANDOM(),2,3) ||
SUBSTRING(RANDOM(),2,4);
```

  The **UPDATE** command will update the **phone_number** column with random numbers based on the **RANDOM** function. The **SUBSTRING** function will start at position two of the random number generated and return three or four numbers, respectively, and prefixing 555 as the area code.

Extracting information and displaying data from the customer table

In this exercise, we extract information and display the data from the customer table:

- **Extracting information from the customer table**: At the **sqlite>** command prompt, type the command to extract the **phone_number** column, and add hyphens to the number. Refer to the following example:

```
SELECT full_name,
```

```
CONCAT(
SUBSTRING(phone_number, 1, 3), '-',
SUBSTRING(phone_number, 4, 3), '-',
SUBSTRING(phone_number, 7, 4)
) AS formatted_phone
        FROM customer
LIMIT 10;
```

The **SELECT** statement will extract the **full_name** column and the **phone_number** column in the format of 555-111-2222. We will use the **LIMIT** function to display only ten results in the query.

Displaying the first name and last name in uppercase

In this exercise, we will use the **UPPER** and **LOWER** functions to display information in a desired format:

- **Displaying information from the customer table**: At the **sqlite>** command prompt, type the command to display the **first_name**, **full_name**, and **last_name** column in **UPPER** and **LOWER** case:

  ```
  SELECT UPPER(first_name), LOWER(last_name), UPPER(full_name)
  ```

  ```
  FROM customer;
  ```

  This **SELECT** statement uses the **UPPER** function on **first_name** and **full_name** to display the text in uppercase. In addition, the **LOWER** function is used to display the **last_name** column in lower case.

Join our Discord space

Join our Discord workspace for latest updates, offers, tech happenings around the world, new releases, and sessions with the authors:

https://discord.bpbonline.com

Advanced Data Retrieval

Introduction

In this chapter, we will explore advanced SQL techniques for retrieving, filtering, and managing data effectively. We will begin by learning how to use aliases to rename columns and tables, which enhances query readability and organization. Next, we will eliminate duplicate rows using the **DISTINCT** keyword, a critical tool for ensuring your results reflect unique data. You will also work with the **GROUP BY** clause and aggregate functions to summarize data, then learn how to write and use subqueries for more complex operations. Towards the end of the chapter, we will learn to handle NULL values, which will enable us to query correctly and manage missing or incomplete data. By the conclusion of this chapter, you will gain the required skills to solve more complex data retrieval tasks with confidence and precision.

Structure

This chapter covers the following topics:

- Using aliases to rename columns and tables
- Eliminating duplicate rows with DISTINCT
- Grouping data with GROUP BY
- Aggregate functions

- Subqueries and nested queries
- Handling NULL values in queries

Objectives

By the end of this chapter, you will be able to apply advanced SQL techniques to retrieve, organize, and manipulate data efficiently. You will understand how to use aliases to rename columns and tables, improving the readability of complex queries. You will also master using the **DISTINCT** keyword to eliminate duplicate rows, ensuring your query results display unique data. In addition, you will learn how to group data using the **GROUP BY** clause and apply aggregate functions to summarize large datasets. You will also learn to write and use subqueries to perform more dynamic and layered queries. Finally, you will develop a deep understanding of handling NULL values, ensuring that your queries account for missing or incomplete data. These techniques will equip you to manage advanced data retrieval challenges accurately and efficiently.

Using aliases to rename columns and tables

Aliases in SQL are temporary names given to columns or tables for the duration of a query. They are not permanent changes to the database structure but make your queries more readable, especially when dealing with complex or lengthy column names or when joining multiple tables. Aliases help you simplify the presentation of results and improve clarity in cases where you have to refer to columns or tables multiple times within the same query.

Using aliases for columns

Column aliases are frequently used to make query results more understandable or user-friendly, particularly when the original column names are long or need to be more intuitive. By assigning an alias to a column, you can rename the column header in the output of your query without affecting the actual structure of the table.

Use the **AS** keyword to create an alias for a column. For example, let us take the **customer** table **first_name**, and you want to make the result more readable by renaming it to just **First Name**, you would write the following code:

```
SELECT first_name AS "First Name", last_name AS "Last Name"
FROM customer;
```

In this query, the **AS First Name** and **AS Last Name** statements create aliases for the **first_name** and **last_name** columns, respectively. When the query runs, the output will display **First Name** and **Last Name** as the headers instead of the original column names.

It is important to note that column aliases are handy when using aggregate functions like **SUM()**, **COUNT()**, or **AVG()**. For instance, consider a query that calculates the total payments from the **payment** table:

```
SELECT SUM(amount) AS "Total Amount"
FROM payment;
```

Without the alias **AS Total Amount**, the result might display the original column name or the function itself as the header, which can be unclear. By assigning a meaningful alias, the output is easier to understand.

Using aliases for tables

Just as you can assign aliases to columns, you can also create aliases for tables in SQL queries. Table aliases are especially helpful when working with multiple tables in joins, subqueries, or other complex operations. Assigning short, descriptive aliases to tables reduces the amount of typing required and improves the readability of your query.

To create a table alias, you write the table name followed by a short alias. For example, consider the following query that selects data from two tables, **customer**, and **payment**, using aliases:

```
SELECT c.first_name as 'First Name', p.amount 'Amount'
FROM customer c
INNER JOIN payment p
ON c.customer_id = p.customer_id;
```

In this example, the **customer** table is aliased as c, and the **payment** table is aliased as p. The aliases allow you to refer to the tables using shorter names, particularly useful when working with large queries or when table names are long. Additionally, aliases can make the query more straightforward to understand, especially when there are multiple joins.

It is also essential to know that when using table aliases, you can still access columns from the table by prefixing the column name with the alias, as shown in the previous example (**c.first_name** and **p.amount**).

Aliases in self-joins

Aliases are especially useful when performing self-joins, where a table is joined with itself. Without aliases, self-joins would be cumbersome and difficult to read because it would be unclear which version of the table each column belongs to. Let us take an example of a self-join using the **staff** table, where you want to find all staff members who work in the same store as a specific staff member:

```
SELECT
s1.first_name AS "Employee",
```

```
s2.first_name as "Colleague", s1.store_id
FROM staff AS s1
JOIN staff AS s2
ON s1.store_id = s2.store_id
WHERE s1.staff_id <> s2.staff_id;
```

In this query, the **staff** table is aliased as **s1** and **s2**, allowing the query to refer to the same table twice, once as **s1** and once as **s2**. The aliases clarify which instance of the table each column belongs to and make the self-join possible. As a result, you will see staff members listed alongside their colleagues from the same store.

Best practices for using aliases

While aliases can simplify your queries, it is important to use them wisely. When assigning aliases, ensure that they are meaningful and help convey the purpose of the query. For example, using s for staff and c for customers is a good practice because the aliases can easily relate to the original table names. On the other hand, using non-descriptive aliases like a or b might make the query harder to follow, especially when revisiting or sharing the code with others.

Consider maintaining a consistent naming convention when you use aliases for multiple tables or columns in the same query. For instance, if your query involves two different tables representing similar data (e.g., **payment_2024** and **payment_2025**), you can use them as o2024 and o2025 for clarity.

Aliases are also particularly useful when working with subqueries. In a subquery, you may need to refer to columns or tables from the outer query, and aliases can make this much simpler and more readable. For instance, consider the following query where we want to get all payments that exceed the average for each customer, along with the total count of payments exceeding the average:

```
SELECT c.customer_id, p1.amount, COUNT(p1.amount)
FROM customer AS c
INNER JOIN payment AS p1 ON c.customer_id = p1.customer_id
WHERE amount >
        (SELECT AVG(amount)
         FROM payment p2
         WHERE p2.customer_id = p1.customer_id)
GROUP BY c.customer_id;
```

In this query, the outer **payment** table is aliased as p1, while the subquery also aliases the **payment** table as p2. Without these aliases, the query would be much harder to follow, especially when referring to the same table multiple times in different contexts.

Aliases in SQL, whether for columns or tables, are powerful tools for improving your queries' clarity, simplicity, and readability. They allow you to give meaningful names to result sets and help make complex queries more understandable. By effectively using aliases, you can make your SQL code cleaner, more maintainable, and easier to work with, especially when dealing with large datasets or complex database structures.

Eliminating duplicate rows with DISTINCT

In SQL, the **DISTINCT** keyword is a powerful tool for eliminating duplicate rows from the results of a query. By default, when you execute a query that retrieves data from a table, it may return multiple identical rows if the same data appears more than once. This can occur frequently in databases with redundant information or where data from different tables is combined. The **DISTINCT** keyword allows you to remove duplicate rows and return only unique results, making your queries more efficient and your results more accurate.

Using DISTINCT with a single column

The simplest use of **DISTINCT** is with a single column. When applied, it ensures that only unique values from that column are returned, even if other columns in the table contain duplicate information. For example, consider our **film** table, which shows multiple films that might have the same rating. If you want to retrieve a list of all unique ratings for films, you would use **DISTINCT** on the rating column. Refer to the following code:

```
SELECT DISTINCT rating

FROM film;
```

In this query, the **DISTINCT** keyword ensures that only one rating instance is returned. This simple application of **DISTINCT** is useful for summarizing data and eliminating unnecessary duplicates in the result set.

Using DISTINCT with multiple columns

You can also use **DISTINCT** with multiple columns to remove duplicates based on the combination of values across those columns. In this case, **DISTINCT** will treat each combination of values in the specified columns as a unique entry. This is the appropriate approach if you only want to eliminate duplicates where all specified columns have the same values.

For example, in our **film** table with columns for **rating** and **special_features**, you might want to retrieve a list of unique ratings with a combined special feature. The query would look like the following:

```
SELECT DISTINCT rating, special_features

FROM film;
```

Here, **DISTINCT** will ensure that only unique combinations of **rating** and **special_feature** are returned. If two films have the same rating but different special features, both rows will appear in the result set. However, if multiple ratings have the same special feature, only one row for that rating-special_feature pair will be returned. This use of **DISTINCT** is helpful when you need to group or summarize data across multiple dimensions.

Performance considerations for DISTINCT

While **DISTINCT** is useful for removing duplicates, it is important to understand its impact on query performance. When **DISTINCT** is used, the database must examine each row in the result set and compare it to the others to identify duplicates. This process can be computationally expensive, especially when dealing with large datasets or complex queries.

For example, in a query that retrieves data from multiple tables using joins, adding **DISTINCT** can significantly increase the processing time because the database has to retrieve and combine data and eliminate duplicates. To ensure optimal performance, it is a good practice to apply **DISTINCT** only when necessary. In some cases, improving the structure of your query, using indexing, or filtering the data more effectively can reduce the need for **DISTINCT**.

Additionally, if you are working with a large dataset and need to apply **DISTINCT**, consider whether the dataset can be filtered or aggregated before using **DISTINCT** to minimize the number of rows the database must process. For example, applying a **WHERE** clause to filter the data before using **DISTINCT** can improve performance if you only need distinct values from a subset of your data.

Combining DISTINCT with aggregate functions

Another common scenario where **DISTINCT** is used is in combination with aggregate functions such as **COUNT()**, **SUM()**, **AVG()**, or **MAX()**. By using **DISTINCT** within an aggregate function, you can ensure that only unique values are included in the calculation. For instance, if you want to count the number of unique ratings in the **film** table, you can use the following query:

```
SELECT COUNT(DISTINCT rating)
FROM film;
```

In this query, **COUNT(DISTINCT rating)** ensures that only distinct ratings are counted. Without **DISTINCT**, the **COUNT()** function would count every row, including those with duplicate rating values. This combination is useful when calculating metrics based on unique values rather than the total number of rows.

Similarly, **DISTINCT** can be used with other aggregate functions like **SUM()** to ensure that only distinct values are included in the calculation. For example, if you want to calculate the total sales from unique payments (where duplicate payments might exist due to data entry errors), you could write the following code:

```
SELECT SUM(DISTINCT amount) AS total_unique_amount
FROM payment;
```

Here, **SUM(DISTINCT order_total)** ensures that duplicate order totals are not included in the calculation, giving you a more accurate total sales figure.

DISTINCT with JOIN operations

DISTINCT is often used in queries that involve **JOIN** operations, where multiple tables are combined, and duplicate rows might be generated. When joining tables, it is common for a query to return multiple rows with identical values if the same data appears in both tables being joined. **DISTINCT** can help eliminate these duplicates and return a cleaner result set.

Consider the scenario for our two tables: **staff** and **store**. Suppose you want to retrieve a list of unique store IDs where staff work. In that case, a **JOIN** query might return multiple rows for the same store if multiple staff belong to that store. In this case, you would use **DISTINCT** to eliminate the duplicate store names. Refer to the following code:

```
SELECT DISTINCT staff.store_id
FROM staff
JOIN store ON staff.store_id = store.store_id;
```

Without **DISTINCT**, the query might return multiple rows for each store, depending on how many staff members belong to each one. By using **DISTINCT**, you ensure that only unique store names are included in the result, regardless of how many staff members work in each store.

Limitations of DISTINCT

While **DISTINCT** is a powerful tool, it has limitations. One key limitation is that **DISTINCT** applies to the entire row in the result set, meaning that it eliminates rows only if all specified columns contain the same values. This means that if even one column in a row contains a different value, **DISTINCT** will treat it as a unique row and not remove it as a duplicate.

For instance, if you use **DISTINCT** on two columns, city and state, and two rows have the same city but different state values, both rows will be returned, even though the city values are the same. In such cases, if you only want to eliminate duplicates based on one column (e.g., city), you would need to adjust your query or use additional filtering techniques.

Another limitation is that **DISTINCT** does not allow you to specify which duplicate row to keep. For example, if multiple rows have the same values in the columns you are filtering by, **DISTINCT** does not provide a way to select which row to keep based on another condition, such as the most recent date or the highest value. To achieve this level of control, you would need to use other SQL techniques, such as **ROW_NUMBER()** or **RANK()** functions, which can be combined with **DISTINCT** for more advanced queries.

Practical use cases for DISTINCT

You will find **DISTINCT** useful in your SQL queries in many practical situations. Some common use cases include generating reports where duplicate data is unnecessary, cleaning up data that contains redundancy, or summarizing data across multiple tables. For example, in a sales report, you might use **DISTINCT** to list all the unique products sold within a certain period, ensuring that each product is listed only once, even if it was sold multiple times.

Additionally, **DISTINCT** can be used when importing data from external sources where duplicates may exist or when merging data from different systems. By applying **DISTINCT**, you can ensure that your final result set contains only the unique records you need, which is particularly important for data accuracy and consistency.

Ultimately, **DISTINCT** is an essential part of SQL that allows you to refine your query results, eliminate redundancy, and focus on the unique data that matters most to your analysis.

Grouping data with GROUP BY

The **GROUP BY** clause in SQL is a powerful tool for grouping rows with the same values in specified columns into summary rows, such as aggregating data into totals, averages, counts, or other summary metrics. This capability is essential for analyzing data and generating meaningful reports from large datasets. By mastering the **GROUP BY** clause, you can transform raw data into valuable insights, making it easier to understand trends, compare groups, and identify patterns within your database.

The basic syntax of the **GROUP BY** clause involves adding it to a **SELECT** statement along with an aggregate function, such as **COUNT**, **SUM**, **AVG**, **MAX**, or **MIN**. These functions calculate the grouped data and return a single result for each group. For example, if you want to find out how many rentals each customer has placed, you would write the following code:

```
SELECT customer_id, COUNT(rental_id) AS rental_count
FROM rental
GROUP BY customer_id;
```

In this query, the **GROUP BY** clause groups the rows in the **rental** table by **customer_id**, and the **COUNT** function counts the number of rentals for each customer. The result is a list of customers and the number of rentals they have placed. This approach is invaluable when generating reports or summaries requiring aggregated data based on specific criteria.

Another common use of the **GROUP BY** clause is calculating each group's total or average values. For instance, to calculate the total sales for each rental, you could use the **SUM** function:

```
SELECT rental_id, SUM(amount) as total_sales

FROM payment

GROUP BY rental_id;
```

Here, the **GROUP BY** clause groups the rows by **rental_id**, and the **SUM** function calculates the total sales for each rental. The resulting data provides a clear picture of how each rental performs in terms of sales, allowing you to make informed decisions about inventory, pricing, and marketing strategies.

You can also use the **AVG** function to find the average value within each group. For example, to determine the average order value for each customer, you might write the following code:

```
SELECT customer_id, AVG(amount) as avg_sales
FROM payment
GROUP BY rental_id;
```

This query groups the rentals by **customer_id** and then calculates the average order value for each customer. This type of analysis helps understand customer behavior, identify high-value customers, and tailor marketing efforts to different segments of your customer base.

The **GROUP BY** clause is not limited to grouping by a single column. You can group by multiple columns to create more granular summaries. For instance, if you want to find out the total sales by inventory and by staff, you could group by both **inventory_id** and **staff_id**:

```
SELECT
r.inventory_id,
p.staff_id,
SUM(amount) as total_sales
FROM payment AS p
INNER JOIN rental AS r
ON p.rental_id = r.rental_id
GROUP BY r.inventory_id, p.staff_id;
```

In this query, the data is grouped first by **inventory_id** and then by **staff_id**, resulting in a summary of total sales for each inventory item by staff. This allows you to analyze sales performance across different markets and identify regional trends requiring different strategies.

One important consideration when using the **GROUP BY** clause is the **HAVING** clause, which allows you to filter groups based on the results of aggregate functions. While the **WHERE** clause filters rows before they are grouped, the **HAVING** clause filters groups after the aggregation has been performed. For example, if you want to find customers who have placed more than five rentals, you could use:

```
SELECT customer_id, COUNT(rental_id) AS rental_count
FROM rental
GROUP BY customer_id
HAVING COUNT(rental_id) > 5;
```

In this query, the **HAVING** clause filters the groups to include only those customers with more than five rentals. This is particularly useful for identifying significant patterns or outliers within your data, such as top-performing product regions or customers with unusually high or low activity.

Another key aspect of using the **GROUP BY** clause is understanding how it interacts with non-aggregated columns in the **SELECT** statement. When you group by one or more columns, any columns in the **SELECT** list that are not part of an aggregate function must be included in the **GROUP BY** clause. This ensures that the query produces valid and meaningful results. For example, refer to the following code:

```
SELECT customer_id, inventory_id, COUNT(rental_id) AS rental_count

FROM rental

GROUP BY customer_id, inventory_id;
```

Here, both **customer_id** and **inventory_id** are included in the **GROUP BY** clause because they are listed in the **SELECT** statement without being part of an aggregate function. This query counts the rentals for each customer's inventory, providing detailed insights into customer purchasing patterns.

It is also important to note that the **GROUP BY** clause can significantly impact query performance, especially when working with large datasets. Grouping requires the database to process and organize large amounts of data, which can be resource-intensive. To optimize performance, consider indexing the columns used in the **GROUP BY** clause, as this can speed up the grouping process and reduce the query execution time.

The **GROUP BY** clause is an essential tool for anyone working with SQL, providing the ability to aggregate and summarize data meaningfully. Whether you are calculating totals, averages, counts, or other metrics, **GROUP BY** allows you to extract valuable insights from your data. By mastering this clause and understanding how to use it effectively, you can transform raw data into actionable information, supporting decision-making processes and driving business success.

Aggregate functions

Aggregate functions are essential tools in SQL that allow you to perform calculations on multiple rows of data and return a single result. These functions are widely used for summarizing, analyzing, and reporting data, making them invaluable for any database professional. By applying aggregate functions, you can quickly gain insights into your data, such as totals, averages, counts, and other statistical measures, all within the context of a single query.

COUNT aggregate function

One of the most used aggregate functions is **COUNT**, which counts the number of rows that match a specified condition. This function is handy when determining the number of entries in a table, the number of NOT NULL values in a column, or the number of unique entries. For example, to count the total number of rentals in a table, you would use the following code:

```
SELECT COUNT(*) AS total_rental
FROM rental;
```

In this query, **COUNT(*)** returns the total number of rows in the **rental** table. The asterisk (*) indicates that every row should be counted, regardless of whether it contains NULL values. If you want to count only the NOT NULL values in a specific column, you can specify the column name:

```
SELECT COUNT(rental_id) AS total_rentals
FROM rental;
```

This query counts only the rows where **rental_id** is not NULL, providing a more accurate count if some rows have NULL values in the **rental_id** column.

SUM aggregate function

Another powerful aggregate function is **SUM**, which adds up the values in a specified numeric column. This function is commonly used in financial and business applications to calculate totals, such as total sales, revenue, or expenses. For instance, to calculate the total sales amount from the **payment** table, you would write the following code:

```
SELECT SUM(amount) AS total_sales
FROM payment;
```

Here, **SUM(amount)** returns the sum of all values in the **amount** column, giving you the total sales figure. The **SUM** function is versatile and can be combined with other SQL clauses, such as **GROUP BY**, to calculate totals for specific groups or categories.

AVG aggregate function

The **AVG** function calculates the average value of a numeric column. This function is handy when you need to determine the central tendency of a dataset, such as the average order value, average salary, or average score. For example, to find the average payment amount in the **payment** table, you would use the following code:

```
SELECT AVG(amount) AS average_payment

FROM payment;
```

In this query, **AVG(amount)** calculates the average value of the **amount** column. The AVG function is especially helpful in identifying trends and making comparisons across different groups or time periods.

MIN and MAX aggregate functions

The **MIN** and **MAX** functions find a column's minimum and maximum values, respectively. These functions are essential for identifying the range of values in a dataset, such as the lowest and highest prices, the earliest and latest dates, or the smallest and largest quantities. For example, to find the lowest and highest payment amounts in the **payment** table, you would write:

```
SELECT MIN(amount) AS smallest_payment, MAX(amount) AS largest_payment

FROM payment;
```

This query returns the smallest and largest values in the **amount** column, providing insight into the dataset's payment amount range. Depending on your analysis needs, the **MIN** and **MAX** functions can be used independently or together.

COUNT DISTINCT aggregate function

Another useful aggregate function is **COUNT(DISTINCT   column_name)**, which counts the number of unique values in a column. This function is particularly valuable when determining the number of distinct entries, such as unique customers, products, or categories. For example, to count the number of unique customers in the **payment** table, you would use the following code:

```
SELECT COUNT(DISTINCT customer_id) AS unique_customers

FROM payment;
```

In this query, **COUNT(DISTINCT customer_id)** returns the number of distinct **customer_id** values, giving you the total number of unique customers who have made payments.

Aggregate functions and GROUP BY

Aggregate functions can also be combined with the **GROUP BY** clause to perform calculations on specific data groups. For instance, to calculate the total sales for each rental in the **payment** table by customer, you would use the following code:

```
SELECT rental_id, SUM(amount) AS total_sales
FROM payment
GROUP BY rental_id;
```

In this query, **GROUP BY** groups the rows by **rental_id**, and **SUM(amount)** calculates the total sales for each rental. The result is a list of rentals with their corresponding total sales, allowing you to compare the performance of different products.

Understanding and effectively using aggregate functions is essential for anyone working with SQL. These functions allow you to summarize large datasets, perform calculations, and generate insights crucial for decision-making and reporting. Whether counting rows, calculating totals, finding averages, or identifying extremes, aggregate functions provide the tools to analyze and interpret your data precisely and clearly.

Subqueries and nested queries

Subqueries, also known as nested queries, are a powerful feature in SQL that allows you to embed one query within another. This technique is essential when performing operations requiring intermediate results, enabling you to break down complex tasks into more manageable parts. Subqueries can be used in various clauses such as **SELECT**, **FROM**, **WHERE**, and **HAVING**, making them incredibly versatile in solving various database challenges.

One of the most common uses of subqueries is within the **WHERE** clause. This type of subquery allows you to filter results based on a secondary query that provides a condition for the main query. For example, if you want to find all customers who have placed an order with an amount greater than the average order amount, you can use a subquery in the **WHERE** clause. Refer to the following example:

```
SELECT
customer_id,
amount
FROM payment
WHERE amount > (SELECT AVG(amount) FROM payment);
```

In this query, the subquery **(SELECT AVG(amount) FROM payment)** calculates the average payment amount. The main query retrieves all rows from the **payment** table where the **amount** is more significant than this average. Subqueries like this are invaluable for comparing values within a table and filtering data based on aggregate conditions.

Subqueries can also be used in the **SELECT** clause to calculate values dynamically for each row in the result set. For instance, if you want to retrieve all orders along with the total sales for the corresponding customer, you can use a subquery in the **SELECT** clause. Refer to the following example:

```
SELECT rental_id,
       amount,
       (SELECT SUM(amount)
        FROM payment p2
```

```
        WHERE p2.customer_id = p1.customer_id) AS total_sales
FROM payment p1;
```

In this query, the subquery calculates the total sales for each customer by summing the amount for all payments placed by that customer. The result is a list of payments, each with the corresponding total sales for the customer who placed the order. This approach is particularly useful when generating reports that combine detailed transaction data with summary statistics.

Another powerful application of subqueries is in the **FROM** clause, where the subquery acts as a virtual table. This is often used when you need to join the results of a complex query with another table or further refine the data before performing additional operations. For example, to find the top-performing rentals by sales, you could use a subquery to calculate total sales for each rental and then join this result with the payment details using the following code:

```
SELECT r.rental_id, sales_data.total_sales
FROM rental r
JOIN (SELECT rental_id, SUM(amount) AS total_sales
    FROM payment
    GROUP BY rental_id) AS sales_data
ON r.rental_id = sales_data.rental_id
ORDER BY sales_data.total_sales DESC;
```

In this example, the subquery **(SELECT rental_id, SUM(amount) AS total_sales FROM payment GROUP BY rental_id)** calculates the total sales for each rental. The main query then joins this result with the **rental** table to retrieve the rental IDs and their corresponding total sales, ordered by the highest sales first. Using subqueries in the **FROM** clause allows you to organize and simplify complex queries, making them easier to understand and maintain.

Subqueries can also be employed in the **HAVING** clause to filter groups based on aggregate results. For example, suppose you want to find all rentals that have generated more revenue than a certain threshold. In that case, you can use a subquery to calculate the total revenue for each rental and then apply a filter. Refer to the following code for a better understanding:

```
SELECT rental_id, SUM(amount) AS total_revenue
FROM payment
GROUP BY rental_id
HAVING SUM(amount) > (SELECT AVG(total_revenue)
FROM (SELECT rental_id, SUM(amount) AS total_revenue
FROM payment
```

```
GROUP BY rental_id) AS category_totals);
```

In this query, the inner subquery calculates the total revenue for each rental. The outer subquery then computes the average revenue across all rentals, and the main query filters out any categories whose total revenue is below this average. This use of subqueries in the **HAVING** clause is particularly effective for performing comparative analysis within grouped data.

Correlated subqueries are another important concept in SQL. Unlike regular subqueries, correlated subqueries depend on the outer query for their values and are executed once for each row processed by the outer query. For example, to find employees who earn more than the average salary in their department, you would use a correlated subquery:

```
SELECT e1.employee_id, e1.salary
FROM employees e1
WHERE e1.salary > (SELECT AVG(e2.salary)
                   FROM employees e2
                   WHERE e2.department_id = e1.department_id);
```

In this query, the subquery calculates the average salary for each employee's department, which is processed by the outer query. The main query then retrieves only those employees whose salary exceeds the departmental average. Correlated subqueries are powerful because they allow you to compare each row against a dynamically calculated value, providing fine-grained control over your query logic.

Finally, subqueries can also be used with **EXISTS** and **NOT EXISTS** operators to check the existence of rows in a subquery. These operators are useful when verifying the presence or absence of related data before including a row in the result set. For instance, to find all customers who have not placed any orders for rentals, you can use a **NOT EXISTS** subquery:

```
SELECT customer_id, first_name, last_name
FROM customer c
WHERE NOT EXISTS (SELECT 1
                  FROM rental r
                  WHERE r.customer_id = c.customer_id);
```

In this query, the subquery checks for the existence of rentals for each customer. The **NOT EXISTS** operator ensures that only customers without corresponding rentals are included in the result set. This query type is particularly useful for identifying gaps or missing relationships in your data.

Subqueries and nested queries are essential tools in SQL that provide the flexibility to handle complex data retrieval and manipulation tasks. By understanding and effectively using subqueries, you can write more powerful, efficient, and maintainable SQL queries, enabling you to tackle even the most challenging database problems confidently.

Handling NULL values in queries

In SQL, NULL represents a missing or undefined value, and it plays a crucial role in database management. It is different from zero, an empty string, or any other value; NULL means that a value is absent. When working with databases, understanding how to handle NULL values in queries is essential for ensuring that your queries return accurate results and that data integrity is maintained. Proper handling of NULL is especially important when filtering results, performing calculations, or working with joins.

Understanding the nature of NULL

The critical aspect of NULL is that it is neither equal to nor not equal to any other value, including itself. This makes comparisons involving NULL different from other types of comparisons. For instance, if you try to compare two NULL values, the result will not be TRUE or FALSE, but instead unknown. This behavior has important implications for filtering and querying data that contains NULL values.

Consider the following example. Suppose you want to use the **customer** table and filter customers based on their **active** status. If some customers have NULL values in the active column (meaning they are not active or inactive), filtering customers with a certain active status becomes tricky:

```
SELECT first_name, last_name, active
FROM customer
WHERE active = 0;
```

This query returns all customers who have an active status of 0. However, it will not return customers with NULL values in the *active* column, as NULL is not treated as a value that can be directly compared to 0. You must explicitly handle NULL values to include customers with no active status (those with NULL).

Using IS NULL and IS NOT NULL

SQL provides the **IS NULL** and **IS NOT NULL** operators to handle NULL values in your queries. These operators allow you to check for NULL values explicitly in a column.

For example, to retrieve all customers who have no active status (i.e., NULL in the **active** column), you can write the query as follows:

```
SELECT first_name, last_name, active
FROM customer
WHERE active IS NULL;
```

In this case, the query returns all rows where the **active** column is NULL, meaning those customers do not receive any status. Conversely, if you want to find all customers who do have an active status (i.e., where the value is not NULL), you can use the **IS NOT NULL** operator. Refer to the following code:

```
SELECT first_name, last_name, active

FROM customer

WHERE active IS NOT NULL;
```

This query filters out customers with NULL values in the active column and returns only those with a specific value.

Using NULL with comparison operators

Since NULL represents an unknown or missing value, it does not behave as a regular value in comparison operations. As mentioned earlier, trying to compare NULL directly to a value using operators like =, !=, <, or > will not return the expected results. For example, the following query will not work as intended:

```
SELECT first_name, last_name, active

FROM customer

WHERE active = NULL;
```

This query will not return any results because commission = NULL does not evaluate to TRUE, FALSE, or unknown. Instead, you must use IS NULL or IS NOT NULL for comparisons involving NULL values.

Using COALESCE to handle NULL values

The **COALESCE** function is a useful tool in SQL for handling NULL values by returning the first non-NULL value from a list of expressions. It is commonly used to provide default values when a column contains NULL. For instance, if you want to display a default value if the column is NULL, you can use **COALESCE**.

Consider the following example where you want to retrieve the customer's first name and active status. However, for customers with no active status (NULL), you want to display a default value of 0. Refer to the following example:

```
SELECT first_name, COALESCE(active, 0) AS active

FROM customer;
```

In this query, the **COALESCE(active, 0)** expression checks if the *active* column contains a NULL value. If it does, the function returns 0 instead of NULL. Otherwise, it returns the actual value in the **active** column. This approach allows you to handle missing data gracefully without having NULL values in your results.

The **COALESCE** function is not limited to two arguments. You can pass multiple arguments, and it will return the first non-NULL value from the list. For example:

```
SELECT first_name, COALESCE(active, create_date, 0) AS compensation
FROM customer;
```

The **COALESCE** function first checks the **active** column in this query. It checks the **create_date** column if it contains a NULL value. If both columns contain NULL, it returns 0 as the default value.

NULL in aggregate functions

When using aggregate functions like **COUNT()**, **SUM()**, **AVG()**, **MIN()**, or **MAX()**, it is important to understand how NULL values are treated, most aggregate functions ignore NULL values by default, with the exception of **COUNT()**, which has a specific behavior regarding NULL.

For instance, consider the following example where you want to calculate the total payment amount for all customers. Refer to the following example:

```
SELECT SUM(amount) AS total_amount
FROM payment;
```

In this query, the **SUM()** function will ignore any NULL values in the **amount** column and only sum the non-NULL values. However, if all values in the **amount** column are NULL, the result will be NULL instead of 0. To handle this, you can use the **COALESCE** function. Refer to the following code:

```
SELECT COALESCE(SUM(amount), 0) AS total_amount
FROM payment;
```

In this case, **COALESCE** ensures that if the sum of the *amount* column is NULL (because all values are NULL), it will return 0 instead of NULL.

Similarly, the **COUNT()** function can be used in two different ways, depending on how you want to handle NULL values. If you want to count all rows, including those with NULL values, you can use **COUNT(*)**. However, if you want to count only the rows where a specific column is not NULL, you can use **COUNT(column_name)**. Refer to the following code:

```
SELECT COUNT(*) AS total_payments, COUNT(amount) AS payment_with_amount
FROM payment;
```

In this query, **COUNT(*)** returns the total number of rows in the table, while **COUNT(commission)** only counts rows where the commission column is not NULL.

NULL in joins

When performing joins, it is important to consider how NULL values in columns will affect the join results. In an **INNER JOIN**, rows with NULL values in the join columns are excluded from the result set because NULL cannot match any value. However, in **LEFT JOIN** or **RIGHT JOIN** operations, rows from the table on the left or right side of the join will be included in the result set, even if the corresponding column contains a NULL value.

For example, in the following **LEFT JOIN** query, staff who do not belong to any store (i.e., their store_id is NULL) will still appear in the result, with NULL values for the department name. Refer to the following code:

```
SELECT staff.first_name, store.store_id
FROM staff
LEFT JOIN store ON staff.store_id = store.store_id;
```

Understanding how NULL values interact with joins is important for ensuring that your queries return the expected results, especially when dealing with incomplete data.

Conclusion

In this chapter, we have explored how to apply key advanced SQL techniques that enhance your ability to retrieve and manipulate data. You began by exploring the foundational tool of using aliases to rename columns and tables. This simple but powerful technique is instrumental in making complex queries more readable and easier to manage. Aliases streamline query writing, especially when working with multiple tables or long and complex column names. They allow for more precise presentation and reduce ambiguity in your SQL results, a crucial aspect of data analysis.

Next, we mastered the **DISTINCT** keyword, a critical tool for eliminating duplicate rows in query results. Whether working with large datasets or merged tables, ensuring that unique data is returned is vital for accurate analysis and reporting. By learning to use **DISTINCT**, you can now efficiently clean and organize your data, ensuring that your query outputs are precise and free from redundancy. This is especially useful in scenarios where data accuracy is critical, such as in reporting systems or data analytics projects.

You also explored the GROUP BY clause and aggregate functions like **SUM()**, **COUNT()**, and **AVG()**, which allow you to summarize and analyze large sets of data by grouping and aggregating specific columns. This powerful capability is essential for reporting and analytics, allowing you to break down data into meaningful segments and perform calculations across them. The chapter also covered subqueries, enabling you to nest queries for more advanced, multi-layered data retrieval. Finally, you understood how to handle NULL values, ensuring that missing or incomplete data does not affect the integrity of your results. These combined skills equip you to handle even the most complex data retrieval tasks confidently and precisely.

In the next chapter, we will focus on data modification, exploring how to insert, update, and delete records effectively in a database. You will learn how to manage and manipulate existing data while maintaining the integrity of your database. Additionally, the chapter will cover techniques for handling NULL values during data modification, ensuring your database remains consistent and reliable. This transition will equip you with the tools to manage your data and dynamically adapt to evolving business requirements.

Exercises

In these exercises, we will explore the Sakila database to learn how to utilize advanced querying techniques to retrieve detailed information.

Grouping data from tables

In this exercise, we will gather information from the **film**, **special_features**, **category**, and **film_category** tables to understand the rating of a film and special features customers like to rent:

- **Querying to find the total number of films by rating**: At the **sqlite>** command prompt, type the command to use the **GROUP BY** function to find the total number of films by each rating in the **film** table:

```
SELECT rating, COUNT(film_id) AS 'total_number_of_films '
FROM film
GROUP BY rating;
```

- **Querying to group special features by customer**: At the **sqlite>** command prompt, type the command to use the **GROUP BY** function to determine the total number of films by **special_feature**:

```
SELECT special_features, COUNT(film_id) as 'total_number_of_films'
FROM film
GROUP BY special_features;
```

- **Querying to find the total number of films by category**: At the **sqlite>** command prompt, type the command to use the **GROUP BY** function in conjunction with **INNER JOIN** to find the total number of films per category by joining three tables **film**, **film_category**, and **category**:

```
SELECT c.name, COUNT(f.film_id) as 'total_number_of_films'
FROM film f
INNER JOIN film_category fc
ON f.film_id = fc.film_id
INNER JOIN category c
ON fc.category_id = c.category_id
GROUP BY c.category_id;
```

Exploring the film table with aggregated functions

In this exercise, we will gather information from the film table to understand the top films rented and how much a film made:

- **Querying to determine the most rented film:** At the **sqlite>** command prompt, type the command to join three tables, **rental**, **inventory**, and **film**, to determine the film **title** with the most rentals:

```
SELECT f.film_id, f.title, COUNT(r.rental_id) as 'count_of_rentals'
FROM rental r
INNER JOIN inventory i
ON r.inventory_id = i.inventory_id
INNER JOIN film f
ON i.film_id = f.film_id
GROUP BY f.title
ORDER BY COUNT(r.rental_id) DESC;
```

- **Querying to determine top-grossing rental:** At the **sqlite>** command prompt, type the command to make it a bit more complex by joining four tables: **film,** **inventory, rental,** and **payment** to retrieve the top-rented films by title:

```
SELECT f.title, SUM(p.amount) as 'sum_of_payment'
FROM film as f
INNER JOIN inventory i
ON f.film_id = i.film_id
INNER JOIN rental r
ON i.inventory_id = r.inventory_id
INNER JOIN payment p
ON r.rental_id = p.rental_id
GROUP BY f.title
ORDER BY SUM(p.amount) DESC;
```

Bringing data together with nesting and subqueries

In this exercise, we will gather information from the film table to understand customer, store, and staff information as it relates to inventory and rentals:

- **Retrieve the most rented films**: At the **sqlite>** prompt, write a query to find the titles of the films that have been rented the most. Use a subquery to count rentals for each film:

```
SELECT title,(SELECT COUNT(*)
FROM rental r
JOIN inventory i ON r.inventory_id = i.inventory_id
```

```
WHERE i.film_id = f.film_id) AS rental_count
FROM film f
ORDER BY rental_count
DESC LIMIT 5;
```

- **Find customers who rented a specific film**: At the **sqlite>** prompt, write a query to retrieve the **first_name** and **last_name** of customers who rented the film ACADEMY DINOSAUR. Use a subquery to filter rentals related to this film:

```
SELECT
DISTINCT
c.first_name,
c.last_name
FROM customer c
WHERE c.customer_id IN (
SELECT r.customer_id
FROM rental r
JOIN inventory i ON r.inventory_id = i.inventory_id
JOIN film f ON i.film_id = f.film_id
WHERE f.title = 'ACADEMY DINOSAUR'
);
```

- **Determine the total revenue generated by each store**: At the **sqlite>** prompt, write a query to calculate the total revenue generated by each store. Use a subquery to sum the rental amounts by store:

```
SELECT s.store_id,
(SELECT SUM(p.amount)
FROM payment p
JOIN rental r ON p.rental_id = r.rental_id
WHERE r.staff_id IN (
SELECT staff_id
FROM staff
WHERE store_id = s.store_id)) AS total_revenue
FROM store s;
```

Average payment amount by customer

In this exercise, we will query the database to determine the average payment per customer using JOIN, GROUP BY, and ORDER BY:

- **Query to determine the average payment per customer**: At the `sqlite>` command prompt, type the command to join two tables, payment and customer, to determine the average payment per customer based on the overall payments made. We will use the subquery to determine the average amount among all customers and get `customer_id` that pays higher than the average:

```
SELECT c.customer_id, p.amount
FROM payment p
INNER JOIN customer c
ON p.customer_id = c.customer_id
WHERE p.amount > (SELECT AVG(amount) FROM payment)
GROUP BY c.customer_id
ORDER BY p.amount DESC;
```

Determining which customers have no rentals

In this exercise, we will query the database to determine the customers with no rentals:

- **Query to determine customer with no rentals:** At the `sqlite>` command prompt, type the command to insert a record into the customer table that is not assigned any rentals. We use a subquery to determine which customer_ids do not exist in the rental table:

```
INSERT INTO customer (
    customer_id,
    store_id,
    first_name,
    last_name,
    email,
    address_id,
    active,
    create_date,
    last_update,
    full_name,
    phone_number)
    VALUES (
    600,
    2,
    'SOPHIA',
    'JONES',
```

```
       'SOPHIA.JONES@sakilacustomer.org',
       605,
       1,
       02-14-2006,
       02-14-2006,
       'SOPHIA JONES',
       '5558135678');
SELECT customer_id, first_name, last_name
    FROM customer c
    WHERE NOT EXISTS (SELECT 1
                        FROM rental r
                        WHERE r.customer_id = c.customer_id);
```

Join our Discord space

Join our Discord workspace for latest updates, offers, tech happenings around the world, new releases, and sessions with the authors:

https://discord.bpbonline.com

CHAPTER 6
Modifying Data

Introduction

In this chapter, you will explore techniques for modifying data in SQL, including how to insert, update, and delete records within a database. You will learn the appropriate syntax and methods for adding new data using the **INSERT INTO** statement, making changes to existing records with the **UPDATE** statement, and removing data using the **DELETE** statement. Additionally, the chapter will cover how to handle NULL values effectively during data modification operations. These skills will provide a solid foundation for managing and maintaining data integrity within your databases.

Structure

This chapter covers the following topics:

- Inserting data with INSERT INTO
- Updating data with UPDATE
- Deleting data with DELETE
- Handling NULL values in data modification

Objectives

By the end of this chapter, you will be able to modify data in SQL using essential commands for inserting, updating, and deleting records. You will understand how to structure **INSERT INTO** statements to add new records efficiently, apply the **UPDATE** statement to modify existing data, and use the **DELETE** statement to remove records while maintaining database integrity. Additionally, you will learn strategies for managing NULL values to prevent inconsistencies and ensure data accuracy. These techniques will enhance your ability to maintain and update relational databases effectively.

Inserting data with INSERT INTO

The **INSERT INTO** statement is a fundamental SQL command used to add new records to a table in a database. Understanding how to use this statement effectively is crucial for managing and maintaining data within any relational database system. By mastering the **INSERT INTO** statement, you can populate your tables with data, whether adding a single row, inserting multiple rows at once, or copying data from another table.

The basic syntax for inserting data into a table involves specifying the table name, the columns you want to populate, and the values you wish to insert. The simplest form of the **INSERT INTO** statement looks like the following:

```
INSERT INTO actor (actor_id, first_name, last_name)
VALUES (1000, 'Penelope', 'Jones');
```

Let us understand this example in detail:

- You insert a new row into the **actor** table, where **actor_id** is set to the number 1000, **first_name** is set to Penelope, and **last_name** is set to Jones.
- Each value corresponds directly to its respective column, and the order of the values must match the order of the columns listed in the statement.

A critical aspect of the **INSERT INTO** statement is that it allows you to specify only the columns you want to populate. If a column is not listed in the **INSERT INTO** statement, SQL will either insert a default value or allow the column to remain NULL, depending on the table's schema and the column's constraints. For example, if **actor_id** has a default value that increments by one based on the last inserted value, you can omit it from the **INSERT INTO** statement. Refer to the following command:

```
INSERT INTO actor (first_name, last_name)
VALUES ('Penelope', 'Jones');
```

SQL will automatically insert the default value for **actor_id** in the new row, in this case, if the default constraint is set up for the column. This flexibility is valuable when you need to insert data into a table where some columns have default values or when you only have partial data available at the time of insertion.

In addition to inserting single rows, the **INSERT INTO** statement also supports the insertion of multiple rows in a single command. This can be a highly efficient way to add large amounts of data to a table, reducing the number of transactions and improving performance.

The syntax for inserting multiple rows is like that of a single row, but you can provide multiple sets of values separated by commas. Refer to the following code:

```
INSERT INTO actor (actor_id, first_name, last_name, last_update)
VALUES
(1001, 'Monica', 'Jones', 07-04-2005),
(1002, 'Sophia', 'Swift', 07-04-2005),
(1003, 'Jennifer', 'Smith', 07-04-2005);
```

Let us understand this example in detail:

- Three new rows are inserted into the actor table, each with its values for **actor_id**, **first_name**, and **last_name**.

Another powerful feature of the **INSERT INTO** statement is inserting data from another table. This is accomplished by combining **INSERT INTO** with a **SELECT** statement, allowing you to copy data from one table to another. For example, if you want to copy all rows from the **actor** table to **actor_backup_table**, you will write. Refer to the following code:

```
CREATE TABLE actor_backup_table (
    actor_id INTEGER PRIMARY KEY,
    first_name TEXT,
    last_name TEXT
);
INSERT INTO actor_backup_table (actor_id, first_name, last_name)
SELECT actor_id, first_name, last_name FROM actor;
```

Let us understand this example in detail:

- This query selects all rows from the actor table and inserts them into the **actor_backup_table**.
- The columns in both tables must match data type and order, ensuring that the data is transferred correctly.
- This method is helpful for data migration, backup operations, or creating summary tables based on existing data.

You can also insert data conditionally using a **SELECT** statement with a **WHERE** clause. For example, if you only want to insert rows from the actor table where **actor_id** meets a certain condition, you will write the following code:

```
INSERT INTO actor_backup_table (actor_id, first_name, last_name)
SELECT actor_id, first_name, last_name
FROM actor
```

```
WHERE actor_id = 1000;
```

Let us understand this example in detail:

- In this case, only the rows from actor, where **actor_id** equals 1000, are inserted into **actor_backup_table**.

- This allows precise control over which data is copied, making the **INSERT INTO** statement versatile for various use cases.

Transaction control with INSERT INTO

Handling errors and maintaining data integrity are important considerations when using the **INSERT INTO** statement. If the data being inserted violates any constraints on the table, such as unique constraints, foreign key constraints, or NOT NULL constraints, SQL will return an error, and the insert operation will fail. To handle such situations, you can use error-handling techniques like transaction control, which allows you to roll back a transaction if an error occurs, ensuring that the database remains consistent.

For example, in a situation where you need to ensure that all rows are inserted correctly or not at all, you can use a transaction. Refer to the following code:

```
BEGIN TRANSACTION;
INSERT INTO actor (actor_id, first_name, last_name, last_update)
VALUES (1010, 'Sophia', 'Swift', 07-04-2005);
INSERT INTO film_actor (actor_id, film_id, last_update)
VALUES (1011, 300, 07-04-2005);
-- Additional insert operations can go here
COMMIT;
```

If an error occurs during the insert operation, you can roll back the transaction to undo all changes, preserving the integrity of the database:

```
ROLLBACK;
```

This approach is crucial for maintaining data integrity in scenarios where multiple related operations must be performed together.

The **INSERT INTO** statement is a fundamental SQL command that allows you to add new data to your database efficiently and effectively. Whether inserting a single row or multiple rows or copying data from another table, mastering **INSERT INTO** is essential for managing the data flow into your tables. By understanding the various features and options available with this statement, you can ensure that your database is populated with accurate, reliable data while maintaining the integrity and performance of your system.

Updating data with UPDATE

The **UPDATE** statement in SQL is a powerful tool for modifying existing data within a table. This capability is crucial for maintaining accurate and up-to-date information in your database. Whether you need to correct errors, reflect changes in real-world data, or implement new business rules, the statement gives you the flexibility to make these changes efficiently.

The basic syntax of the **UPDATE** statement involves specifying the table you want to update, the columns to be modified, and the new values to be assigned. Additionally, you typically use a **WHERE** clause to ensure that only the intended rows are affected. For example, to update the **rental_rate** of a film in the film table, you would write the following code:

```
UPDATE film
SET rental_rate = 4.99
WHERE film_id = 101;
```

Let us understand this example in detail:

- In this query, the **UPDATE** statement targets the film table.
- The **SET** clause specifies that the **rental_rate** column should be updated to 4.99 for the film with **film_id** 101.
- In this context, the **WHERE** clause ensures that only the row corresponding to **film_id** 101 is updated.
- Without the **WHERE** clause, the **UPDATE** statement would modify the **rental_rate** for every film in the table, which is usually not the desired outcome.

When updating multiple columns within a single row, you can specify each column and its new value within the **SET** clause, separated by commas. For instance, if you need to update both the **rental_rate** and the rating of the film, you would use the following code:

```
UPDATE film
SET rental_rate = 5.99, rating = 'PG-13'
WHERE film_id = 102;
```

Let us understand this example in detail:

- This query updates the **rental_rate** to 5.99 and the rating to PG-13 for the film with **film_id** 102.
- The ability to update multiple columns at once is useful when multiple attributes of a record need to be changed in a coordinated manner.

The **UPDATE** statement can also modify data across multiple rows by omitting or broadening the **WHERE** clause. For example, if the rental company decides to have a 5% raise for all films in the category of Action, you could write the following code:

```
UPDATE film
SET rental_rate = rental_rate * 1.05
```

```
WHERE film_id IN (
    SELECT film_id
    FROM film_category
    JOIN category ON film_category.category_id = category.category_id
    WHERE category.name = 'Action'
);
```

Let us understand this example in detail:

- In this query, all films in the **Action** category receive a 5% increase.
- The **WHERE** clause ensures that only rows with films that have the category of **Action** are updated, while the expression **rental_rate * 1.05** recalculates the new rate based on the existing value.
- This efficient approach allows you to apply bulk updates to a subset of rows that meet specific criteria.

Using conditional logic within an **UPDATE** statement is another powerful feature that allows more complex data modifications. This can be achieved by combining the **UPDATE** statement with CASE expressions. For example, suppose the rental company wants to give different **rental_rate** raises based on the film's current rate. You could write the following code:

```
UPDATE film
SET rental_rate = CASE
    WHEN rental_rate < 2.99 THEN rental_rate * 1.10
    WHEN rental_rate BETWEEN 2.99 AND 4.99 THEN rental_rate * 1.07
    ELSE rental_rate * 1.05
END;
```

Let us understand this example in detail:

- This query updates the **rental_rate** for each film based on the film's current rental rate range.
- Films with a rate less than 2.99 receive a 10% increase, those earning between 2.99 and 4.99 receive a 7% increase, and those films **rental_rates** that are more than 4.99 receive a 5% raise.
- The **CASE** expression provides a way to apply different updates to different rows within the same statement based on specified conditions.

It is important to be cautious when using the **UPDATE** statement, especially when data integrity is critical. To prevent unintended updates, always ensure that your **WHERE** clause is correctly defined and targets only the rows you intend to modify. If the **WHERE** clause is omitted, the **UPDATE** statement will apply changes to every row in the table, which can lead to significant and sometimes irreversible data errors.

In scenarios where you need to update data based on values from another table, you can use a correlated subquery within the **UPDATE** statement. For example, say we have a hypothetical **film_performance** table with a **bonus_rate** column that represents the additional rate to be added based on each film's performance. Here is how the adapted query would look like:

```
UPDATE film
SET rental_rate = rental_rate + (
    SELECT bonus_rate FROM film_performance
    WHERE film_performance.film_id = film.film_id
)
WHERE EXISTS (
    SELECT 1 FROM film_performance
    WHERE film_performance.film_id = film.film_id
);
```

Let us understand this example in detail:

- In this query, the subquery **(SELECT bonus_rate FROM film_performance WHERE film_performance.film_id = film.film_id)** retrieves the **bonus_rate** for each film.
- The **EXISTS** clause ensures that only films with a corresponding record in **film_ performance** are updated.

The **UPDATE** statement can also be combined with transaction control to ensure data modifications are performed safely. Using transactions, you can group multiple **UPDATE** statements, ensuring that all changes are applied or not, depending on whether the transaction is committed or rolled back. For example:

```
BEGIN;
UPDATE film
SET rental_rate = rental_rate * 1.05
WHERE film_id IN (
    SELECT film_id
    FROM film_category
    JOIN category ON film_category.category_id = category.category_id
    WHERE category.name = 'Drama'
);
UPDATE film
SET rental_rate = rental_rate * 1.03
WHERE film_id IN (
    SELECT film_id
    FROM film_category
    JOIN category ON film_category.category_id = category.category_id
```

```
        WHERE category.name = 'Comedy'
);
COMMIT;
```

Let us understand this example in detail:

- The transaction ensures that both **UPDATE** operations are treated as a single unit of work.

- If any error occurs during the transaction, you can roll back the changes, preventing partial updates and maintaining the consistency of your data.

The **UPDATE** statement is a critical tool for managing and maintaining data accuracy within a database. Whether updating a single row, applying bulk changes, or using complex conditional logic, understanding how to use the **UPDATE** statement effectively ensures that your database reflects the most current and accurate information.

Deleting data with DELETE

SQL's **DELETE** statement is a powerful command that removes rows from a table. It plays a crucial role in maintaining the accuracy and relevance of data within a database. Whether you need to remove outdated information, clean up duplicate records, or eliminate data that no longer meets specific criteria, the **DELETE** statement allows you to do so efficiently and effectively. However, given its irreversible nature, it is essential to use this command carefully to avoid unintended data loss.

The basic syntax of the **DELETE** statement involves specifying the table from which you want to delete rows and defining a **WHERE** clause to target the specific rows to be removed. For example, if you need to delete a record for a film, you would write the following command:

```
DELETE FROM film
WHERE film_id = 123;
```

Let us understand this example in detail:

- In this query, the **DELETE** statement targets the film table and removes the row where the **film_id** is 123.

- In this context, the **WHERE** clause only deletes the intended row.

- Without a **WHERE** clause, the **DELETE** statement would remove all rows from the table, which could lead to catastrophic data loss.

When deleting multiple rows meeting specific criteria, the **DELETE** statement can target a broader data set. For example, if you need to delete all records of films that have not been rented in over a year, you could write the following code:

```
DELETE FROM film
WHERE film_id IN (
    SELECT film_id
```

```
     FROM rental
     WHERE rental_date < DATE_SUB(CURDATE(), INTERVAL 1 YEAR)
);
```

Let us understand this example in detail:

- In this query, the **WHERE** clause targets films that have not been rented in over a year.
- The subquery retrieves **film_ids** from the rental table with a **rental_date** older than one year.
- This approach is particularly useful for regular maintenance tasks, such as cleaning up inactive accounts, removing expired promotions, or purging old data that is no longer needed.

It is important to note that the **DELETE** statement permanently removes the specified rows from the table, meaning that once the deletion is executed, the data cannot be recovered unless a backup is available. To mitigate the risk of accidental data loss, it is a good practice first to perform a **SELECT** query using the same **WHERE** clause to review the rows that will be deleted. Refer to the following code:

```
SELECT *
FROM film
WHERE film_id IN (
     SELECT film_id
     FROM rental
     WHERE rental_date < date('now', '-1 year')
);
```

Let us understand this example in detail:

- Running this **SELECT** statement first ensures that the **DELETE** operation only affects the intended rows.
- This extra step is especially important in production environments where the impact of data loss can be significant.

The **DELETE** statement can also be combined with subqueries to target rows based on data from other tables. For example, if you want to delete records from the rental table where the **customer_id** no longer exists in the customer table, you could write the following code:

```
DELETE FROM rental
WHERE customer_id NOT IN (SELECT customer_id FROM customer);
```

Let us understand this example in detail:

- In this query, the subquery **(SELECT customer_id FROM customer)** retrieves all valid **customer_id** values from the **customer** table.
- The **DELETE** statement removes any rows in the **rental** table where the **customer_id** does not match these valid values.

- This approach helps maintain referential integrity and removes orphaned records from the database.

In scenarios where you need to delete data across multiple related tables, you can use cascading deletes, provided your database schema supports foreign key constraints with ON DELETE CASCADE. Cascading deletes automatically remove related rows in child tables when a parent row is deleted. For example, we can use a similar approach to set up a cascading delete between the customer and rental tables. This would ensure that deleting a customer would automatically delete all their related rentals:

```
ALTER TABLE rental
ADD CONSTRAINT fk_customer
FOREIGN KEY (customer_id) REFERENCES customer(customer_id)
ON DELETE CASCADE;
```

With this foreign key constraint in place, any time a row in the customer table is deleted, all related rows in the rental table will also be deleted. Cascading deletes are powerful but should be used carefully, as they can lead to widespread data removal if not correctly configured.

Another important aspect of using the DELETE statement is transaction control. In cases where you need to delete data from multiple tables or where the deletion operation is critical, it is advisable to use transactions to ensure that the operation is atomic. This means that either all deletions are successfully executed or none are, preserving the integrity of your database. For example, refer to the following code:

```
BEGIN;
DELETE FROM customer
WHERE last_update < date('now', '-1 year');
DELETE FROM rental
WHERE customer_id NOT IN (SELECT customer_id FROM customer);
COMMIT;
```

Let us understand this example in detail:

- The transaction ensures that both DELETE operations are treated as a single unit of work.

- If any error occurs during the transaction, you can roll back the changes to undo the deletions and maintain the consistency of your data:

  ```
  ROLLBACK;
  ```

This approach is crucial in scenarios where partial deletions, such as removing records from one table but not their corresponding records from related tables, could leave your database inconsistent.

Lastly, it is worth noting that the DELETE statement can be optimized for performance by using indexes on the columns involved in the WHERE clause. Indexes help the database quickly locate the rows to be deleted, reducing the time required for the operation.

However, it is important to balance indexing with overall database performance, as maintaining too many indexes can slow down other operations like inserts and updates.

The **DELETE** statement is a fundamental SQL command that efficiently removes data from your database. Whether deleting individual rows, performing bulk deletions, or maintaining referential integrity, understanding how to use the **DELETE** statement effectively is essential for managing your database's data lifecycle. By following best practices such as using **WHERE** clauses, reviewing deletions with **SELECT** statements, employing transaction control, and optimizing with indexes, you can ensure that your data deletions are performed safely and effectively.

Handling NULL values in data modification

In SQL, NULL represents the absence of a value or a placeholder for missing information. NULL is distinct, unlike zero, an empty string, or other default values, because it signifies no data is present. This unique status can impact how data is inserted, updated, and even deleted in a database. Effectively managing NULL values during data modification is essential to maintain data accuracy and consistency within your tables. This section explores how to effectively handle NULL values when performing data insertions, updates, and deletions, along with best practices for using NULL to represent missing data accurately.

Inserting NULL values

When inserting new data into a table, there may be instances where complete information is not available for all columns. Rather than inserting arbitrary placeholder values, SQL allows inserting NULL to indicate missing information. Inserting NULL helps avoid using misleading data (e.g., setting default values like zero or empty strings), which could be mistaken for valid information. Consider the **INSERT INTO** example where NULL is used for the **special_features** column to represent the absence of data rather than using an empty string or placeholder text. Refer to the following code:

```
INSERT INTO film (film_id, title, description, language_id, film_id, last_
update, special_features)

VALUES (101, 'Mystery Movie', 'An exciting thriller with unknown twists',
1, 1,  07-04-2005, NULL);
```

Let us understand this example in detail:

- NULL is used for the **special_features** column, accurately reflecting the absence of a **special_feature** rather than inserting an empty string or a placeholder text.

- It is crucial to ensure that columns accepting NULL values are defined as such in the table schema. By default, columns in SQL can accept NULL, but inserting a NULL value will result in an error if a column is set to NOT NULL.

- Thus, when designing tables, it is good practice to identify which columns might have missing values and allow NULL for those specific fields.

Updating values to NULL

In addition to inserting NULL values, there may be instances where existing data becomes invalid or unnecessary, requiring the value to be set to NULL. The **UPDATE** statement enables you to modify data in one or more columns, and setting a column to NULL can effectively mark information as unavailable. For instance, if a film's **replacement_cost** is unknown or no longer applicable, and you want to update this column to NULL for a specific film. Here is how that would look:

```
UPDATE film
SET replacement_cost = NULL
WHERE film_id = 101;
```

The **replacement_cost** for the film with **film_id** 101 is set to NULL, indicating the absence of a replacement cost rather than deleting the entire row.

However, if the entire row of data becomes obsolete, deletion may be more appropriate. Using NULL in updates also allows future updates when added information becomes available, making it a flexible approach to data management.

Handling NULL values in conditional updates

Handling NULL values becomes more complex when conditional updates with SQL operators are used. Since NULL does not equal any value (including itself), comparisons involving NULL require special handling. To update records conditionally where columns contain NULL, use IS NULL or IS NOT NULL operators rather than equality comparisons. For example, if we want to add a default value for all films missing a rating assignment, we could write the query like the following:

```
UPDATE film
SET rating = 'Unrated'
WHERE rating IS NULL;
```

Let us understand this example in detail:

- In this query, the **rating** column is updated to the string *Unrated* for rows where the **rating** is currently NULL.

- Using IS NULL ensures only films without a specified rating are updated, as = NULL would not return any results.

- By using IS NULL, you ensure that your condition correctly identifies rows with missing values and applies updates appropriately. Understanding these nuances is essential for accurately managing NULL values in conditional updates.

Deleting records with NULL values

When deleting records from a database, NULL values may influence your choice of conditions. Suppose you need to delete records containing incomplete data or indicate certain information is missing; it is important to use IS NULL to accurately identify rows with NULL values. For instance, one approach could be applied to delete films that lack certain key information. For example, if we want to delete films that have no description and no `special_features`, we could write the query as follows:

```
DELETE FROM film
WHERE description IS NULL AND special_features IS NULL;
```

Let us understand this example in detail:

- In this case, the `DELETE` statement removes only those rows where the `description` and `special_features` columns are NULL.

- Using NULL as a condition in deletions helps you focus on incomplete records without affecting rows with valid data.

- It also lets you maintain data quality by removing unnecessary entries that may skew analysis or reporting.

Best practices for managing NULL values

Effectively managing NULL values in SQL is essential for maintaining data integrity and ensuring that queries return accurate results. The following are key best practices to handle NULL values efficiently:

- Design database schema thoughtfully
  - o Specify which columns can accept NULL values based on data requirements.
  - o Use NOT NULL constraints on columns where values must always be present to enhance data reliability.
- Use NULL intentionally
  - o Assign NULL only when data is genuinely missing or unknown instead of using arbitrary placeholders.
  - o Avoid using values like 0, N/A, or unknown as substitutes for NULL, as they can lead to misinterpretation.
- Handle NULL conditions correctly
  - o Use IS NULL and IS NOT NULL in queries instead of comparison operators like = or !=, which do not work with NULL values.
  - o Ensure conditional updates and deletions account for NULL values appropriately.

- Use default values where applicable
    - ○ Define default values for columns when feasible to minimize NULL occurrences.
    - ○ Implement the **COALESCE()** function to replace NULL values with meaningful defaults in query results, improving report clarity.

With these best practices, you can minimize issues related to NULL values, maintain data integrity, and ensure your SQL queries produce accurate and insightful results.

Conclusion

In this chapter, we learned how to modify data within a SQL database using key data manipulation techniques. Additionally, we explored how to add new records with the INSERT INTO statement to ensure data is accurately introduced into tables. Then, we mastered the pivotal UPDATE statement, a key technique in database management that allows you to modify existing records and keep your database current. The DELETE statement helps remove no longer needed data, providing a method for maintaining a clean and efficient database. Finally, we learned how to handle NULL values during data modification, ensuring data consistency and preventing errors. With these skills, you can manage data precisely, keeping your database well-maintained and accurate.

In the next chapter, we will look into the power of SET operators in SQL. You will learn to combine and compare data from multiple result sets using commands like UNION, UNION ALL, INTERSECT, and EXCEPT. We will explore their applications and nuances, and examine how to use them effectively for data analysis. This transition will further expand your ability to work with complex data scenarios and extract valuable insights from your queries.

Exercises

In these exercises, we will explore the Sakila database to understand how to modify data in the database.

Inserting data

In this exercise, you will practice adding new records to the Sakila sample database, specifically to the actor and film tables:

- **Insert data into the actor table:** At the **sqlite>** prompt, insert a new record into the actor table with an **actor_id** of 201, **first_name** of **Alex**, and **last_name** of **Green**. Refer to the following example:

```
INSERT INTO actor (actor_id, first_name, last_name, last_update)
VALUES (201, 'Alex', 'Green', 07-04-2005);
```

- **Insert data into the film table:** At the **sqlite>** prompt, insert a new film record in the film table with the following values: **film_id** of 1001, title of *Tech Thriller*, description as *A suspenseful tech drama*, and **rental_rate** of 3.99. Refer to the following example:

INSERT INTO film (film_id, title, description, language_id, rental_
rate, last_update)

VALUES (1001, 'Tech Thriller', 'A suspenseful tech drama', 1, 3.99,
07-04-2005);

- **Insert data into the customer table:** At the **sqlite>** prompt, add a new row to the customer table. Set the **customer_id** to 601, **first_name** to **Taylor**, **last_name** to **Smith**, and leave email as NULL. Refer to the following example:

IINSERT INTO customer (customer_id, first_name, last_name, address_
id, store_id, create_date, last_update, email)

VALUES (601, 'Taylor', 'Smith', 1, 1, 07-04-2005, 07-04-2005, NULL);

Updating data

In this exercise, you will practice updating existing records, using the actor and film tables to modify the Sakila sample database data:

- **Updating the actor table:** At the **sqlite>** prompt, update the **last_name** of the actor with **actor_id** 201 to **Brown**. Refer to the following example:

UPDATE actor

SET last_name = 'Brown'

WHERE actor_id = 201;

- **Updating the film table:** At the **sqlite>** prompt, increase the **rental_rate** by 10% for all films in the film table that have a **rental_rate** below 3.00. Refer to the following example:

UPDATE film

SET rental_rate = rental_rate * 1.10

WHERE rental_rate < 3.00;

- **Updating data in the customer table:** At the **sqlite>** prompt, update the **last_update** date of the customer with **customer_id** 601 to the current date (for SQLite, you can use **CURRENT_TIMESTAMP** for the current date and time). Refer to the following example:

UPDATE customer

SET last_update = CURRENT_TIMESTAMP

WHERE customer_id = 601;

Deleting data

In this exercise, you will practice deleting records in the Sakila sample database from the customer and film tables:

- **Delete data in the film table:** At the **sqlite>** prompt, delete the film record with a **film_id** of 1001. Refer to the following example:

```
DELETE FROM film

WHERE film_id = 1001;
```

- **Delete data in the actor table:** At the **sqlite>** prompt, delete all actors from the **actor** table whose **last_name** is **Doe**. Refer to the following example:

```
DELETE FROM actor

WHERE last_name = 'Doe';
```

- **Delete data in the customer table:** At the **sqlite>** prompt, remove all customer records from the **customer** table where both **email** and **address_id** are NULL. Refer to the following example:

```
DELETE FROM customer

WHERE email IS NULL AND address_id IS NULL;
```

NULL handling

In this exercise, you will practice handling NULL values in the Sakila sample database using the **actor**, **film**, and **customer** tables:

- **Updating data with NULLs:** At the **sqlite>** prompt, update the description of any film with a NULL description in the **film** table to **Description unavailable**. Refer to the following example:

```
UPDATE film

SET description = 'Description unavailable'

WHERE description IS NULL;
```

- **Inserting data with NULLs:** At the **sqlite>** prompt, insert a new customer into the **customer** table with the following details: **customer_id** of 602, **first_name** of **Jordan**, **last_name** of **Lee**, and leave the email field as NULL to indicate the **email** is unknown. Refer to the following example:

```
INSERT INTO customer (customer_id, first_name, last_name, email)

VALUES (602, 'Jordan', 'Lee', NULL);
```

- **Deleting data with NULLs:** At the **sqlite>** prompt, delete all records from the **actor** table where both the **first_name** and **last_name** are NULL, representing actors with incomplete information. Refer to the following example:

```
DELETE FROM actor

WHERE first_name IS NULL AND last_name IS NULL;
```

CHAPTER 7
Working with SET Operators

Introduction

In this chapter, we will explore the powerful capabilities of **SET** operators in SQL, which allow you to combine and manipulate results from multiple queries to produce complex datasets. Beginning with foundational operators like **UNION**, **UNION ALL**, **INTERSECT**, and **EXCEPT**, we will learn how each operator uniquely combines data to meet different requirements. Moving into advanced usage, we will see how to apply multiple **SET** operators together, use parentheses to control their order, and understand how these operators interact in complex queries. By mastering these techniques, you will enhance your ability to perform sophisticated data retrieval, gaining flexibility and precision in handling large and diverse datasets.

Structure

This chapter covers the following topics:

- Introduction to SET operators
- Using UNION and UNION ALL
- Using INTERSECT
- Using EXCEPT
- In-depth usage of SET operators

Objectives

By the end of this chapter, you will be equipped to use **SET** operators in SQL to effectively combine and manipulate data from multiple queries. Depending on your data requirements, you will understand how to apply **UNION**, **UNION ALL**, **INTERSECT**, and **EXCEPT** to merge, intersect, and differentiate result sets. You will also learn advanced techniques for combining multiple **SET** operators in a single query, controlling their execution order with parentheses, and understanding how SQL processes them. Additionally, you will gain insight into using **SET** operators in complex scenarios, enabling you to refine data retrieval with precision and flexibility. These skills will allow you to tackle more advanced data manipulation tasks and streamline data analysis processes.

Introduction to SET operators

SET operators in SQL are powerful tools that allow you to combine the results of two or more queries into a single result set. These operators are essential for performing complex data manipulations and comparisons between datasets, enabling you to unify, intersect, or differentiate the data retrieved from multiple queries. The primary **SET** operators used in SQL include **UNION**, **UNION ALL**, **INTERSECT**, and **EXCEPT** (or **MINUS** in some SQL dialects). Each operator serves a distinct purpose, allowing you to handle different scenarios with relational data.

The **UNION** operator is the most commonly used **SET** operator. It combines the results of two queries and returns a single result set that includes all the unique rows from both queries. When you use **UNION**, SQL automatically removes duplicate rows, ensuring that each row in the result set is distinct. The basic syntax for using **UNION** is as follows:

```
SELECT first_name, last_name
FROM actor
UNION
SELECT first_name, last_name
FROM customer;
```

Let us understand this example in detail:

- The **UNION** operator combines the results from the **actor** and **customer** tables. SQL ensures that only unique rows appear in the result set, even if some **first_name** and **last_name** pairs are present in both tables.

- This is particularly useful when merging data from similar tables or queries, such as combining customer lists from different regions or aggregating product inventories across multiple warehouses.

Note: **It is important to note that when using UNION, the number of columns and the data types in the corresponding query columns must be the same.**

SQL will return an error if there is a mismatch, as it cannot reconcile the differences between the datasets. Ensuring that the columns align correctly is crucial for successfully using **SET** operators.

While **UNION** removes duplicates, there are scenarios where you might want to retain all rows from both queries, including duplicates. This is where the **UNION ALL** operator comes into play. Unlike **UNION**, **UNION ALL** does not remove duplicate rows, making it more efficient in cases where duplicates are acceptable or necessary for the analysis. The syntax for **UNION ALL** is similar to that of **UNION**:

```
SELECT
first_name, last_name
FROM customer;
```

Let us understand this example in detail:

- **UNION ALL** returns all rows from both **actor** and **customer**, including any duplicates.
- This operator is handy when you must include all data points in the analysis, such as when tracking all transactions, even if some are repeated, or when aggregating logs from different systems where identical events might occur.

Another important **SET** operator is **INTERSECT**, which returns only the standard rows to both queries. For example, you can use the **INTERSECT** operator to find overlapping data between two datasets. For instance, if you want to find **first_name** and **last_name** values that appear in both the **actor** and **customer** tables, you could write the following code:

```
SELECT first_name, last_name
FROM actor
INTERSECT
SELECT first_name, last_name
FROM customer;
```

Let us understand the example in detail:

- The **INTERSECT** operator returns only the rows that are common to both the **actor** and **customer** tables.
- This operation is particularly useful for identifying records that exist in both datasets, making it ideal for tasks like data validation and auditing.

The **EXCEPT** operator (or **MINUS** in some SQL dialects) finds the difference between two queries, returning the rows from the first query that do not appear in the second. The **EXCEPT** operator can be used to identify discrepancies between tables. For example, if you want to find **first_name** and **last_name** values that are present in the **actor** table but not in the **customer** table, you could write the following code:

```
SELECT first_name, last_name
FROM actor
```

```
EXCEPT
SELECT first_name, last_name
FROM customer;
```

Let us understand the example in detail:

- The **EXCEPT** operator returns the rows from the **actor** table that do not appear in the **customer** table.

- This is particularly useful for spotting records that exist in one dataset but are missing from another, which is helpful for data integrity checks, audits, or ensuring consistency after data migrations.

Using **SET** operators effectively requires a solid understanding of how they interact with the underlying data. For example, the order of the queries in **EXCEPT** or **MINUS** is critical, as reversing the order will yield different results. Similarly, while **UNION** and **INTERSECT** remove duplicates by default, you should know the potential performance implications, especially when working with large datasets.

Another key consideration when using **SET** operators is combining consistent data types across the columns. If the columns have different data types, SQL will attempt to convert them to a common type, which can lead to errors or unexpected results. Ensuring that the columns in each query have compatible data types is essential for avoiding these issues and ensuring accurate query results.

SET operators are powerful tools for manipulating and comparing data in SQL. Whether merging datasets, finding commonalities, or identifying differences, understanding how to use **UNION**, **UNION ALL**, **INTERSECT**, and **EXCEPT** allows you to perform complex data operations precisely and efficiently. By mastering these operators, you can enhance your ability to analyze, aggregate, and manage data across multiple sources, making them an indispensable part of your SQL toolkit.

Using UNION and UNION ALL

Earlier in the chapter, we explored **UNION** and **UNION ALL**. Let us understand in more detail how to use these operators with other tables and different SQL clauses you learned in *Chapter 3, Basic SQL Queries*. SQL's **UNION** and **UNION ALL** operators are powerful tools that allow you to combine the results of two or more queries into a single result set.

These operators are handy when aggregating data from multiple tables or queries with a similar structure. While both **UNION** and **UNION ALL** merge datasets, they differ in handling duplicate rows, and understanding this difference is crucial for using them effectively.

The **UNION** operator is designed to combine the results of two or more queries and return a single result set that includes only unique rows. When you use **UNION**, SQL automatically removes any duplicate rows from the final result set, ensuring each row appears only once. This makes **UNION** an ideal choice when you need to merge datasets but want to avoid any repetition of identical rows. The basic syntax for using **UNION** is straightforward, but we will add a twist. Refer to the following code:

```
SELECT title, release_year
FROM film
UNION
SELECT name AS title, NULL AS release_year
FROM category;
```

Let us understand the example in detail:

- The **UNION** operator combines the **title** and **release_year** columns from the **film** table with the **name** column from the **category** table.

- The **name** from category is aliased as **title**, and NULL is used for **release_year** since the category table does not have a corresponding column.

- This feature is handy in scenarios where you must create a consolidated list from multiple sources without duplicates, such as combining customer lists from different regions or merging product inventories from different warehouses.

One of the key requirements when using **UNION** is that the queries involved must have the same number of columns, and the corresponding columns must have compatible data types. SQL will return an error if the columns do not align in terms of number or type. Ensuring the columns match is essential for successfully executing a **UNION** operation.

While **UNION** helps eliminate duplicates, there are scenarios where you might want to retain all rows, including duplicates, in the final result set. This is where **UNION ALL** comes into play. Unlike **UNION**, **UNION ALL** does not remove duplicate rows but returns all rows from both queries, including duplicates. This makes **UNION ALL** a more efficient option when you need to combine datasets and are not concerned about duplicates, or when duplicates are expected and necessary for your analysis. The syntax for **UNION ALL** is nearly identical to that of **UNION**. Refer to the following code:

```
SELECT rental_id, rental_date
FROM rental
UNION ALL
SELECT payment_id AS rental_id, payment_date AS rental_date
FROM payment;
```

Let us understand the example in detail:

- The **UNION ALL** operator combines **rental_id** and **rental_date** from the **rental** table with **payment_id** and **payment_date** from the **payment** table.

- All rows from both tables are included, even if there are duplicates. This can be useful when you need to account for every record, such as analyzing all transaction timestamps from both rentals and payments.

One of the advantages of using **UNION ALL** over **UNION** is performance. Since **UNION ALL** does not have to remove duplicates, it is generally faster, especially when working with large datasets. This makes **UNION ALL** the preferred choice when the presence of duplicates is either irrelevant or desired. However, the trade-off is that the final result set may include redundant data, which could complicate further analysis if not appropriately managed.

It is also essential to consider the order of the queries when using **UNION** or **UNION ALL**. The order in which the queries are combined determines the order of the rows in the final result set. If you need to ensure a specific order in the combined results, you should use the **ORDER BY** clause after the final **UNION** or **UNION ALL**. Refer to the following code:

```
SELECT title, rental_rate
FROM film
UNION ALL
SELECT name AS title, NULL AS rental_rate
FROM category
ORDER BY title;
```

Let us understand the example in detail:

- The **UNION ALL** operator combines `title` and `rental_rate` from the `film` table with `name` (aliased as `title`) and NULL for `rental_rate` from the `category` table.

- The **ORDER BY title** clause ensures that the final combined result set is sorted alphabetically by `title`, regardless of the original order of rows in each query.

- This use of **ORDER BY** helps present the combined data in a clear and meaningful way, making it easier to review or analyze.

Another practical application of **UNION** and **UNION ALL** is in scenarios where you must create a summary or a consolidated view of data from multiple sources. For instance, if you manage data from various departments or regions and need to generate a company-wide report, you can use these operators to merge the data into a single, unified result set. This allows you to perform analysis and report on the combined data as if from a single source, simplifying the process and providing a more comprehensive view.

In cases where you need to ensure that the combined result set adheres to specific constraints or business rules, you can use the **WHERE** clause within each query before applying the **UNION** or **UNION ALL** operator. For example, if you wanted to combine data from different tables while filtering results only to include certain records, you could adapt the example as follows:

```
SELECT store_id, total_amount
FROM payment
WHERE total_amount > 50
UNION
SELECT store_id, NULL AS total_amount
FROM rental
WHERE rental_date > DATE('2006-01-01');
```

Let us understand the example in detail:

- In this query, the **UNION** operator combines **store_id** and **total_amount** from the **payment** table with **store_id** and NULL as **total_amount** from the **rental** table.

- Only records with **total_amount** greater than 50 are included from the **payment** table, and only rentals after January 1, 2006, are included from the **rental** table.

- The **UNION** ensures that the result set contains only unique **store_id** and **total_ amount** combinations.

In summary, both **UNION** and **UNION ALL** are invaluable tools in SQL for combining datasets from multiple queries. By understanding when to use each operator and how to manage the resulting data, you can perform complex data manipulations with precision and efficiency. Whether you need to eliminate duplicates or retain all instances of your data, these operators provide the flexibility and power required to handle a wide range of data aggregation tasks.

Using INTERSECT

The **INTERSECT** operator in SQL is a powerful tool for identifying commonalities between two or more datasets. By using **INTERSECT**, you can combine the results of multiple queries and return only the rows that appear in all of them. This makes **INTERSECT** an essential tool when comparing datasets and focusing on the shared data points. Whether you are cross-referencing lists, finding overlapping entries, or ensuring consistency across different sources, **INTERSECT** provides a straightforward and efficient way to achieve these goals.

The basic syntax of **INTERSECT** is simple and mirrors that of other SQL set operators like **UNION** and **EXCEPT**. You execute two **SELECT** queries and place the **INTERSECT** operator between them. The result is a set of rows that are common to both queries. For example, you could use the **INTERSECT** operator to find records that are present in both the rental and payment tables, such as identifying rental transactions that also have an associated payment. You would write the following code:

```
SELECT rental_id, customer_id
FROM rental
INTERSECT
SELECT rental_id, customer_id
FROM payment;
```

Let us understand the example in detail:

- In this query, the **INTERSECT** operator returns only the rows with matching **rental_ id** and **customer_id** values in both the **rental** and **payment** tables.

- This helps identify rental transactions that have corresponding payments, useful for verifying that all rentals have been paid for.

- This approach is ideal for pinpointing common records between datasets, such as in data validation or auditing scenarios.

- Any row in only one of the tables or with different values in these columns will be excluded from the result set. This functionality is handy in scenarios where you need to ensure that the data in multiple sources is consistent or when you need to find records that meet criteria across different datasets.

One of the most common use cases for **INTERSECT** is data validation and quality control. Suppose you have two lists of customer orders, one from an online store and one from an in-store **point of sale** (**POS**) system. You want to identify the orders in both lists, indicating that the same customers have purchased through both channels. You could use the **INTERSECT** operator to identify customers who have made rentals across different locations, assuming we have two tables representing rentals from two separate stores:

```
SELECT rental_id, customer_id, rental_date
FROM rental_store1
INTERSECT
SELECT rental_id, customer_id, rental_date
FROM rental_store2;
```

In this query:

- The **INTERSECT** operator returns only the rows with matching **rental_id**, **customer_id**, and **rental_date** in **rental_store1** and **rental_store2**.

- This allows you to identify customers who have rented from both store locations, which can be useful for analyzing customer engagement across different branches.

- This kind of analysis helps identify high-engagement customers and ensure data consistency across multiple locations.

Another critical application of **INTERSECT** is in auditing and compliance. For instance, you can use the **INTERSECT** operator to find customers who have rented a film and paid. This ensures that the customers in both the **rental** and **payment** tables are accounted for in both activities:

```
SELECT customer.customer_id, customer.first_name || ' ' || customer.last_
name AS full_name
FROM customer
JOIN rental ON customer.customer_id = rental.customer_id
INTERSECT
SELECT customer.customer_id, customer.first_name || ' ' || customer.last_
name AS full_name
FROM customer
JOIN payment ON customer.customer_id = payment.customer_id;
```

Let us understand this query in detail:

- In this query, the **INTERSECT** operator returns only those customers who appear in both the **rental** and **payment** tables, indicating they have both rented a film and completed a payment.

- This helps you focus on customers who are fully active in renting and paying, while any customer appearing only in one table but not the other will be excluded.

- This approach is practical for verifying consistency across customer transactions and ensuring all eligible customers have complete records.

When using **INTERSECT**, it is essential to ensure that the **SELECT** statements on either side of the operator have the same number of columns and that the data types of these columns are compatible.

If the columns do not match, SQL will return an error, as it cannot correctly compare and intersect the datasets. Ensuring that your columns align is essential for successfully using the **INTERSECT** operator.

Another critical point is that **INTERSECT** removes duplicates from the result set, like other SQL set operators. This means that even if a row appears multiple times in both queries, it will only appear once in the final result. This behavior is beneficial when focusing on unique records and eliminating redundancy from your analysis.

Performance is another consideration when using **INTERSECT**, especially with large datasets. It can be resource-intensive because **INTERSECT** compares the results of two queries and returns only the standard rows.

To optimize performance, ensure that the columns used in the **INTERSECT** operation are indexed. This can significantly speed up the comparison process and reduce the time required to generate the result set.

In addition to simple comparisons, **INTERSECT** can be used in more complex queries where multiple conditions must be met. For example, you can use the **INTERSECT** operator to find find inventory that hasn't been returned, helping to identify popular films that are actively circulating. Refer to the following code:

```
SELECT inventory_id
FROM inventory
INTERSECT
SELECT inventory_id
FROM rental
WHERE rental_date IS NULL;
```

Let us understand the example in detail:

- The **INTERSECT** operator combines inventory marked as available in the **inventory** table with films with a **rental_date** NULL in the **rental** table.

- This returns only inventory that are both available in stock and have been rented recently, helping you focus on inventory not returned.

- This query type is especially useful for aligning inventory management with customer demand by identifying in-stock films with recent rental activity.

INTERSECT is also useful when validating complex data relationships. For example, here is how you could identify customers who have both rented regular and special feature films. Refer to the following code:

```
SELECT customer_id, film_id
FROM rental
JOIN film ON rental.film_id = film.film_id
WHERE special_features IS NU
INTERSECT
SELECT customer_id, film_id
FROM rental
JOIN film ON rental.film_id = film.film_id
WHERE special_features IS NOT NULL;
```

Let us understand the components of the preceding code:

- In this query, the **INTERSECT** operator identifies customers who have rented both regular and special feature films.

- The first **SELECT** statement retrieves **customer_id** and **film_id** for rentals where the film has no **special_features** (considered regular films).

- The second **SELECT** statement retrieves **customer_id** and **film_id** for rentals where the film has **special_features**, identifying it as a special feature film.

- Only customers who appear in both result sets are returned, showing those who have rented both films. This is useful for identifying customers with diverse rental preferences and potentially informing targeted recommendations or promotions.

INTERSECT is a powerful tool for identifying commonalities between datasets in SQL. Whether performing data validation, ensuring consistency across systems, or analyzing overlapping records, **INTERSECT** allows you to focus on the data points that meet specific criteria across multiple queries. By mastering **INTERSECT**, you can enhance your ability to manage and analyze relational data precisely and efficiently.

Using EXCEPT

The **EXCEPT** operator in SQL is a powerful tool for identifying differences between two datasets. By using **EXCEPT**, you can compare the results of two queries and return only the rows present in the first query but not in the second. This makes **EXCEPT** particularly useful when finding discrepancies, detecting missing data, or validating that one dataset fully encompasses another. Understanding how to use **EXCEPT** effectively allows you to perform precise and targeted analyses, ensuring data accuracy and integrity across your database.

The basic syntax of **EXCEPT** is straightforward and similar to other SQL set operators like **UNION** and **INTERSECT**. You execute two **SELECT** queries and place the **EXCEPT** operator between them. The result is a set of rows that appear in the first query but are absent from the second query. For example, using the **EXCEPT** operator to find rows in one table that do not exist in another, you would write the following code:

```
SELECT film_id
FROM film
EXCEPT
SELECT film_id
FROM inventory;
```

Let us understand this query in detail:

- In this query, the **EXCEPT** operator returns **film_id** and **title** values from the **film** table that do not have matching entries in the **inventory** table.

- Any **film_id** and **title** combination that exists in both the **film** and **inventory** tables is excluded from the result set.

Data validation is one of the most common use cases for **EXCEPT**. You could adapt this example to check for discrepancies between two tables. Refer to the following code:

```
SELECT film_id, title
FROM film
EXCEPT
SELECT film_id, title
FROM rental;
```

The **EXCEPT** operator returns **film_id** and **title** values from the **film** table that do not have matching entries in the **rental** table. This query helps identify films listed in the film table but never rented, highlighting discrepancies between the film catalog and actual rentals. This method is valuable for ensuring data consistency between records of available items and their use or tracking, such as validating stock records against transactions or rentals.

Another important application of **EXCEPT** is in auditing and compliance. For instance, you can use a similar **EXCEPT** query to ensure consistency between related tables, such as identifying customers who are in the **customer** table but have never made a payment. Refer to the following code:

```
SELECT customer_id, first_name || ' ' || last_name AS full_name
FROM customer
```

EXCEPT

```
SELECT customer_id, first_name || ' ' || last_name AS full_name
FROM payment;
```

Let us understand this example in detail:

- In this query, the **EXCEPT** operator returns **customer_id** and the concatenated **full_name** of customers from the **customer** table who do not have a corresponding record in the **payment** table.

- This helps identify customers who are listed in the customer database but have never made a payment, highlighting potential discrepancies.

- By using this query, you can ensure that all customers who should have payment records are correctly accounted for, helping maintain consistency across the system.

- When using **EXCEPT**, it is essential to ensure that the **SELECT** statements on either side of the operator have the same number of columns and that the data types of these columns are compatible. SQL will return an error if the columns do not match, as it cannot accurately compare the datasets. Ensuring that your columns align correctly is essential for successfully using the **EXCEPT** operator.

- Another key point is that **EXCEPT** removes duplicates from the result set like other SQL set operators. This means that even if a row appears multiple times in the first query but is absent from the second query, it will appear only once in the final result. This behavior is advantageous when focusing on unique records and eliminating redundancy from your analysis.

- Performance is another consideration when using **EXCEPT**, especially with large datasets. It can be resource-intensive because **EXCEPT** compares the results of two queries and returns only the non-overlapping rows. To optimize performance, ensure that the columns used in the **EXCEPT** operation are indexed, as this can significantly speed up the comparison process and reduce the time required to generate the result set.

In addition to simple comparisons, **EXCEPT** can also be used in more complex queries where you must ensure that one dataset fully encompasses another. For example, focusing on customers who have rented films within the last year but are not yet part of a hypothetical **loyalty_program** table, you can use **EXCEPT**. Refer to the following code:

```
SELECT customer_id, first_name || ' ' || last_name AS full_name
FROM rental
JOIN customer ON rental.customer_id = customer.customer_id
WHERE rental_date > DATE('2006-01-01')
EXCEPT
```

```
SELECT customer_id, first_name || ' ' || last_name AS full_name
FROM loyalty_program;
```

Let us understand the example in detail:

- In this query, the **EXCEPT** operator returns **customer_id** and **full_name** of customers who have rented a film in 2006 and beyond but do not have a corresponding record in the **loyalty_program** table.

- This helps identify active customers who are eligible but not enrolled in the loyalty program.

- By using this query, you can take targeted actions to invite these customers to join the loyalty program and enhance engagement with eligible members.

EXCEPT is also useful when auditing data migrations or updates. For example, suppose you can use a similar approach to compare data between two related tables, such as ensuring that all films listed in an old inventory system have been correctly transferred to a new system:

```
SELECT film_id, title
FROM old_inventory
EXCEPT
SELECT film_id, title
FROM new_inventory;
```

Let us understand the example in detail:

- In this query, the **EXCEPT** operator returns **film_id** and **title** from the **old_inventory** table that does not match entries in the **new_inventory** table.

- This helps identify films that were not successfully transferred during the migration process, ensuring the data migration was complete and accurate.

- By running this query, you can quickly pinpoint missing records and take corrective action to ensure all necessary data is in the new system.

EXCEPT is a powerful tool for identifying and addressing discrepancies between datasets in SQL. Whether you are performing data validation, auditing records, or ensuring consistency across systems, **EXCEPT** allows you to focus on the data points that are missing or misaligned. This enables you to take corrective action and maintain the integrity of your database. By mastering **EXCEPT**, you can enhance your ability to manage and analyze relational data with precision and confidence.

In-depth usage of SET operators

SET operators in SQL, such as **UNION, UNION ALL, INTERSECT,** and **EXCEPT,** can combine and manipulate data from multiple queries. While the basic use of these operators is essential for standard data retrieval tasks, understanding their advanced usage allows you to handle complex data scenarios more effectively. This section explores in-depth applications, including combining multiple SET operators, using parentheses for complex operations, and leveraging order and precedence to create precise query results.

Combining multiple SET operators

A common requirement in data analysis is to combine the results of multiple operations in a single query. SQL allows you to use multiple SET operators in the same query, provided you understand the order of precedence and how the results will be processed. For instance, here is how you could find unique actors and staff members who have been involved in a film while filtering out those who are no longer active. Refer to the following code:

```
SELECT first_name, last_name
FROM actor
UNION
SELECT first_name, last_name
FROM staff
INTERSECT
SELECT first_name, last_name
FROM film_actor
EXCEPT
SELECT first_name, last_name
FROM inactive_staff;
```

This query performs the following:

- The **UNION** operation combines actors and staff, eliminating duplicates to get unique individuals.

- The **INTERSECT** operation then finds common entries between this combined set and the **film_actor** table, identifying those involved in a film.

- Finally, the **EXCEPT** operation removes any individuals listed in the **inactive_staff** table, ensuring that only active actors and staff involved in films remain.

SQL processes the **UNION**, **INTERSECT**, and **EXCEPT** operators from left to right in this query. This approach is beneficial for managing a diverse dataset, where understanding each operator's role is key to achieving accurate, filtered results.

Using parentheses for complex operations

When multiple **SET** operators are used in a single query, controlling the order of operations is important to achieve the desired results. SQL follows a default precedence for **SET** operators, typically processing **INTERSECT** first, followed by **UNION** and **EXCEPT**. To override this default behavior and create more complex logic, you can use parentheses to group specific parts of the query and control their evaluation.

Here is an example where we want to find active actors who have worked on films and include additional active staff members:

```
(SELECT first_name, last_name
FROM actor
EXCEPT
SELECT first_name, last_name
FROM inactive_actors)  -- Assuming inactive_actors lists actors no longer active
UNION
SELECT first_name, last_name
FROM staff
WHERE active = 'Y';
```

This query performs the following:

- The **EXCEPT** operation within parentheses is executed first, returning active actors by excluding any listed in the **inactive_actors** table.

- The result of this **EXCEPT** operation is then combined with active staff members from the staff table using the **UNION** operator, ensuring unique entries from both sets are included.

Using parentheses, we can control which operations occur first, allowing for precise filtering. This approach is essential when building complex queries that need to follow specific logic to meet analytical goals, ensuring that active and relevant entries are captured accurately.

Order and precedence of SET operators

Understanding the precedence of **SET** operators is essential for interpreting query results accurately. By default, SQL evaluates **INTERSECT** before **UNION** and **EXCEPT**, affecting how results are combined and filtered. If you write a query without parentheses, SQL processes the operations in the default order, which might lead to unexpected results.

For instance, refer to the following code:

```
SELECT first_name, last_name
FROM actor
UNION
SELECT first_name, last_name
FROM film_directors
INTERSECT
```

```
SELECT first_name, last_name
FROM active_cast;
```

This query performs the following:

- The **INTERSECT** operation is processed first, finding common entries between **film_directors** and **active_cast**.

- The result is combined with actors using **UNION**, producing a unique list of actors and active directors.

We would need parentheses if you intended to combine actors and directors first, and then find which are active. Refer to the following code:

```
(SELECT first_name, last_name
FROM actor
UNION
SELECT first_name, last_name
FROM film_directors)
INTERSECT
SELECT first_name, last_name
FROM active_cast;
```

Let us understand this example in detail:

- The **UNION** operation between **actor** and **film_directors** is processed first, combining actors and directors into one set.

- The **INTERSECT** operation then filters this combined result with **active_cast**, ensuring only active actors or directors are included.

Using parentheses to control precedence helps create accurate queries that align with specific goals, avoiding unexpected results from default evaluation orders. This is crucial in complex data scenarios where precise filtering and combination are needed.

Practical applications of in-depth SET operations

Advanced use of **SET** operators can streamline complex reporting and data analysis tasks. For example, you could use a query structure to identify active staff members who are both involved in a film project and part of the management team, while excluding those on leave. Refer to the following code:

```
(SELECT first_name || ' ' || last_name AS name
FROM staff_projects
INTERSECT
SELECT first_name || ' ' || last_name AS name
FROM management_team)
```

```
EXCEPT
SELECT first_name || ' ' || last_name AS name
FROM leave_list;
```

This query performs the following:

- The **INTERSECT** operation first identifies individuals who are both in the **staff_projects** table and the **management_team** table, finding staff involved in projects and part of management.

- The **EXCEPT** operation then excludes any individuals in the **leave_list** table, ensuring that only active project members who are not on leave are included.

This layered approach with **INTERSECT** and **EXCEPT** allows for precise filtering, helping to focus on specific groups based on multiple criteria. This method is ideal for extracting insights aligned with nuanced requirements, like monitoring project involvement while accounting for team status.

SET operators with ORDER BY clause

Applying the **ORDER BY** clause when using **SET** operators requires careful consideration. The **ORDER BY** clause can only be applied to the final result set of a query that uses **SET** operators like **UNION**, **INTERSECT**, or **EXCEPT**. Attempting to use **ORDER BY** within the individual subqueries will result in an error.

For example:

```
SELECT first_name, last_name FROM actor
UNION
SELECT first_name, last_name FROM staff
ORDER BY last_name;
```

In this query, the **ORDER BY last_name** clause applies to the final combined result of the **UNION** operation between the **actor** and **staff** tables. This means the combined list of actors and staff members will be sorted by **last_name**.

If you need to sort individual subqueries before combining them, consider using **common table expressions** (**CTEs**) or temporary tables, which we will discuss in-depth in *Chapter 11, Advanced SQL Techniques*. However, remember that the final **ORDER BY** still applies to the overall result set.

Here is how you might use CTEs:

```
WITH actor_list AS (
    SELECT first_name, last_name
    FROM actor
),
staff_list AS (
```

```
    SELECT first_name, last_name
    FROM staff
)
SELECT * FROM actor_list
UNION
SELECT * FROM staff_list
ORDER BY last_name;
```

This query performs the following:

- CTEs **actor_list** and **staff_list** are defined without **ORDER BY** clauses.

- The **UNION** operator combines the two lists.

- The **ORDER BY last_name** clause sorts the final result set.

If you attempt to include **ORDER BY** within the subqueries used in a **UNION**, use the following code:

```
SELECT first_name, last_name FROM actor ORDER BY last_name
UNION
SELECT first_name, last_name FROM staff ORDER BY last_name;
```

You will encounter an error because **ORDER BY** is not allowed within subqueries when using **SET** operators.

To control the sort order of the individual datasets before combining them, you might need to include an additional column to indicate the source of each row and then sort accordingly:

```
SELECT first_name, last_name, 'Actor' AS source
FROM actor
UNION ALL
SELECT first_name, last_name, 'Staff' AS source
FROM staff
ORDER BY source, last_name;
```

This query does a few different things. Let us do a breakdown:

- An additional column source is added to identify each row's origin.

- **UNION ALL** is used to include all records, including duplicates if any.

- The result set is sorted first by source (either **'Actor'** or **'Staff'**), and then by **last_name**.

There are a few things to note with the **UNION ALL** operator. It is used here because it preserves all rows from both queries, including duplicates, which might be necessary depending on your data.

If you require sorting within the individual datasets and the database supports it, you might consider using subqueries or temporary tables to store and sort the individual results before performing the **SET** operation. However, this approach can be more complex and may impact performance.

Overall, when working with **SET** operators keep these points in mind:

- Apply the **ORDER BY** clause only to the result set.
- Use additional columns or markers if you need to sort based on the origin of the data.
- Consider alternative methods like CTEs or temporary tables if you need more control over the sorting of individual subqueries.

Understanding these nuances allows you to construct complex queries that meet your specific data analysis requirements while avoiding common pitfalls associated with **SET** operators and sorting.

Combining SET operators with subqueries

Advanced usage of **SET** operators can also involve subqueries to refine data retrieval further. You could use advanced **SET** operator techniques with subqueries to combine filtered data from multiple sources. For example, suppose you want to retrieve a list of actors involved in films from a specific category and staff members working on high-budget projects:

```
SELECT first_name, last_name
FROM actor
WHERE actor_id IN (
    SELECT actor_id
    FROM film_actor
    JOIN film_category ON film_actor.film_id = film_category.film_id
    JOIN category ON film_category.category_id = category.category_id
    WHERE category.name = 'Action'
)
UNION
SELECT first_name, last_name
FROM staff
WHERE staff_id IN (
    SELECT staff_id
    FROM project_staff
    JOIN projects ON project_staff.project_id = projects.project_id
    WHERE projects.budget > 100000
);
```

This query performs the following:

- The first subquery filters actor records to only those associated with films in the *Action* category. This is achieved by joining **film_actor**, **film_category**, and **category** tables.

- The second subquery filters staff records to those associated with projects where the budget exceeds 100,000 by joining **project_staff** and **projects**.

- The **UNION** operator then combines the filtered results, returning unique names of actors involved in action films and staff members engaged in high-budget projects.

This method allows you to create a refined final result set by combining data that meets specific conditions across various sources. Mastering such techniques enables you to tackle complex data analysis tasks with accuracy, tailoring your results to meet detailed criteria.

Conclusion

In this chapter, we explored the versatility and power of SQL SET operators. You learned how to combine and compare result sets using **UNION**, **UNION ALL**, **INTERSECT**, and **EXCEPT**, mastering their applications for solving complex data analysis challenges. These operators enable us to merge, compare, and filter data effectively across multiple queries, providing new ways to handle diverse datasets.

Additionally, the in-depth usage of **SET** operators demonstrated their potential to simplify complex questions and enhance data retrieval efficiency. We can confidently tackle advanced scenarios by understanding how to manage duplicates, deal with NULL values, and optimize query results.

In the next chapter, we will focus on managing database objects. We will learn how to create and modify tables, work with indexes to improve query performance, and use views to simplify complex queries. Furthermore, we will explore stored procedures, functions, and triggers to automate database tasks and enhance functionality. This chapter will deepen our understanding of database management, providing practical tools to structure, optimize, and maintain a high-performing database.

Exercises

In these exercises, we will explore the Sakila database to understand how to work with SET operators in the database.

Using UNION

In this exercise, you will practice using the **UNION** operator to combine results from different tables or queries:

- **Removing duplicates**: At the **sqlite>** prompt, write a query that returns a combined list of **first_name** from the **actor** table and the **customer** table, ensuring no duplicate names are in the result:

```
SELECT first_name FROM actor
UNION
SELECT first_name FROM customer;
```

- **Combining data**: At the **sqlite>** prompt, write a query combining the titles of films from the film table and the names of categories from the category table into a single column, ensuring unique values:

```
SELECT title AS name FROM film
UNION
SELECT name FROM category;
```

- **Distinct values with UNION**: At the **sqlite>** prompt, create a query to list all distinct **address_id** values from the **address** table and **store** table:

```
SELECT address_id FROM address
UNION
SELECT address_id FROM store;
```

UNION ALL

In this exercise, you will practice using the **UNION ALL** operator to combine query results, including duplicates:

- **Including duplicates with UNION ALL**: At the **sqlite>** prompt, create a query that returns all **first_name** values from the **actor** table and the **customer** table, including duplicates:

```
SELECT first_name FROM actor
UNION ALL
SELECT first_name FROM customer;
```

- **Include duplicates and combining data**: At the **sqlite>** prompt, write a query that combines the **description** from the **film** table and the **special_features** from the film table, allowing duplicates:

```
SELECT description FROM film
UNION ALL
SELECT special_features FROM film;
```

INTERSECT

In this exercise, you will practice using the **INTERSECT** operator to find common values between query results:

- **Finding common datasets with INTERSECT**: At the `sqlite>` prompt, write a query to find common **first_name** values that exist in both the **actor** and **customer** tables.

```
SELECT first_name FROM actor
INTERSECT
SELECT first_name FROM customer;
```

EXCEPT

In this exercise, you will practice using the **EXCEPT** operator to find rows from one query that are not in another:

- **Finding missing values**: At the `sqlite>` prompt, create a query that lists **first_name** values from the **actor** table that do not appear in the **customer** table:

```
SELECT first_name FROM actor
EXCEPT
SELECT first_name FROM customer;
```

Join our Discord space

Join our Discord workspace for latest updates, offers, tech happenings around the world, new releases, and sessions with the authors:

https://discord.bpbonline.com

CHAPTER 8
Managing Database Objects

Introduction

In this chapter, you will learn about managing database objects in SQL, focusing on creating, modifying, and organizing critical structures within your database. You will learn how to create and alter tables to suit evolving data requirements, use indexes to improve query performance, and simplify complex queries by defining views. Additionally, you will explore stored procedures, functions, and triggers, which help automate tasks and streamline database operations.

Structure

This chapter covers the following topics:

- Creating and modifying tables
- Improving queries with indexes
- Simplifying complex queries with views
- Stored procedures and functions
- Automating database tasks with triggers

Objectives

By the end of this chapter, you will be able to manage essential database objects in SQL confidently. You will learn how to create and modify tables to meet changing data requirements, and you will understand how to utilize indexes to optimize query performance. Additionally, you will learn to create views to simplify and streamline complex queries, making data retrieval more efficient. You will also gain experience with stored procedures and functions, enabling you to automate repetitive tasks and encapsulate logic within the database. Ultimately, you will learn how to configure triggers to automate actions based on specific events. These skills will equip you to maintain and optimize your database for improved functionality and performance.

Creating and modifying tables

In *Chapter 2, Understanding Databases*, we briefly explored creating and altering tables in SQL. These fundamental operations form the backbone of database design and management. In this section, we will explore creating and modifying tables further.

Tables are where data is stored, and their structure defines how data is organized, accessed, and manipulated. Whether designing a new database or maintaining an existing one, understanding how to create and modify tables effectively is crucial for ensuring that your database meets the needs of your applications and users.

Use the **CREATE TABLE** statement to create a new SQL table. This statement allows you to define the table's name, its columns, and the data types of each column. As we explored in previous chapters, you can specify constraints, such as primary keys, foreign keys, unique constraints, and default values, which help enforce data integrity and consistency. For example, if you wanted to create a table to store information about film crew members, you would write the following code:

```
CREATE TABLE film_crew (
crew_id INT PRIMARY KEY,
first_name VARCHAR(50),
last_name VARCHAR(50),
hire_date DATE,
nickname VARCHAR(50),
department_id INT,
bonus_rate INT
);
```

Let us understand this example in detail:

- The **crew_id** column is defined as an integer and designated as the primary key, ensuring that each crew member has a unique identifier and that this field cannot contain NULL values.

- The **first_name** and **last_name** columns are set as variable character fields with a maximum length of 50 characters, providing adequate space for storing names.

- The **hire_date** column is defined as a date, which allows for the storage of the crew member's hire date in a standard format.

- This structure provides a solid framework for managing film crew data, ensuring consistency in identifiers, names, and dates.

Creating tables with well-defined constraints is essential for maintaining data integrity. The primary key constraint ensures that each row in the table can be uniquely identified, which is critical for referencing and linking data across different tables. Additionally, foreign keys can enforce referential integrity, ensuring that relationships between tables remain consistent. For example, if you have a **departments** table and want to link it to the **film_crew** table, you would add a foreign key constraint using the following code:

```
CREATE TABLE departments (
department_id INT PRIMARY KEY,
department_name VARCHAR(100)
);
CREATE TABLE employees (
employee_id INT PRIMARY KEY,
first_name VARCHAR(50),
last_name VARCHAR(50),
hire_date DATE,
department_id INT,
FOREIGN KEY (department_id) REFERENCES departments(department_id)
);
```

Let us understand this example in detail:

- The **department_id** column in the **film_crew** table is a foreign key that references the **department_id** column in the **departments** table.

- This constraint ensures that each crew member is linked to a valid department, helping to prevent orphaned records and maintain data integrity in the relationship between **film_crew** and **departments**.

- By defining this foreign key, you ensure that each crew member's department assignment is valid, reinforcing the structure and consistency of your database.

Modifying existing tables is another critical aspect of database management. As requirements evolve, you may need to add new columns, change data types, or update constraints to accommodate new data or improve performance. SQL provides the **ALTER TABLE** statement to modify the structure of an existing table without losing the data it contains. For instance, if you wanted to add an **email** column to the **film_crew** table, you would use the following command:

```
ALTER TABLE film_crew
ADD email VARCHAR (100);
```

Let us understand this example in detail:

- The command adds a new **email** column to the **film_crew** table, enabling the storage of email addresses for each crew member.
- This new column will be added to all existing rows by default, with NULL as the default value unless otherwise specified.
- This enables us to add email information without altering or impacting current records, providing a straightforward way to expand the table's data capacity.

In addition to adding columns, you can modify an existing column's data type using the **ALTER TABLE** statement. For example, if you initially defined the **phone_number** column in the **film_crew** table as an integer but later decided to change it to a string to allow for different formats, you would use the following command:

```
ALTER TABLE film_crew
MODIFY phone_number VARCHAR(15);
```

Note: **MODIFY statements are common in other database systems. SQLite 3 does not support this function. It is important, however, to understand these statements with SQL.**

Let us understand this example in detail:

- The command changes the data type of the **phone_number** column to **VARCHAR(15)**, allowing phone numbers to be stored in various formats, including country codes or hyphens.
- This flexibility helps accommodate international formats and ensures that the data can be stored accurately without restrictions on number-only formats.

If you need to remove an unused column from the **film_crew** table, you can use the **DROP COLUMN** clause. For example, if the nickname column is no longer needed, you would write the following command:

```
ALTER TABLE film_crew
DROP COLUMN nickname;
```

Let us understand this example in detail:

- The command removes the **nickname** column from the **film_crew** table, deleting all associated data and freeing up storage space.

- It is essential to carefully assess the impact of dropping a column, as this action is irreversible and can result in the permanent loss of information.

- Ensuring that the data is truly unnecessary before proceeding helps maintain data integrity.

Constraints can also be added or modified using the **ALTER TABLE** statement. For example, if you want to enforce a unique constraint on the **email** column in the **film_crew** table to prevent duplicate email addresses, you would write the following code:

```
ALTER TABLE film_crew
ADD CONSTRAINT unique_email UNIQUE (email);
```

Let us understand this example in detail:

- The command adds a unique constraint to the **email** column in the **film_crew** table, ensuring that no two crew members can have the same email address.

Adding such constraints is crucial for maintaining data integrity and enforcing business rules, as it prevents duplicate entries and ensures each email is unique across the table. This approach helps in scenarios where unique identifiers, like emails, are essential for accurate record-keeping.

Sometimes, you may need to rename a table or a column to reflect changes in the business context or improve clarity. SQL provides the **RENAME** clause within the **ALTER TABLE** statement. For example, if you want to rename the **film_crew** table to **crew_members** for better clarity, you would write the following command:

```
ALTER TABLE film_crew
RENAME TO crew_members;
```

Let us understand this example in detail:

- The command renames the **film_crew** table to **crew_members** without impacting the data or structure within the table.

Renaming tables can improve the readability and consistency of your database schema, mainly as your data model grows and evolves. This ensures table names align with their contents and are easy to understand for future reference and maintenance.

Creating and modifying tables in SQL requires a thorough understanding of the database schema and the relationships between different data entities. By carefully designing tables with appropriate columns, data types, and constraints, you can ensure that your database is well-structured, scalable, and capable of supporting your application's data needs. Additionally, modifying tables as requirements change allows you to maintain flexibility and adaptability in your database design, ensuring that it continues to meet your organization's evolving needs.

Improving queries with indexes

Indexes are one of the most effective tools available in SQL to improve query performance. An index is a data structure that enhances the speed of data retrieval operations on a database table. Creating indexes on columns frequently searched, sorted, or used in join operations can significantly reduce the time it takes to execute queries, particularly on large datasets. Understanding how to create, manage, and optimize indexes is essential for maintaining a responsive and efficient database system.

When a query is executed, the database engine typically performs a full table scan to find the requested data, which means it checks each row in the table sequentially. This process can be slow, especially in large tables.

An index, however, allows the database to quickly locate the rows that match the query conditions, much like a book's index helps you quickly find a specific topic without reading every page.

To create an index, you use the **CREATE INDEX** statement, specifying the table and the columns to be indexed.

For example, if you need to search for crew members in the **film_crew** table by their **last_name**, you would create an index on the **last** column like the following command:

```
CREATE INDEX idx_last_name
ON film_crew (last_name);
```

Let us understand this example in detail:

- The command creates an index named **idx_last_name** on the **last_name** column of the **film_crew** table.
- With this index in place, any query filtering or sorting by **last_name** will execute more quickly, as the database can rapidly locate the relevant rows.

Indexing is especially useful for improving performance on columns frequently used in search or sort operations, enhancing the efficiency of database queries.

Indexes are also useful in speeding up queries that involve **WHERE** clauses, **ORDER BY** clauses, and joins. For instance, if your application frequently retrieves records of crew members based on their **hire_date**, you can create an index on the **hire_date** column in the **film_crew** table to improve query performance. You can use the following command:

```
CREATE INDEX idx_hire_date
ON film_crew (hire_date);
```

In this example, the command creates an index named **idx_hire_date** on the **hire_date** column of the **film_crew** table. With this index in place, the following queries will speed up the retrieval of data from the **film_crew** table:

```
SELECT * FROM film_crew
WHERE hire_date > '2020-01-01';
```

Let us understand this example in detail:

- This will execute faster, as the database can use the index to locate rows with the desired **hire_date** quickly.

- Indexing columns frequently used in filtering criteria enhances performance, making data retrieval more efficient, especially for large datasets.

Compound indexes, or multi-column indexes, are another powerful feature that allow you to index multiple columns within a single index. This is particularly beneficial when multiple columns often filter your queries. For example, if you frequently search for crew members based on both **last_name** and **first_name**, you can create a compound index on the **film_crew** table like the following command:

```
CREATE INDEX idx_name
ON film_crew (last_name, first_name);
```

In this example, the command creates a compound index named **idx_name** on the **last_name** and **first_name** columns of the **film_crew** table. This compound index improves performance for queries that filter on both **last_name** and **first_name**,. Refer to the following code:

```
SELECT * FROM film_crew
WHERE last_name = 'Smith'
AND first_name = 'John';
```

Let us understand this example in detail:

- The order of columns in a compound index is crucial, as the index is most effective when the query filters by the first column (**last_name** in this case) before filtering by the second (**first_name**).

- If a query filters by **first_name** alone, the index might not provide as much benefit.

- Compound indexes like this are particularly helpful when you often query multiple columns together, optimizing retrieval efficiency for those specific search patterns.

- While indexes improve query performance, they also have some trade-offs that must be carefully managed. Let us look at them in detail:

  o One of the main drawbacks of indexes is that they require additional storage space.

  o The more indexes you create, the more disk space is needed to store them.

  o Additionally, indexes can slow down write operations, such as **INSERT**, **UPDATE**, and **DELETE**, because the database must update the indexes every time the data in the indexed columns changes. Therefore, it is important to strike a balance between read performance and the overhead introduced by maintaining indexes.

You can use **EXPLAIN** to check whether the database is utilizing an index for optimized query performance. For example, if you want to verify that the **idx_last_name** index on the **film_crew** table's **last_name** column is being used, you would write the following command:

```
EXPLAIN SELECT * FROM film_crew WHERE last_name = 'Doe';
```

Let us understand this example in detail:

- The **EXPLAIN** command provides the execution plan for the query, showing whether the **idx_last_name** index is being utilized.
- If the execution plan indicates that the index is not being used, this could suggest that the query is not optimized for the index, or the index itself may not be fully optimized for this search pattern.
- Regularly analyzing query performance with tools like **EXPLAIN** helps you identify opportunities for optimization, whether by adjusting indexes or refining query structure to better leverage existing indexes.

This proactive approach is key to maintaining efficient database performance, especially as data and usage patterns evolve.

It is also important to periodically review and maintain indexes on tables like **film_crew** can help keep performance optimal, especially as the data grows and changes over time. If the **idx_last_name** index on the **last_name** column becomes fragmented, you can rebuild it with the following command:

```
ALTER INDEX idx_last_name REBUILD;
```

Let us understand this example in detail:

- The command reorganizes the data within the **idx_last_name** index, reducing fragmentation and enhancing query performance.
- As data is inserted, updated, or deleted, indexes can become inefficient due to fragmentation.
- Scheduling regular index maintenance as part of database management helps ensure that indexes remain efficient, supporting faster queries and minimizing slowdowns over time.

By rebuilding or reorganizing indexes periodically, you can maintain the database's responsiveness and ensure indexes continue to support data retrieval effectively.

In some cases, if an index on the **last_name** column of the **film_crew** table, such as **idx_last_name**, is no longer beneficial or causing more overhead, you can remove it with the following command:

```
DROP INDEX idx_last_name
ON film_crew;
```

Let us understand this example in detail:

- The **DROP INDEX** command removes the **idx_last_name** index from the **film_crew** table, freeing up storage space and potentially improving performance for write operations, like inserts and updates.

- Indexes can sometimes become a liability if they are not frequently used in queries or if their maintenance costs outweigh the performance benefits for read operations.

Removing unnecessary indexes helps optimize database performance and resource utilization. Regularly reviewing and adjusting indexes to match usage patterns ensures a balanced approach to data retrieval efficiency and system responsiveness.

Finally, you might want to enforce data integrity on the email column in the **film_crew** table by creating a unique index. This would prevent duplicate email addresses and ensure each crew member has a unique email. Here is how to set it up:

```
CREATE UNIQUE INDEX idx_unique_email
ON film_crew (email);
```

Let us understand this example in detail:

- The command creates a unique index named **idx_unique_email** on the **email** column of the **film_crew** table.

- This index enhances query performance and ensures data integrity by preventing duplicate email addresses.

- Using unique indexes on columns like email addresses or usernames is particularly useful when uniqueness is required, as it enforces business rules and helps avoid data inconsistencies within the table.

Indexes are a critical component of SQL performance optimization. By understanding how and when to create indexes, monitor their effectiveness, and maintain them over time, you can significantly enhance the speed and efficiency of your queries.

However, it is essential to balance the benefits of faster query performance with the costs associated with storage and write operation overhead, ensuring that your database remains fast and responsive to the needs of your applications.

Simplifying complex queries with views

Views in SQL are powerful tools that allow you to simplify complex queries by encapsulating them in a virtual table. A view is a saved query you can reference like a table, providing an abstraction layer that hides the complexity of the underlying SQL code.

By using views, you can present data in a more accessible and organized way, making it easier to work with complex datasets, enforce security, and maintain consistency across your applications.

Creating a view is straightforward. You define the view using the **CREATE VIEW** statement, followed by the name of the view and the **SELECT** query that specifies the data it should include. For example, if you frequently need to retrieve data about film crew members and their departments, you can create a view that simplifies this process by combining the **film_crew** and **departments** tables using the following code:

```
CREATE VIEW crew_details AS
SELECT fc.crew_id, fc.first_name, fc.last_name, d.department_name
FROM film_crew fc
JOIN departments d ON fc.department_id = d.department_id;
```

In this example, the **crew_details** view joins the **film_crew** table with the **departments** table, providing a result set that includes each crew member's ID, first name, last name, and the name of their department. With this view in place, retrieving the combined data becomes straight forward:

```
SELECT * FROM crew_details;
```

Let us understand this example in detail:

- This query returns the same result set as the original join query, but with much less effort.

- The view simplifies queries, reduces repetition of complex joins and logic, and minimizes the potential for errors and inconsistencies.

- Using views is particularly valuable in scenarios where combined data is frequently accessed, as it streamlines data retrieval and improves maintainability.

Views are beneficial for breaking down complex queries into manageable components. The SQL code can quickly become difficult to read and maintain when dealing with multi-step calculations, intricate joins, or extensive filtering.

Encapsulating these operations in a view isolates the complexity and presents a clean interface to users or developers who need to interact with the data.

For example, if you want to calculate the total rentals for each crew member and their bonus based on a bonus rate, you could encapsulate the logic in a view you can use the following code:

```
CREATE VIEW crew_rentals AS
SELECT fc.crew_id, fc.first_name, fc.last_name,
       COUNT(r.rental_id) AS total_rentals,
       COUNT(r.rental_id) * fc.bonus_rate AS total_bonus
FROM film_crew fc
JOIN rental r ON fc.crew_id = r.staff_id  -- Assuming crew members are
linked to rentals via staff_id
GROUP BY fc.crew_id, fc.first_name, fc.last_name, fc.bonus_rate;
```

Now, instead of writing the complex query every time you need this data, you can query the **crew_rentals** view:

```
SELECT * FROM crew_rentals;
```

Let us understand this example in detail:

- This approach simplifies data access by avoiding repeated complex query logic, improving code readability, and making it easier to maintain and update your queries.

- Views like this are invaluable for streamlining workflows and ensuring consistency in complex calculations across multiple use cases.

Views also play a role in enforcing security and access control within a database. By granting users access to views instead of the underlying tables, you can restrict what data they view and query. For example, if you want to control access to sensitive information in the **film_crew** table, such as email addresses or hire dates, you can create a view that excludes these columns:

```
CREATE VIEW public_crew_details AS
SELECT crew_id, first_name, last_name, department_id
FROM film_crew;
```

Let us understand this example in detail:

- In this scenario, the **public_crew_details** view includes only non-sensitive columns like **crew_id**, **first_name**, **last_name**, and **department_id**.

- Sensitive information such as **email** or **hire_date** is excluded from the view. By granting access to this view instead of the underlying **film_crew** table, you ensure that users can access relevant crew information without exposing sensitive details.

- This approach could help you align with security best practices, allowing you to enforce data access policies more effectively and reduce the risk of unauthorized access to sensitive data.

Another advantage of using views is maintaining consistent business logic across multiple queries and applications. When business rules or calculations need to change, updating a view is often more straightforward and less error-prone than updating multiple queries scattered across different parts of an application. For example, if your organization changes the formula for calculating crew bonuses, you can update the **crew_rentals** view to reflect the new calculation without altering the queries that rely on it.

Here is how you perform the update:

```
crew_rentals;
CREATE VIEW crew_rentals AS
SELECT
    fc.crew_id,
    fc.first_name,
```

```
    fc.last_name,
    COUNT(r.rental_id) AS total_rentals,
    COUNT(r.rental_id) * fc.new_bonus_rate AS total_bonus
FROM
    film_crew fc
JOIN
    rental r ON fc.crew_id = r.staff_id
GROUP BY
    fc.crew_id, fc.first_name, fc.last_name, fc.new_bonus_rate;
```

Let us understand this example in detail:

- With this update, the **CREATE OR REPLACE VIEW** statement updates the **crew_rentals** view to use the **new_bonus_rate** column for bonus calculations instead of the old formula.

- This ensures that all queries relying on the **crew_rentals** view automatically reflect the updated bonus calculation.

- By centralizing the business logic in the view, you prevent discrepancies and reduce maintenance overhead.

- Any change to the calculation logic is managed in a single place, ensuring consistency across all dependent queries and simplifying system updates.

- This approach enhances scalability and reduces the risk of errors in your database operations.

Views can also present data in a more user-friendly format, particularly when working with complex or poorly structured tables. For example, suppose you have data stored in a normalized format across multiple tables, such as rental, customer, and film. In that case, you can create a view to present the data in a denormalized and user-friendly format.

Here is an example you can refer to:

```
CREATE VIEW rental_summary AS
SELECT r.rental_id, c.first_name || ' ' || c.last_name AS customer_name,
       f.title AS film_title, r.rental_date, r.return_date
FROM rental r
JOIN customer c ON r.customer_id = c.customer_id
JOIN inventory i ON r.inventory_id = i.inventory_id
JOIN film f ON i.film_id = f.film_id;
```

Let us understand this example in detail:

- The **rental_summary** view joins the rental, customer, inventory, and film tables.

- It provides a denormalized result set that includes the **rental_id**, **first_name**, the film **title**, and the **rental** and **return_date**.

With this view, users can easily retrieve rental details without needing to understand or query the normalized table structure directly. For example, they can simply run the following command:

```
SELECT * FROM rental_summary WHERE rental_date > '2005-01-01';
```

Let us understand this example in detail:

- This abstraction simplifies data interaction, reduces the learning curve for users, and ensures consistent queries across the system.

- It is particularly beneficial in environments where data relationships are complex, and users need a more intuitive way to access information.

- In addition to simplifying queries, views can improve performance in certain situations by optimizing how data is retrieved. For example, if a view encapsulates a frequently used complex query, the database engine may cache the result, reducing the time required to execute the query in the future.

- However, it is important to note that views only sometimes improve performance, especially if they involve complex operations on large datasets. In some cases, materialized views, which store the result of the query physically, might be a better option, though there are things to consider, like storage and maintenance.

Overall, views are a powerful feature in SQL that helps simplify complex queries, enforce security, maintain consistent business logic, and present data in a more accessible format. By understanding how to create and effectively use views, you can streamline your database operations, reduce redundancy, and enhance the usability and maintainability of your SQL queries.

Stored procedures and functions

Stored procedures and functions are essential components of SQL that enhance the capabilities of a database by allowing you to encapsulate and reuse complex logic. These constructs help you streamline database operations, improve performance, and enforce consistency across your database applications. Using stored procedures and functions, you can automate repetitive tasks, implement business logic directly within the database, and ensure that operations are executed efficiently and securely.

Stored procedures are precompiled collections of SQL statements and control-of-flow logic stored within some database management systems. SQLite 3 does not support stored procedures like MySQL, Microsoft SQL Server do. It is important to understand they they exist and how to utilize them. They can be executed as needed, allowing you to encapsulate complex sequences of operations and run them with a single call. Stored procedures are particularly useful for tasks that require multiple steps, such as data validation, transformation, and integration processes.

To create a stored procedure, use the **CREATE PROCEDURE** statement, followed by the procedure's name and the SQL code it should execute. For example, if you frequently need to update crew member bonuses based on their performance levels, you can create a stored procedure to automate this task. Refer to the following code:

```
CREATE PROCEDURE UpdateCrewBonuses AS
BEGIN
    UPDATE film_crew
    SET bonus = bonus * 1.15
    WHERE performance_level = 'Outstanding';
    UPDATE film_crew
    SET bonus = bonus * 1.10
    WHERE performance_level = 'Exceeds Expectations';
    UPDATE film_crew
    SET bonus = bonus * 0.90
    WHERE performance_level = 'Needs Improvement';
END;
```

This stored procedure, `UpdateCrewBonuses` adjusts the bonus values in the `film_crew` table based on each crew member's `performance_level`.

The logic is encapsulated within the procedure, ensuring consistent execution of the updates. To execute this procedure, you run the following command:

```
EXEC UpdateCrewBonuses;
```

Stored procedures offer several advantages. First, they improve performance by reducing the data transfer between the database and the application. Since the procedure is executed on the server, only the results must be returned to the client, minimizing network traffic:

- By using a stored procedure, you centralize the logic for bonus adjustments, ensuring that updates are consistent, repeatable, and efficient.

- It also makes the process easier to maintain and reduces the risk of errors in manually written queries. This is particularly useful for periodic tasks or complex update logic tied to specific business rules.

- Additionally, stored procedures are precompiled, meaning that the database engine optimizes them during creation, leading to faster execution times than repeatedly executing raw SQL statements.

- Another significant benefit of stored procedures is their ability to enforce security and control access to data. By permitting users to execute stored procedures rather than directly accessing the underlying tables, you can ensure that sensitive operations are controlled.

- This approach helps prevent unauthorized access and maintains data integrity, as users cannot modify the procedure's logic or access data outside the procedure's scope.

- Stored procedures can also accept input parameters, allowing you to pass values to the procedure at runtime. This feature adds flexibility and reusability, as the same procedure can perform different operations based on the input provided.

For example, you could modify the **UpdateCrewBonuses** procedure to accept a percentage increase as a parameter, allowing dynamic adjustments based on the input. Here is how it could look:

```
CREATE PROCEDURE UpdateCrewBonuses
    @PercentIncrease DECIMAL(5, 2)
AS
BEGIN
    UPDATE film_crew
    SET bonus = bonus * (1 + @PercentIncrease / 100)
    WHERE performance_level = 'Outstanding';
    UPDATE film_crew
    SET bonus = bonus * (1 + (@PercentIncrease / 100) / 2)
    WHERE performance_level = 'Exceeds Expectations';
    UPDATE film_crew
    SET bonus = bonus * (1 - (@PercentIncrease / 100) / 2)
    WHERE performance_level = 'Needs Improvement';
END;
```

In this version, the procedure **UpdateCrewBonuses** accepts a parameter **@PercentIncrease**, which defines the percentage change to apply. The bonus values are dynamically updated based on the **performance_level**, with greater increases for better performance levels and decreases for those needing improvement. To execute this procedure with a 10% increase, you would use the following command:

```
EXEC UpdateCrewBonuses @PercentIncrease = 10;
```

Let us understand this example in detail:

- This version of the procedure provides flexibility by allowing you to adjust the bonus updates dynamically, ensuring that changes align with current business needs.

- It simplifies management and ensures consistent application of the bonus adjustment logic across all applicable records.

In addition to stored procedures, SQL functions provide another way to encapsulate reusable logic. Unlike stored procedures, functions return a single value and are typically used for calculations, data transformations, or retrieving specific data. Functions can be called within SQL queries, making them ideal for operations that must be applied to individual rows or columns.

To create a function, you use the **CREATE FUNCTION** statement, specifying the function's name, parameters, return type, and the logic it should execute. For example, you could create a function to calculate the annual bonus of a crew member based on their monthly bonus.

Refer to the following code:

```
CREATE FUNCTION CalculateAnnualBonus
(@MonthlyBonus DECIMAL(10, 2))
RETURNS DECIMAL(10, 2)
AS
BEGIN
    RETURN @MonthlyBonus * 12;
END;
```

Let us understand this example in detail:

- This function, **CalculateAnnualBonus**, takes the monthly bonus as input (@ *MonthlyBonus*) and returns the annual bonus.
- This encapsulates the calculation logic, making it reusable across multiple queries.

You can then use the function in a query to calculate the annual bonus for all crew members:

```
SELECT crew_id, first_name, last_name,
       CalculateAnnualBonus(bonus) AS annual_bonus
FROM film_crew;
```

Let us understand this example in detail:

- This query retrieves the **crew_id**, **first_name**, and **last_name** of each crew member and calculates their annual bonus using the **CalculateAnnualBonus** function.
- By centralizing the calculation logic in a function, you simplify and standardize calculations across your database, reducing redundancy and ensuring consistency.

Functions enhance the modularity and maintainability of your SQL code by allowing you to reuse complex calculations or transformations across multiple queries. They also improve readability, as the logic is abstracted into a named function, making your queries cleaner and easier to understand.

SQL functions can be categorized into scalar functions and table-valued functions. Scalar functions, like **CalculateAnnualSalary**, return a single value, while table-valued functions return a result set.

Table-valued functions are particularly useful when you need to return a set of rows based on some input parameters. For example, you could create a table-valued function to return all crew members in a specific department. It would look like the following code:

```
CREATE FUNCTION GetCrewByDepartment
(@DepartmentID INT)
```

```
RETURNS TABLE
AS
RETURN
(
    SELECT crew_id, first_name, last_name
    FROM film_crew
    WHERE department_id = @DepartmentID
);
```

The **GetCrewByDepartment** function takes a parameter **@DepartmentID** to specify the department. It returns a table of **crew_id**, **first_name**, and **last_name** for all crew members in the given department. You can use this function in a query like a regular table:

```
SELECT * FROM GetCrewByDepartment(2);
```

This query retrieves all crew members in the department with an ID of 2. Table-valued functions like this are useful for encapsulating reusable logic that returns subsets of data, simplifying complex queries, and improving maintainability.

Stored procedures and functions are powerful tools that enhance the flexibility, performance, and maintainability of your SQL code. By encapsulating complex logic and reusing it across your database operations, you can reduce redundancy, enforce consistency, and improve the overall efficiency of your database applications. Whether you are automating routine tasks, implementing business logic, or performing calculations, stored procedures and functions provide the necessary infrastructure to build robust and scalable database solutions.

Automating database tasks with triggers

Triggers in SQL are powerful mechanisms that allow you to automate database tasks by executing predefined actions in response to specific events within the database. These events typically include data modifications such as **INSERT**, **UPDATE**, or **DELETE** operations. Using triggers, you can enforce business rules, maintain data integrity, and perform automatic logging or auditing without requiring manual intervention. Triggers provide a way to embed logic directly within the database, ensuring that critical processes are executed consistently and efficiently whenever the specified events occur.

A trigger is a set of SQL statements automatically executed when a particular event occurs on a specified table. To create a trigger, you use the **CREATE TRIGGER** statement, defining the event that will activate the trigger and the actions that the trigger will perform. For example, you can create a similar trigger to log additions of new crew members to the **film_crew** table by inserting records into a **crew_log** table. Here is how you can implement it:

```
CREATE TRIGGER log_crew_insert
```

```
AFTER INSERT ON film_crew
FOR EACH ROW
BEGIN
    INSERT INTO crew_log (crew_id, action, action_date)
    VALUES (NEW.crew_id, 'INSERT', CURRENT_TIMESTAMP);
END;
```

Let us understand this example in detail:

- The **log_crew_insert** trigger is fired after an **INSERT** operation is performed on the **film_crew** table.

- It inserts a new record into the **crew_log** table, capturing the **crew_id** of the new entry, the action performed (**INSERT**), and the current date and time using **CURRENT_TIMESTAMP.**

- The **NEW** keyword refers to the new row being inserted into the **film_crew** table. This trigger automates logging for new crew member additions, ensuring that the **crew_log** table maintains a consistent audit trail.

- This approach improves data integrity and reduces the risk of missed or inconsistent logging compared to manual processes.

Triggers can be classified into two main types: **BEFORE** triggers and **AFTER** triggers. A **BEFORE** trigger is executed before the triggering event occurs, allowing you to validate or modify data before it is committed to the database. For instance, you could create a **BEFORE INSERT** trigger to enforce a rule that prevents crew members from being added with a hire date in the future. It would look like the following code:

```
CREATE TRIGGER check_crew_hire_date
BEFORE INSERT ON film_crew
FOR EACH ROW
WHEN NEW.hire_date > DATE('now')
BEGIN
  SELECT RAISE(FAIL, 'Hire date cannot be in the future');
END;
```

Let us understand this example in detail:

- The **check_crew_hire_date** trigger is executed before an **INSERT** operation on the **film_crew** table.

- It checks if the **hire_date** of the new row is greater than the current date (**CURRENT_ DATE**).

- If the condition is true, the trigger raises an error with **SIGNAL SQLSTATE '45000'** and provides a custom message: *Hire date cannot be in the future.*

- This prevents the insertion of records with invalid **hire_date** values.

BEFORE triggers like this are excellent for enforcing validation rules directly within the database, ensuring that only valid data enters the table and maintaining the integrity of the data model without relying solely on application logic.

AFTER triggers, however, are executed after the triggering event has occurred. These triggers are commonly used for tasks such as updating related tables, maintaining summary data, or triggering other processes. For example, if you want to maintain the count of crew members in each department within the departments table whenever a crew member is added or removed from the **film_crew** table, you could create **AFTER INSERT** and **AFTER DELETE** triggers like the following code:

```
DROP TRIGGER IF EXISTS update_department_count_after_insert;
CREATE TRIGGER update_department_count_after_insert
AFTER INSERT ON film_crew
FOR EACH ROW
BEGIN
  UPDATE departments
  SET crew_count = crew_count + 1
  WHERE department_id = NEW.department_id;
END;
DROP TRIGGER IF EXISTS update_department_count_after_delete;
CREATE TRIGGER update_department_count_after_delete
AFTER DELETE ON film_crew
FOR EACH ROW
BEGIN
  UPDATE departments
  SET crew_count = crew_count - 1
  WHERE department_id = OLD.department_id;
END;
```

Let us understand this example in detail:

- The **update_department_count_after_insert** trigger fires after a new row is added to the **film_crew** table.
- It increases the **crew_count** in the corresponding department by one (1) using the **NEW.department_id** from the newly inserted row.
- The **update_department_count_after_delete** trigger fires after a row is deleted from the **film_crew** table.
- It decreases the **crew_count** in the corresponding department by one (1) using the **OLD.department_id** from the deleted row.

- By automating the maintenance of the **crew_count** column in the **departments** table, you ensure that the count always reflects the current state of the database.

- You eliminate the need for manual updates or additional logic in application code to manage these changes.

Triggers can also be used for auditing purposes, tracking changes to data, and capturing who made the changes and when they occurred. This is especially important in environments where data security and compliance are critical. For example, you can create an **AFTER UPDATE** trigger to track crew member bonus updates by logging changes in a **bonus_audit** table. The trigger, named **audit_bonus_changes**, runs after any update to the **film_crew** table. It checks if the bonus value has changed by comparing the old value (**OLD.bonus**) with the new value (**NEW.bonus**). The trigger inserts a record into the **bonus_audit** table if a change is detected. This record includes the **crew_id** of the updated crew member, the old bonus value, the new bonus value, and the date and time of the change.

To implement this, you can define the trigger as follows:

```
DROP TRIGGER IF EXISTS audit_bonus_changes;
CREATE TRIGGER audit_bonus_changes
AFTER UPDATE ON film_crew
FOR EACH ROW
WHEN OLD.bonus <> NEW.bonus
BEGIN
  INSERT INTO bonus_audit (crew_id, old_bonus, new_bonus, change_date)
  VALUES (NEW.crew_id, OLD.bonus, NEW.bonus, CURRENT_TIMESTAMP);
END;
```

Let us understand this example in detail:

- This trigger ensures that every update to the bonus column is automatically recorded in the **bonus_audit** table, providing a clear and consistent audit trail for bonus changes.

- Automating this process simplifies record-keeping and supports accountability, enabling you to track adjustments reliably and efficiently.

Triggers also allow for the enforcement of referential integrity between related tables. For example, you could create a **BEFORE DELETE** trigger on the **departments** table to prevent the deletion of a department that still has crew members assigned to it. This trigger ensures that referential integrity is maintained between the **departments** and **film_crew** tables. Here is how it can be implemented:

```
DROP TRIGGER IF EXISTS prevent_department_deletion;
CREATE TRIGGER prevent_department_deletion
BEFORE DELETE ON departments
FOR EACH ROW
```

```
WHEN EXISTS (
  SELECT 1
  FROM film_crew
  WHERE department_id = OLD.department_id
)
BEGIN
  SELECT RAISE(FAIL, 'Cannot delete department with assigned crew
members');
END;
```

This trigger prevents the deletion of departments that still have crew members assigned to them, ensuring that the relationship between departments and crew members remains consistent. Automating this check helps maintain data integrity without requiring additional application-level logic, making it a reliable solution for managing database constraints.

While triggers are powerful, they should be used judiciously. Since they operate automatically and often behind the scenes, they can complicate debugging and troubleshooting if they are not well-documented or introduce unintended side effects. It is important to ensure that triggers are carefully designed, thoroughly tested, and properly documented to avoid any negative impact on database performance or maintainability.

Triggers provide an efficient and reliable way to automate tasks, enforce business rules, and maintain data integrity within a SQL database. By understanding how to create and implement triggers effectively, you can ensure that critical database operations are carried out automatically and consistently, reducing the risk of human error and enhancing the overall functionality of your database applications.

Conclusion

In this chapter, you developed a comprehensive understanding of managing database objects. You explored how to create and modify tables, ensuring your database structure aligns with organizational needs. Additionally, you learned the importance of indexes in improving query performance and the role of views in simplifying complex queries. The chapter also introduced you to stored procedures, functions, and triggers, which automate repetitive tasks and enhance the functionality of your database. These tools are essential for building efficient, well-organized, and scalable database systems, equipping you to handle diverse data management challenges confidently.

In the next chapter, we will look into SQL performance optimization. You will learn to analyze query execution plans, implement effective indexing strategies, and optimize joins and subqueries for better performance. We will also explore common performance pitfalls and how to avoid them. This chapter will provide the knowledge and techniques to refine your SQL queries and ensure your database operates efficiently, setting the stage for handling large-scale datasets and complex analytical tasks.

Exercises

In these exercises, you will gain practical experience managing database objects, covering operations for tables, indexes, views, functions, and triggers.

Managing tables

In this exercise, you will create, modify, and drop tables to manage the structure of your database:

- **Create a table**: At the **sqlite>** prompt, create a table named **rental_log** to log rental activities with columns for **log_id**, **rental_id**, **customer_id**, and **log_date**. Refer to the following code:

```
CREATE TABLE rental_log (
    log_id INTEGER PRIMARY KEY AUTOINCREMENT,
    rental_id INTEGER,
    customer_id INTEGER,
    log_date TEXT
);
```

- **Alter a table:** At the **sqlite>** prompt, add a new column, notes, to the **rental_log** table:

```
ALTER TABLE rental_log
ADD COLUMN notes TEXT;
```

- **Drop a table:** At the **sqlite>** prompt, drop the **rental_log** table when it is no longer needed:

```
DROP TABLE rental_log;
```

Managing indexes

In this exercise, you will create and manage indexes to optimize performance:

- **Creating an index**: At the **sqlite>** prompt, create an index on the title column of the film table to improve searches by film title:

```
CREATE INDEX idx_film_title ON film (title);
```

- **Using EXPLAIN:** At the **sqlite>** prompt, use **EXPLAIN** to check if the index is used for a query searching for a specific film:

```
EXPLAIN QUERY PLAN SELECT * FROM film WHERE title = 'ACADEMY
DINOSAUR';
```

- **Dropping an index**: At the **sqlite>** prompt, drop the **idx_film_title** index if it is no longer required:

```
DROP INDEX idx_film_title;
```

Using views

In this exercise, you will create views to simplify commonly used queries:

- **Creating a view:** At the **sqlite>** prompt, create a view named **rental_summary** to show **rental_id**, **customer_id**, **title**, and **rental_date** by joining **rental**, **customer**, and **film** tables:

```
CREATE VIEW rental_summary AS
        SELECT r.rental_id, c.customer_id, f.title, r.rental_date
        FROM rental r
        JOIN customer c ON r.customer_id = c.customer_id
        JOIN inventory i ON r.inventory_id = i.inventory_id
        JOIN film f ON i.film_id = f.film_id;
```

- **Querying the view**: At the **sqlite>** prompt, query the **rental_summary** view to retrieve the combined data:

```
SELECT * FROM rental_summary WHERE rental_date > '2005-01-01';
```

- **Dropping the view**: At the **sqlite>** prompt, drop the **rental_summary** view when it is no longer needed:

```
DROP VIEW rental_summary;
```

Using functions

In this exercise, you will simulate a function to calculate rental revenue for a customer:

- **Creating the table**: At the **sqlite>** prompt, create a table **customer_revenue** with columns for **customer_id** and **monthly_revenue**:

```
CREATE TABLE customer_revenue (
     customer_id INTEGER PRIMARY KEY,
     monthly_revenue REAL
     );
```

- **Perform a query**: At the **sqlite>** prompt, calculate the annual revenue for each customer by multiplying **monthly_revenue** by **12**:

```
SELECT customer_id, monthly_revenue * 12 AS annual_revenue
FROM customer_revenue;
```

- **Alter the table and update**: At the **sqlite>** prompt, update the **customer_revenue** table to store annual revenue:

```
ALTER TABLE customer_revenue
ADD COLUMN annual_revenue REAL;
UPDATE customer_revenue
SET annual_revenue = monthly_revenue * 12;
```

Using triggers

In this exercise, you will create triggers to automate database actions:

- **Create trigger**: At the **sqlite>** prompt, create a trigger **log_rental_insert** to log new rentals in the **rental_log** table:

```
CREATE TRIGGER log_rental_insert
AFTER INSERT ON rental
BEGIN
INSERT INTO rental_log (rental_id, customer_id, log_date)
VALUES (NEW.rental_id, NEW.customer_id, DATETIME('now'));
END;
```

- **Activate the trigger by inserting a record**: At the **sqlite>** prompt, insert a new rental and check the **rental_log** table for the log entry:

```
INSERT INTO rental (rental_id, customer_id, inventory_id, rental_
date, staff_id, last_update)
VALUES (990022, 2, 3, '2023-11-01', 1, 07-04-2005);
```

- **Drop the trigger**: At the **sqlite>** prompt, drop the **log_rental_insert** trigger when it is no longer needed:

```
DROP TRIGGER log_rental_insert;
```

Join our Discord space

Join our Discord workspace for latest updates, offers, tech happenings around the world, new releases, and sessions with the authors:

https://discord.bpbonline.com

CHAPTER 9

SQL Performance Optimization

Introduction

In this chapter, you will focus on SQL performance optimization techniques that enhance query efficiency and improve overall database performance. You will begin by understanding query execution plans, a critical tool for analyzing how your queries interact with the database. You will then explore indexing strategies to speed up data retrieval, optimize joins for complex table relationships, and refine subqueries for better resource management. Additionally, you will learn to identify and avoid common performance pitfalls that can slow down your queries. By mastering these techniques, you will gain the skills to write efficient SQL queries that handle large datasets with precision and speed.

Structure

This chapter covers the following topics:

- Understanding execution plans
- Indexing strategies
- Optimizing joins
- Optimizing subqueries
- Avoiding common pitfalls

Objectives

By the end of this chapter, you will be equipped with the knowledge and skills to optimize SQL queries for maximum performance and efficiency. You will understand how to interpret query execution plans to identify bottlenecks and make informed improvements. You will learn effective indexing strategies to enhance data retrieval speed and optimize joins, thereby streamlining complex table relationships. Additionally, you will refine your use of subqueries, minimizing resource consumption and improving query execution times. Ultimately, you will be able to identify and avoid common performance pitfalls, ensuring that your SQL queries execute efficiently, even when working with large datasets. These optimization techniques will enable you to manage database performance with confidence and precision.

Understanding execution plans

A query execution plan is a detailed breakdown of how a **database management system** (**DBMS**) processes a SQL query. It reveals the database engine's steps for retrieving or manipulating data and provides valuable insight into the query's efficiency. Understanding query execution plans is essential for optimizing SQL performance, as it helps identify potential bottlenecks and inefficiencies in query processing.

Accessing query execution plans

In most relational databases, including the Sakila sample database, you can generate an execution plan using commands specific to the database system. For example, in SQLite, you use the **EXPLAIN** keyword to obtain an execution plan for a query. Consider the following query to retrieve rental data from the Sakila database:

```
EXPLAIN
SELECT rental_id, customer_id, rental_date
FROM rental
WHERE rental_date > '2005-05-25';
```

The output of this command provides information about how the database processes the query, including details about table access methods, indexes used, and the estimated number of rows scanned. Understanding these details is the first step toward identifying areas for improvement.

Key elements of an execution plan

An execution plan typically consists of several essential components that describe how the query is executed. Let us look at them in detail:

- **Table access methods:** This indicates how the database retrieves rows from a table. Common methods include full table scans, index scans, and range scans. For example, in the Sakila database, if the **rental_date** column in the rental table is indexed, the preceding query above may use an index range scan to optimize performance.

- **Join methods**: For queries involving multiple tables, the execution plan outlines the join method used, such as nested loop joins, hash joins, or merge joins. For instance, consider a query that retrieves rental and customer information:

```
EXPLAIN
SELECT r.rental_id, c.first_name, c.last_name
FROM rental r
JOIN customer c ON r.customer_id = c.customer_id
WHERE r.rental_date > '2005-05-25';
```

  The execution plan for this query will specify how the database joins the rental and customer tables, including the order of the joins and whether indexes are used.

- **Filter conditions:** This shows the conditions applied to filter rows, such as **WHERE** clauses or join conditions. Understanding how these conditions are evaluated helps ensure that only necessary rows are processed.

- **Cost estimates:** Many databases provide an estimated cost for each query step, reflecting the expected resource usage. High-cost steps indicate areas where optimization is needed.

Analyzing common performance issues

Execution plans can help identify several common performance issues. One frequent problem is using a full table scan, which occurs when the database reads every row in a table to find matching results. This is often inefficient for large tables, as seen in the following query:

```
SELECT rental_id, customer_id
FROM rental
WHERE rental_date = '2005-05-25';
```

If the **rental_date** column lacks an index, the database must scan the entire rental table to locate matching rows. Adding an index on **rental_date** can significantly reduce the number of rows scanned, as shown in an updated execution plan.

Another area for improvement is efficient joins, where the database uses a suboptimal method to combine tables. For example, a nested loop may perform poorly if the join condition does not use indexed columns. By examining the join order and method in the execution plan, you can determine whether adding indexes or restructuring the query will improve performance.

Using indexes to improve execution plans

Indexes play a critical role in optimizing query performance, and their impact is often reflected in the execution plan. When an index is available for a query condition, the database can use an index scan instead of a full table scan, reducing the number of rows processed. For instance, adding an index on the **rental_date** column in the **rental** table improves the performance of queries filtering by date:

```
CREATE INDEX idx_rental_date ON rental (rental_date);
```

After adding this index, running the **EXPLAIN** command on queries with conditions on **rental_date** will show an index range scan in the execution plan, indicating that the database is leveraging the index for faster row retrieval.

Interpreting key metrics in the plan

When analyzing an execution plan, focus on specific metrics that indicate query performance. The rows column, for example, shows the estimated number of rows the database expects to process at each step. Lower row counts generally indicate more efficient queries.

The type column in SQLite's **EXPLAIN** output describes the access method used, such as **ALL,** for a full table scan or ref for an index scan. A plan showing **ALL** in the type column for a large table often signals the need for optimization. Similarly, the extra column provides additional details, such as whether temporary tables or file sorts are used, which can negatively impact performance.

Optimizing query plans

Once you understand the execution plan, you can take steps to optimize the query. For example, consider the following inefficient query that retrieves customer rental data:

```
SELECT c.first_name, c.last_name, r.rental_date
FROM customer c
JOIN rental r ON c.customer_id = r.customer_id
WHERE r.rental_date > '2005-05-25';
```

If the execution plan reveals a full table scan on the **rental** table, adding an index on the **rental_date** column improves performance. Reviewing the join order and ensuring that indexed columns are used in the join condition further enhances efficiency.

By iterating on the query and re-evaluating the execution plan after each change, you can progressively refine performance and ensure optimal resource usage.

Indexing strategies

Indexes are essential tools in SQL for optimizing query performance by providing faster access to rows in a table. They act as pointers, enabling the database to locate data without scanning every row. Choosing the right indexing strategy can significantly enhance query performance, especially in large databases like the Sakila sample database. Understanding how to design, implement, and maintain indexes is critical for ensuring your queries run efficiently.

Basic indexing concepts

An index is a database object that stores a subset of a table's data in a sorted order, allowing quick lookups. Primary keys and unique constraints automatically create indexes, but you can also define additional indexes based on query requirements. For example, consider the **rental** table. If you frequently query rentals by **rental_date**, creating an index on this column can improve performance. Refer to the following command:

```
CREATE INDEX idx_rental_date ON rental (rental_date);
```

This index allows the database to perform an index range scan instead of a full table scan when executing queries such as the following:

```
SELECT rental_id, customer_id
FROM rental
WHERE rental_date > '2005-05-25';
```

The database uses the sorted index to locate rows matching the condition, reducing the number of rows scanned and speeding up the query.

Choosing the right columns to index

One of the most important aspects of the indexing strategy is selecting the right columns to index. Focus on columns frequently used in **WHERE** clauses, join conditions, and sorting operations. For example, queries that join the **rental** and **customer** tables based on **customer_id** will benefit from an index on this column:

```
CREATE INDEX idx_customer_id ON rental (customer_id);
```

Avoid indexing rarely queried columns with low cardinality (few unique values), such as binary flags or columns with repeated values. Indexing such columns often provides minimal benefit while increasing storage requirements and slowing down write operations.

Composite indexes

Sometimes, more than a single column index may be required, especially for queries involving multiple conditions. Composite indexes, which include multiple columns, are useful for optimizing such queries. For instance, if you frequently query rentals by both

customer_id and **rental_date**, a composite index can improve performance. Refer to the following command:

```
CREATE INDEX idx_customer_rental_date ON rental (customer_id, rental_date);
```

This index optimizes queries that filter by both columns or only the leading column (**customer_id**). For example:

```
SELECT rental_id
FROM rental
WHERE customer_id = 5 AND rental_date > '2005-05-25';
```

However, composite indexes must be designed carefully. The order of columns in a composite index matters because the database uses the leading column to narrow down rows before evaluating subsequent columns. If the leading column is not part of the query conditions, the index may not be used effectively.

Covering indexes

A covering index is an advanced indexing strategy where the index contains all the columns required for a query. This eliminates the need to access the table itself, as the database retrieves all necessary data directly from the index. For example, consider a query that retrieves rental IDs and dates for a specific customer:

```
SELECT rental_id, rental_date
FROM rental
WHERE customer_id = 5;
```

You can create a covering index to optimize the following query:

```
CREATE INDEX idx_covering_rental ON rental (customer_id, rental_id, rental_date);
```

This index lets the database fetch the requested columns without scanning the rental table, resulting in faster query execution.

Index maintenance and monitoring

Indexes require regular maintenance to ensure they remain efficient. Over time, as data in a table changes, indexes can become fragmented, leading to reduced performance. Monitoring index usage and fragmentation is an important part of database optimization. In SQLite, you can use the **PRAGMA** command to examine existing indexes. Refer to the following command:

```
PRAGMA index_list('rental')
```

For fragmented indexes, rebuilding them can restore efficiency. In SQLite, this can be done by dropping the index and recreating it or with the **ANALYZE** and **REINDEX** commands. Refer to the following code:

```
ANALYZE;
REINDEX idx_convering_rental; -- Rebuild the index
REINDEX rental; -- Rebuilds all indexes on rental
```

Monitoring query performance to identify underutilized or unused indexes is also essential. Unused indexes consume storage and slow down write operations without providing any benefit. Removing unnecessary indexes can help maintain overall database performance.

Balancing indexing trade-offs

While indexes improve read performance, they come with trade-offs. Indexes increase storage requirements and can slow down write operations, such as **INSERT**, **UPDATE**, and **DELETE**, because the database must update the indexes in addition to the table data. Balancing the number and type of indexes is critical to maintaining optimal database performance.

For example, excessive indexing on the rental table could slow down **INSERT** operations in a highly transactional system, where new rentals are frequently added. In such cases, prioritize indexes on columns that significantly impact query performance and remove those that provide minimal benefits.

Using indexes in joins

Indexes are especially beneficial for optimizing joins between tables. When joining two tables, indexing the columns used in the join condition can reduce the number of rows the database processes. For example, consider a query that joins the **rental** and **customer** tables:

```
SELECT r.rental_id, c.first_name, c.last_name
FROM rental r JOIN customer c
ON r.customer_id = c.customer_id
WHERE r.rental_date > '2005-05-25';
```

Indexes on **rental.customer_id** and **customer.customer_id** improve the join's performance by allowing the database to quickly match rows between the tables. Without these indexes, the database may resort to a slower nested loop join or a full table scan.

Dynamic indexing strategies

Dynamic indexing strategies involve creating or dropping indexes based on changing query patterns. For instance, if you notice a surge in queries filtering rentals by **inventory_id**, you could create an index on this column:

```
CREATE INDEX idx_inventory_id ON rental (inventory_id);
```

Conversely, if the query patterns change and an index is no longer used, removing it can improve database performance. Refer to the following command:

```
DROP INDEX idx_inventory_id ON rental;
```

Monitoring query performance and adjusting indexes ensures your database remains optimized for its current workload.

Optimizing joins

Joins are a fundamental component of SQL queries, enabling you to combine data from multiple tables based on related columns. However, poorly optimized joins can significantly impact query performance, especially in large databases. Optimizing joins involves selecting the appropriate join type, indexing effectively, and structuring queries to minimize the number of rows processed. These strategies ensure efficient data retrieval and improve overall database performance.

Understanding join types and their impact

The join used in a query has a direct impact on performance. Standard join types include **INNER JOIN**, **LEFT JOIN**, **RIGHT JOIN**, and **FULL OUTER JOIN**. Each serves a specific purpose, but some are more performance-intensive than others. For example, an **INNER JOIN** retrieves only matching rows between two tables and is generally faster than a **FULL OUTER JOIN**, which retrieves all rows from both tables and combines them. Consider a query that joins the **rental** and **customer** tables to retrieve customer information for rentals:

```
SELECT r.rental_id, c.first_name, c.last_name
FROM rental r
INNER JOIN customer c ON r.customer_id = c.customer_id;
```

In this case, the **INNER JOIN** is efficient because it retrieves only rows where a match exists in both tables. Using the right join type for your data requirements is crucial for optimizing performance.

Indexing join columns

Indexes on the columns used in join conditions are critical for improving performance. When a join condition references indexed columns, the database can quickly locate matching rows, reducing the time and resources required. For example, adding the following indexes to the **customer_id** columns in both the **rental** and **customer** tables optimizes the join in the previous query:

```
CREATE INDEX idx_rental_customer_id ON rental (customer_id);
```

```
CREATE INDEX idx_customer_id ON customer (customer_id);
```

With these indexes, the database engine can use index lookups instead of full table scans, significantly speeding up the join operation. A best practice is to ensure that join columns are indexed in all participating tables.

Reducing the number of rows processed

Minimizing the number of rows processed in a join is another key strategy for optimization. Filtering data before performing a join can reduce the workload on the database engine. For instance, if you want to retrieve rental information for customers who rented movies after a specific date, include a **WHERE** clause to filter the rental table before joining it with the customer table. Refer to the following code:

```
SELECT r.rental_id, c.first_name, c.last_name
FROM rental r
INNER JOIN customer c ON r.customer_id = c.customer_id
WHERE r.rental_date > '2005-05-25';
```

This query processes only rows in the rental table where the **rental_date** condition is met, reducing the number of rows involved in the join.

Optimizing multi-table joins

When joining multiple tables, the order of joins and using indexes play a critical role in performance. The database engine determines the join order based on query complexity and table size, but you can influence this behavior by structuring your query logically. For example, always join smaller tables first to minimize intermediate results.

Consider a query that joins the rental, customer, and inventory tables:

```
SELECT r.rental_id, c.first_name, c.last_name, i.film_id
FROM rental r
INNER JOIN customer c ON r.customer_id = c.customer_id
INNER JOIN inventory i ON r.inventory_id = i.inventory_id;
```

If the rental table is the largest, ensuring that the customer and inventory tables are joined first helps reduce the number of rows processed in subsequent joins. Indexing all join columns in these tables further enhances performance.

Avoiding Cartesian products

Cartesian products occur when no join condition is specified, combining every row from one table with every row from another. This is usually unintended, leading to result sets that consume significant resources. To prevent Cartesian products, always include explicit join conditions in your queries. Refer to the following example:

```
SELECT r.rental_id, c.first_name
FROM rental r, customer c;
```

The preceding query creates a Cartesian product because it lacks a **WHERE** clause or **ON** condition. Adding a proper join condition ensures that only relevant rows are combined.

Refer to the following example:

```
SELECT r.rental_id, c.first_name
FROM rental r INNER JOIN customer c ON r.customer_id = c.customer_id;
```

Using EXPLAIN to analyze join performance

The **EXPLAIN** command is a valuable tool for understanding how the database processes join. It details the join order, access methods, and estimated rows processed. Consider the following example in SQLite:

```
EXPLAIN
SELECT r.rental_id, c.first_name, c.last_name
FROM rental r
INNER JOIN customer c ON r.customer_id = c.customer_id;
```

The output indicates whether the join uses an index or a full table scan. If the type column shows **ALL**, a full table scan is being performed, signaling the need for optimization. Adding indexes or restructuring the query can improve performance.

Using temporary tables for complex joins

For complex joins, temporary tables can be an effective optimization strategy. By storing intermediate results in a temporary table, you can simplify the final join operation and reduce redundant processing. For instance, refer to the following example:

```
CREATE TEMPORARY TABLE temp_rentals AS
SELECT rental_id, customer_id
FROM rental WHERE rental_date > '2005-05-25';
SELECT tr.rental_id, c.first_name, c.last_name
FROM temp_rentals tr
JOIN customer c ON tr.customer_id = c.customer_id;
```

This approach reduces the complexity of the main query and allows the database to focus on a smaller subset of data, improving performance.

Using modern join techniques

Modern SQL dialects support advanced join techniques like hash and merge joins, which can be more efficient than nested loop joins in certain scenarios. While SQLite primarily uses nested loop joins, databases like PostgreSQL and Oracle automatically select the most efficient join algorithm based on query conditions and data distribution. Understanding how your database handles joins allows you to structure queries that leverage these advanced techniques for optimal performance.

Optimizing subqueries

Subqueries, known as nested queries, are a powerful tool in SQL for performing complex operations by embedding one query within another. While subqueries provide flexibility and functionality, they can also impact performance if not used efficiently. Optimizing subqueries involves restructuring queries, using alternatives like joins or **common table expressions** (**CTEs**), and minimizing the resources required to process them. By following best practices, you can ensure that subqueries enhance rather than hinder query performance.

Understanding the role of subqueries

Subqueries are often used to filter data, perform calculations, or retrieve intermediate results for the main query. For example, consider the following query that retrieves customer names who have made rentals in the Sakila sample database:

```
SELECT first_name, last_name
FROM customer
WHERE customer_id IN (
SELECT customer_id
FROM rental
WHERE rental_date > '2005-05-25' );
```

Here, the subquery retrieves the `customer_id` values from the rental table where the rental date is after May 25, 2005, and the main query filters customers based on this list. While functional, subqueries like this can lead to performance issues when working with large datasets.

Replacing subqueries with joins

One effective way to optimize subqueries is by replacing them with joins. Joins often perform better than subqueries because they allow the database engine to process relationships between tables more efficiently. The previous query can be rewritten as a join. Refer to the following example:

```
SELECT DISTINCT c.first_name, c.last_name
FROM customer c JOIN rental r ON c.customer_id = r.customer_id
WHERE r.rental_date > '2005-05-25';
```

This approach avoids the overhead of executing the subquery separately, as the join retrieves all matching rows in a single operation. Using `DISTINCT` ensures that duplicate rows are eliminated if the customer appears in multiple rentals.

Using correlated subqueries efficiently

Correlated subqueries, which reference columns from the outer query, are particularly resource-intensive because they execute repeatedly for each row in the outer query. Refer to the following example:

```sql
SELECT first_name, last_name
FROM customer c
WHERE EXISTS (
SELECT 1
FROM rental r
WHERE r.customer_id = c.customer_id AND r.rental_date > '2005-05-25' );
```

In this query, the subquery is evaluated for every row in the customer table, which can potentially lead to significant performance issues with large datasets.

Rewriting such queries using joins or CTEs is often more efficient. For example, the preceding query can be rewritten as:

```sql
SELECT DISTINCT c.first_name, c.last_name
FROM customer c JOIN rental r ON c.customer_id = r.customer_id
WHERE r.rental_date > '2005-05-25';
```

This approach reduces the number of executions and leverages the database engine's ability to optimize joins.

Using CTEs for complex subqueries

Using CTEs can simplify query structure and improve performance for complex queries involving multiple subqueries. CTEs allow you to define intermediate result sets that can be referenced in the main query. For example, refer to the following code:

```sql
WITH RecentRentals AS (
SELECT customer_id
FROM rental
WHERE rental_date > '2005-05-25'
)
SELECT c.first_name, c.last_name
FROM customer c JOIN RecentRentals rr
ON c.customer_id = rr.customer_id;
```

The **RecentRentals** CTE calculates the list of customers with recent rentals, and the main query retrieves their names. This approach improves readability and allows the database to optimize the execution plan more effectively.

Avoiding SELECT * in subqueries

Using **SELECT** * in subqueries can increase resource usage unnecessarily, as it retrieves all columns when only specific ones are required. For example, consider this inefficient query:

```
SELECT first_name, last_name
FROM customer WHERE customer_id
IN (
SELECT * FROM rental
WHERE rental_date > '2005-05-25' );
```

This subquery retrieves all columns from the rental table, even though only **customer_id** is needed. Optimizing it to select only the required column reduces overhead:

```
SELECT first_name, last_name FROM customer WHERE customer_id IN ( SELECT
customer_id FROM rental WHERE rental_date > '2005-05-25' );
```

This small change reduces the amount of data processed and transferred during query execution.

Minimizing nested subqueries

Deeply nested subqueries can be challenging when optimizing the database engine, leading to longer execution times. Flattening nested subqueries by combining conditions or restructuring the query can improve performance. Refer to the following example:

```
SELECT first_name, last_name
FROM customer
WHERE customer_id IN (
SELECT customer_id
FROM rental WHERE rental_date > '2005-05-25' AND inventory_id IN
(
SELECT inventory_id
FROM inventory WHERE film_id = 1
)
);
```

This query uses a nested subquery to filter rentals by inventory items belonging to a specific film. It can be rewritten using joins. Refer to the following example:

```
SELECT DISTINCT c.first_name, c.last_name
FROM customer c
JOIN rental r ON c.customer_id = r.customer_id
```

```
JOIN inventory i ON r.inventory_id = i.inventory_id
WHERE r.rental_date > '2005-05-25' AND i.film_id = 1;
```

The rewritten query processes fewer steps and allows the database to optimize join operations more effectively.

Indexing columns used in subqueries

Indexes are critical in optimizing subqueries, especially when filtering large datasets. For example, adding an index on the **rental_date** column in the rental table enhances the performance of subqueries filtering by date:

```
CREATE INDEX idx_rental_date ON rental (rental_date);
```

With this index, the database can more efficiently locate rows matching the condition **rental_date > '2005-05-25'**. Ensuring that indexed columns are used in subquery conditions minimizes the number of rows scanned and speeds up execution.

Using EXPLAIN to analyze subquery performance

The **EXPLAIN** command provides insights into how the database executes a query, including subqueries. Refer to the following example:

```
EXPLAIN
SELECT first_name, last_name
FROM customer
WHERE customer_id IN (
SELECT customer_id
FROM rental
WHERE rental_date > '2005-05-25'
);
```

The output reveals whether the subquery uses an index, performs a full table scan, or generates temporary tables. By analyzing the execution plan, you can identify bottlenecks and optimize your subqueries accordingly.

Avoiding common pitfalls

SQL queries can become inefficient if common performance pitfalls are not addressed during query design and execution. These pitfalls often arise from unoptimized data structures, improper query construction, or overreliance on resource-intensive operations. Understanding and avoiding these issues is crucial for maintaining a high-performing database environment, especially in systems like the Sakila sample database that involve large datasets and frequent queries.

Overuse of SELECT *

Using **SELECT** * in queries retrieves all columns from a table, even when only specific columns are needed. This approach increases the amount of data processed and transferred, leading to unnecessary resource consumption. For example, consider the following query:

```
SELECT *
FROM rental
WHERE rental_date > '2005-05-25';
```

This query retrieves all columns from the rental table, even if only the **rental_id** and **rental_date** columns are required. A more efficient version of the query specifies the required columns. Refer to the following example:

```
SELECT rental_id, rental_date
FROM rental
WHERE rental_date > '2005-05-25';
```

Limiting the query to only the necessary columns reduces data transfer and improves query performance, mainly when dealing with large tables.

Neglecting indexes

One of the most significant performance pitfalls is failing to use indexes effectively. Without indexes, the database engine performs full table scans, which are resource-intensive and slow. For example, if you frequently query rentals by **rental_date** in the Sakila database, but the column lacks an index, the query performance suffers:

```
SELECT rental_id, customer_id
FROM rental
WHERE rental_date > '2005-05-25';
```

Adding an index to the **rental_date** column significantly improves performance:

```
CREATE INDEX idx_rental_date ON rental (rental_date);
```

This index enables the database to perform an index range scan, reducing the number of rows processed and speeding up the query. Ensuring that frequently queried columns are indexed is a critical best practice for avoiding performance bottlenecks.

Improper use of joins

Joins are a powerful feature of SQL, but can become a performance pitfall when not optimized. A common mistake is joining large tables without indexing the join columns. For example:

```
SELECT r.rental_id, c.first_name, c.last_name
FROM rental r JOIN customer c ON r.customer_id = c.customer_id
WHERE r.rental_date > '2005-05-25';
```

If the `customer_id` column is not indexed in both tables, the join operation requires a full table scan, which could be more efficient. Adding indexes to the join columns improves performance. Refer to the following example:

```
CREATE INDEX idx_rental_customer_id
ON rental (customer_id);
CREATE INDEX idx_customer_id
ON customer (customer_id);
```

Additionally, always filter data as early as possible in the query to reduce the number of rows involved in the join operation.

Ignoring query execution plans

Query execution plans provide insights into how the database processes a query, highlighting inefficiencies such as full table scans, unoptimized joins, or redundant operations. Ignoring execution plans can result in undetected performance issues. For instance, using the `EXPLAIN` command in SQLite reveals how a query interacts with the database. Refer to the following example:

```
EXPLAIN
SELECT r.rental_id, c.first_name, c.last_name
FROM rental r JOIN customer c ON r.customer_id = c.customer_id
WHERE r.rental_date > '2005-05-25';
```

The execution plan shows whether indexes are used, the number of rows processed, and potential bottlenecks. Regularly reviewing execution plans helps you identify and resolve performance issues proactively.

Relying on nested subqueries

Nested subqueries can be resource-intensive, especially when evaluated for every row in the outer query. Refer to the following example:

```
SELECT first_name, last_name
FROM customer
WHERE customer_id IN (
SELECT customer_id
FROM rental
WHERE rental_date > '2005-05-25'
);
```

This query can be optimized by replacing the subquery with a join. Refer to the following example:

```
SELECT DISTINCT c.first_name, c.last_name
FROM customer c JOIN rental r ON c.customer_id = r.customer_id
WHERE r.rental_date > '2005-05-25';
```

Joins are often more efficient than nested subqueries because they allow the database engine to process relationships between tables in a single step, reducing redundancy and execution time.

Overuse of temporary tables

While temporary tables simplify complex queries, overusing them can lead to performance degradation. Temporary tables consume memory and disk space, and excessive use can strain database resources. For example, creating a temporary table for intermediate results in every query can slow down overall performance. Instead, consider using CTEs or subqueries for one-time data transformations:

```
WITH RecentRentals AS (
SELECT customer_id
FROM rental
WHERE rental_date > '2005-05-25'
)
SELECT c.first_name, c.last_name
FROM customer c
JOIN RecentRentals rr ON c.customer_id = rr.customer_id;
```

CTEs often provide a more efficient and readable alternative to temporary tables.

Using wildcards in LIKE clauses

The **LIKE** operator is commonly used for pattern matching, but using leading wildcards (%) in the search pattern turns off index usage, leading to full table scans. For example:

```
SELECT first_name, last_name
FROM customer
WHERE first_name LIKE '%John%';
```

This query cannot leverage an index on the **first_name** column because the wildcard at the beginning of the pattern forces the database to scan all rows. Optimizing the pattern or using full-text search features can improve performance. Refer to the following example:

```
SELECT first_name, last_name
FROM customer
WHERE first_name LIKE 'John%';
```

This query uses the index on **first_name** for faster results.

Failing to optimize aggregate functions

Aggregate functions like **SUM()**, **COUNT()**, and **AVG()** can be slow when applied to large datasets without filters or indexes. For example, to calculate the total rentals without narrowing the dataset, refer to the following example:

```
SELECT COUNT(*)
FROM rental;
```

Adding filters or indexing frequently queried columns reduces the dataset size and improves performance:

```
SELECT COUNT(*)
FROM rental
WHERE rental_date > '2005-05-25';
```

Additionally, materialized views or pre-aggregated data tables can optimize frequently used aggregate calculations.

Conclusion

This chapter focused on essential techniques for optimizing SQL query performance, empowering you to manage large datasets efficiently. You began by exploring query execution plans, a vital tool for understanding how your database processes queries. This knowledge helps identify performance bottlenecks and guides you in making informed adjustments to your queries. You then explored indexing strategies, learning to create and maintain indexes to improve data retrieval speed while balancing their impact on write operations.

The chapter also covered optimizing joins, highlighting the importance of indexing join columns and structuring queries to minimize processed rows. These strategies ensure that joins, a fundamental component of many SQL queries, execute quickly and efficiently. Additionally, you learned to optimize subqueries by replacing them with joins or CTEs and minimizing nested queries to reduce resource consumption.

Finally, the chapter addressed common performance pitfalls, such as overusing **SELECT ***, failing to filter data early, and neglecting to index frequently queried columns. By mastering these optimization techniques, you can write SQL queries that deliver fast and accurate results, ensuring your database performs optimally even under demanding conditions.

In the next chapter, we will focus on data generation and conversions. We will learn how to manipulate string, numeric, and temporal data and convert data between different types while avoiding common pitfalls. These skills are crucial for transforming raw data into meaningful insights and ensuring data consistency across your database. By mastering these techniques, we can handle a wide range of data transformation challenges and prepare datasets for analysis and reporting.

Exercises

In these exercises, you will explore key strategies for optimizing SQL queries, including analyzing execution plans, creating and using indexes, optimizing joins and subqueries, and avoiding common performance pitfalls. Working with the Sakila sample database will give you practical experience in enhancing query efficiency and applying best practices to real-world scenarios.

Understanding query execution plans

In this exercise, you will analyze query execution plans to understand how SQLite processes queries and identify opportunities for optimization:

- At the **sqlite>** prompt, analyze the execution plan for a query retrieving all films with a rental rate greater than 2.99. Refer to the following example:

```
EXPLAIN
SELECT *
FROM film WHERE rental_rate > 2.99;
```

- At the **sqlite>** prompt, compare the execution plans for two queries using a direct condition and a subquery. Refer to the following example:

```
EXPLAIN
SELECT *
FROM rental
WHERE rental_date > '2023-01-01';
EXPLAIN
SELECT *
FROM rental
WHERE rental_id IN (SELECT rental_id FROM rental WHERE rental_date > '2023-01-01');
```

- At the **sqlite>** prompt, optimize the execution plan of a query by adding a condition to narrow down results. Refer to the following example:

```
EXPLAIN
SELECT *
FROM film
WHERE rental_rate > 2.99 AND title LIKE 'A%';
```

Indexing strategies

In this exercise, you will create and use indexes to optimize query performance:

- At the **sqlite>** prompt, create an index on the title column of the film table and verify its effect on query performance:

```
CREATE INDEX idx_film_title ON film (title);
EXPLAIN
SELECT *
FROM film
WHERE title = 'ACADEMY DINOSAUR';
```

- At the **sqlite>** prompt, create a compound index on the **category_id** and **film_id** columns of the **film_category** table and test its usage. Refer to the following example:

```
CREATE INDEX idx_film_category ON film_category (category_id, film_id);
EXPLAIN
SELECT *
FROM film_category
      WHERE category_id = 1 AND film_id = 100;
```

- At the **sqlite>** prompt, drop an unused index to improve write performance. Refer to the following example:

```
DROP INDEX idx_film_title;
```

Optimizing joins

In this exercise, you will optimize join queries by reducing unnecessary rows and using appropriate conditions:

- At the **sqlite>** prompt, perform a join between the rental and film tables, including only columns needed for analysis. Refer to the following example:

```
SELECT r.rental_id, f.title
FROM rental r
JOIN inventory i ON r.inventory_id = i.inventory_id
JOIN film f ON i.film_id = f.film_id;
```

- At the **sqlite>** prompt, use an indexed column in a join query to enhance performance:

```
CREATE INDEX idx_inventory_film ON inventory (film_id);
EXPLAIN
SELECT r.rental_id, f.title
FROM rental r
JOIN inventory i ON r.inventory_id = i.inventory_id
JOIN film f ON i.film_id = f.film_id;
```

- At the **sqlite>** prompt, analyze the performance difference when filtering rows before joining:

```
EXPLAIN
SELECT r.rental_id, f.title
FROM rental r JOIN inventory i
ON r.inventory_id = i.inventory_id
JOIN film f ON i.film_id = f.film_id
WHERE f.rental_rate > 2.99;
```

Optimizing subqueries

In this exercise, you will rewrite subqueries to improve efficiency and compare their performance:

- At the **sqlite>** prompt, analyze the execution plan of a query using a correlated subquery:

```
EXPLAIN
SELECT *
FROM film
WHERE film_id IN (
SELECT film_id
FROM inventory WHERE inventory_id < 100
);
```

- At the **sqlite>** prompt, rewrite the above query as a join to optimize performance:

```
SELECT f.*
FROM film f
JOIN inventory i ON f.film_id = i.film_id
WHERE i.inventory_id < 100;
```

- At the **sqlite>** prompt, use a **WITH** clause CTE to simplify and optimize a subquery:

```
WITH recent_rentals AS (
SELECT rental_id, rental_date
FROM rental
WHERE rental_date > '2023-01-01'
)
SELECT r.rental_id, f.title
FROM recent_rentals r
JOIN inventory i ON r.rental_id = i.inventory_id
JOIN film f ON i.film_id = f.film_id;
```

Avoiding common performance pitfalls

In this exercise, you will identify and address common issues that slow down queries:

- At the **sqlite>** prompt, demonstrate the impact of retrieving unnecessary columns by comparing two queries. Refer to the following example:

```
SELECT * FROM film;
SELECT title, rental_rate FROM film;
```

- At the **sqlite>** prompt, rewrite a query with an **ORDER BY** clause to leverage an index for sorting. Refer to the following example:

```
CREATE INDEX idx_film_rental_rate ON film (rental_rate);

SELECT *

FROM film

ORDER BY rental_rate;
```

- At the **sqlite>** prompt, fix a query that uses a **LIKE** condition without an index. Refer to the following example:

```
CREATE INDEX idx_film_title_prefix ON film (title);

SELECT *

FROM film

WHERE title LIKE 'A%';
```

Join our Discord space

Join our Discord workspace for latest updates, offers, tech happenings around the world, new releases, and sessions with the authors:

https://discord.bpbonline.com

CHAPTER 10
Data Generation and Conversions

Introduction

In this chapter, you will explore techniques for generating, manipulating, and converting data types in SQL, focusing on practical applications for handling string, numeric, and temporal data. You will learn how to generate and manipulate string data to create custom outputs, perform precise arithmetic operations on numeric data, and effectively handle temporal data for time-based queries. Additionally, the chapter will guide you through data type conversions, addressing common pitfalls and best practices for transforming data seamlessly. By mastering these techniques, you will gain the flexibility to work efficiently with diverse data types and prepare them for analysis or reporting.

Structure

This chapter covers the following topics:

- Generation and manipulation of string data
- Arithmetic functions and handling numeric data
- Generation and manipulation of temporal data
- Converting between data types and pitfalls

Objectives

By the end of this chapter, you will have a solid understanding of how to generate, manipulate, and convert data types in SQL for practical applications. You will learn to create and customize string data, leveraging functions to effectively clean, transform, and format text. You will gain proficiency in performing arithmetic operations and managing numeric data precisely, ensuring accurate calculations in your queries. Additionally, you will explore techniques for generating and manipulating temporal data, enabling you to work with dates and times in a dynamic and meaningful manner. Ultimately, you will learn how to perform data type conversions, identify common pitfalls, and implement best practices to seamlessly transform data between formats. These skills will equip you to handle diverse data scenarios and prepare data for analysis or reporting with confidence and precision.

Generation and manipulation of string data

String data is critical in SQL, often representing names, addresses, descriptions, and other textual information. SQL provides various functions and techniques for generating and manipulating string data to meet diverse requirements. Whether creating new string values, modifying existing ones, or analyzing text data, mastering string manipulation is essential for handling real-world databases like the Sakila sample database.

Generating strings dynamically

SQL allows the dynamic generation of strings using concatenation and literal values. The **CONCAT()** function is commonly used to combine multiple strings or column values into a single output. For example, in the Sakila database, you might generate a full name for each customer by combining their **first_name** and **last_name**. Refer to the following example:

```
SELECT CONCAT(first_name, ' ', last_name) AS full_name
FROM customer;
```

Let us understand this example in detail:

- This query combines the **first_name** and **last_name** columns with a space in between, creating a readable full name for each customer.
- Depending on your database system, concatenation operators like || (in PostgreSQL) or + (in some SQL Server configurations) may also be available.

In addition to concatenation, string literals can generate new text values dynamically. For instance, you might create a message for each film in the film table to highlight its rental cost:

```
SELECT CONCAT('The rental cost for "', title, '" is $', rental_rate) AS
rental_message
FROM film;
```

This query creates a custom string for each film by combining text literals with column values, providing a tailored output.

Extracting substrings

Substring functions allow you to extract portions of a string based on position and length. The **SUBSTRING()** function is widely used to retrieve parts of strings. For example, if you need to extract the first three letters of each customer's first name, you can use the following code:

```
SELECT first_name, SUBSTRING(first_name, 1, 3) AS short_name
FROM customer;
```

Let us understand this example in detail:

- In this query, **SUBSTRING(first_name, 1, 3)** retrieves the first three characters of the **first_name** column, starting at position 1 of the string and ending at position 3, generating a shorter version of each name. This is particularly useful for creating identifiers or abbreviations.

Transforming string case

SQL provides functions to change the case of string data, ensuring consistency or meeting specific formatting requirements. The **UPPER()** function converts text to uppercase, while **LOWER()** converts it to lowercase. For example, to standardize customer names in uppercase, you can use the following code:

```
SELECT
UPPER(first_name) AS first_name_upper,
UPPER(last_name) AS last_name_upper
FROM customer;
```

Trimming and padding strings

Trimming functions remove unwanted whitespace or characters from strings, enhancing the cleanliness and usability of text data. The **TRIM()** function removes leading and trailing spaces by default. Refer to the following code:

```
SELECT TRIM(first_name) AS trimmed_first_name
FROM customer;
```

Let us understand this example in detail:

- In this query, **TRIM()** removes extraneous spaces in the **first_name** column, providing cleaner data.
- If specific characters need removal, you can specify them explicitly using the **TRIM()** function's additional parameters.

- Padding functions, such as **LPAD()** and **RPAD()**, add characters to the left or right of a string to reach a specified length. These functions help align text or formatting output for reports.

For example, to ensure customer IDs are always displayed as five characters. Refer to the following code:

```
SELECT LPAD(customer_id, 5, '0') AS padded_customer_id
FROM customer;
```

This query pads the **customer_id** column with leading zeros, ensuring a consistent five-character format.

Replacing and searching within strings

The **REPLACE()** function substitutes specific string parts with new values. For instance, to update the descriptions of films in the film table to replace **rental** with **lease**, you can use the following code:

```
SELECT
title,
REPLACE(description, 'rental', 'lease') AS updated_description
FROM film;
```

This query creates a modified version of the description column, replacing every occurrence of **rental** with **lease**.

To find the position of the pattern in a string, the **POSITION()** or **LOCATE()** function identifies the starting position of a substring. For example, to find where the word **action** appears in film descriptions, you can use the following code:

```
SELECT
title,
POSITION('action' IN description) AS action_position
FROM film;
```

This query identifies the position of the substring **action** within the description column, allowing you to analyze the occurrence of specific terms.

Using regular expressions for advanced manipulation

Many SQL systems support regular expressions for more complex string operations through functions like **REGEXP**. These tools enable pattern matching and sophisticated transformations. For instance, to identify customers with numeric characters in their names, you can use the following code:

```
SELECT first_name, last_name
FROM customer
WHERE first_name REGEXP '[0-9]';
```

This query filters customers whose **first_name** contains any numeric characters, leveraging the power of regular expressions for precise matching.

Combining string functions for advanced use cases

Combining multiple string functions allows you to perform advanced transformations and customizations. For example, to standardize customer names in uppercase, remove spaces, and add a unique identifier, you can use the following code:

```
SELECT CONCAT(UPPER(TRIM(first_name)), '_', UPPER(TRIM(last_name)), '_ID',
customer_id) AS customer_identifier
FROM customer;
```

This query applies **TRIM()**, **UPPER()**, and **CONCAT()** functions to create a standardized and unique identifier for each customer, demonstrating how string functions can work together to produce complex results.

Mastering string generation and manipulation equips you to handle diverse text-related challenges in SQL. Whether cleaning up messy data, creating customized outputs, or analyzing text patterns, these tools enhance your ability to work effectively with string data in any database scenario.

Arithmetic functions and handling numeric data

Numeric data is a cornerstone of SQL, representing prices, quantities, and measurements. SQL provides a suite of arithmetic functions and operators to perform calculations, transform data, and ensure numeric precision. Mastering these tools allows you to manipulate numeric data effectively, whether for financial reports, statistical analysis, or general data processing.

Performing basic arithmetic operations

SQL supports fundamental arithmetic operators such as addition (+), subtraction (-), multiplication (*), and division (/). These operators can be used in queries to calculate derived values directly within result sets. For example, in the Sakila sample database, you can calculate the total revenue for each rental by multiplying the rental rate by the rental duration. Refer to the following code:

```
ALTER TABLE rental ADD COLUMN rental_rate REAL;
ALTER TABLE rental ADD COLUMN duration INT;
UPDATE rental
SET rental_rate =
  CASE ABS(RANDOM()) % 3
    WHEN 0 THEN 2.99
    WHEN 1 THEN 3.99
    ELSE 4.99
  END;
UPDATE rental
SET duration =
  CASE ABS(RANDOM()) % 3
    WHEN 0 THEN 1
    WHEN 1 THEN 4
    ELSE 8
  END;
SELECT rental_id, rental_rate, duration, rental_rate * duration AS total_
revenue
FROM rental;
```

Let us understand this example in detail:

- In this query, the expression **rental_rate * duration** dynamically generates a new column, **total_revenue**, for each rental.
- By leveraging these basic operations, you can compute key metrics on the fly without modifying the underlying data.

Using aggregate functions for summary calculations

Aggregate functions like **SUM()**, **AVG()**, **MIN()**, **MAX()**, and **COUNT()** are essential for summarizing numeric data. For instance, to calculate the total revenue generated across all rentals, you can use the following code:

```
SELECT SUM(rental_rate * duration) AS total_revenue
FROM rental;
```

This query combines multiplication with the **SUM()** function to aggregate the revenue from all rows. Similarly, you can use **AVG()** to calculate the average rental rate:

```
SELECT AVG(rental_rate) AS average_rental_rate
FROM rental;
```

In addition, you can use **MIN()** and **MAX()** to find the minimum and maximum values in a table. The following queries find the **MIN** of the **rental_rate** and **MAX rental_rate** from the rental table:

```
SELECT MIN(rental_rate) as min_rental_rate
     FROM rental;
     SELECT MAX(rental_rate) AS max_rental_rate
     FROM rental;
```

Lastly, you can use **COUNT()** to find the total number of records in a given table or view. The following query finds the total **COUNT** of rentals in the rental table:

```
     SELECT COUNT(rental_id) as count_rentals
     FROM rental;
```

These functions enable you to extract meaningful insights from large datasets, such as identifying trends, averages, and ranges.

Handling precision and decimal points

Precision is critical when working with numeric data, particularly in financial calculations. SQL ensures precision using data types like **DECIMAL** and **NUMERIC**, which allow you to specify the total number of digits and the number of digits after the decimal point. For example, refer to the following code:

```
CREATE TABLE financials (
    amount DECIMAL(10, 2)
);
```

In this schema, **DECIMAL(10, 2)** ensures that the **amount** column stores values with up to 10 digits, two after the decimal point. To control precision in queries, use functions like **ROUND()**. For instance, to round total revenue to two decimal places, you can use the following code:

```
SELECT ROUND(rental_rate * duration, 2) AS rounded_revenue
FROM rental;
```

This function ensures consistent results and prevents discrepancies caused by excessive decimal places.

Handling division and NULL values

Division operations can introduce specific challenges, such as handling zero or NULL values. Dividing by zero results in an error, so queries must include safeguards. For example, to calculate a price-per-minute metric without risking a division error, use the following code:

```
SELECT rental_id,
      CASE
            WHEN duration > 0 THEN rental_rate / duration
            ELSE 0
      END AS price_per_minute
FROM rental;
```

The **CASE** statement checks whether the *duration* value exceeds zero before performing the division, ensuring the query runs without errors.

Similarly, when handling NULL values in arithmetic operations, use the **COALESCE()** function to substitute default values. Refer to the following code:

```
SELECT
rental_id,
rental_rate + COALESCE(discount, 0) AS adjusted_rate
FROM rental;
```

In this query, **COALESCE(discount, 0)** replaces NULL values in the discount column with 0, preventing invalid calculations.

Advanced numeric functions

SQL offers advanced numeric functions for specialized use cases. The **POWER()** function raises a number to a specific power, while **SQRT()** calculates the square root. For instance, to calculate the square root of the rental duration, you can use the following code:

```
SELECT rental_id, SQRT(duration) AS sqrt_duration
FROM rental;
```

Similarly, the **MOD()** function computes the remainder of a division operation, which is useful for categorizing numeric data. For example, to determine whether rental IDs are even or odd, you can use the following code:

```
SELECT rental_id, MOD(rental_id, 2) AS is_odd
FROM rental;
```

These functions expand the range of numeric operations available in SQL, enabling complex calculations and analyses.

Formatting numeric data

In some cases, numeric data needs to be formatted for presentation or reporting. SQL functions, such as **FORMAT()**, allow you to control the appearance of numeric values. For example, to format rental rates with commas and two decimal places:

```
SELECT FORMAT(rental_rate, 2) AS formatted_rate
```

```
FROM rental;
```

This ensures the data is accurate, visually appealing, and easily interpretable.

Combining numeric functions for advanced use cases

Combining multiple numeric functions allows for more sophisticated calculations. For instance, to calculate the total cost of rentals with a discount applied and round the result, you can use the following code:

```
SELECT rental_id,
      ROUND((rental_rate * duration) * (1 - COALESCE(discount, 0.1)), 2)
AS discounted_revenue
FROM rental;
```

In this query, multiplication, subtraction, **COALESCE()**, and **ROUND()** are used together to calculate the discounted revenue for each rental, even when discount values are missing. This demonstrates the power of combining SQL functions for advanced data manipulation.

Best practices for numeric data handling

When working with numeric data, adhere to best practices to ensure accuracy and performance. Always choose appropriate data types, such as **DECIMAL** for monetary values, to avoid rounding errors. Use functions like **ROUND()** or **TRUNCATE()** to explicitly control precision, especially in calculations that feed into financial reports or dashboards. Additionally, validate inputs with conditions or defaults to handle unexpected or incomplete data gracefully.

Generation and manipulation of temporal data

Temporal data, which includes dates and times, plays a critical role in SQL for tracking, analyzing, and predicting time-based events. SQL provides robust tools for generating and manipulating temporal data, allowing you to perform operations like calculating intervals, filtering by date ranges, and formatting output. Understanding these tools is essential for working effectively with real-world databases where temporal data is often tied to transactions, rentals, or other activities.

Generating temporal data

SQL provides functions for generating temporal data dynamically, ensuring that queries remain relevant and adaptable. The **CURRENT_DATE** and **CURRENT_TIMESTAMP** functions retrieve the current date and timestamp, respectively. For example, to retrieve all rentals made today in the database, you can use the following code:

```
SELECT rental_id, rental_date
FROM rental
WHERE rental_date = CURRENT_DATE;
```

This query ensures the results are always updated based on the system date, making it ideal for daily reporting. Similarly, **NOW()** is a commonly used function to retrieve the current date and time in a single value:

```
SELECT NOW() AS current_datetime;
```

This is particularly useful for logging or capturing the exact timestamp of an event.

SQL also supports the generation of custom date and time values using the **DATE** or **TIMESTAMP** literals. For example, to retrieve all rentals made on May 25, 2005, you can use the following code:

```
SELECT
rental_id,
rental_date
FROM rental
WHERE rental_date = DATE('2005-05-25');
```

This approach is helpful in defining specific temporal data points in queries.

Extracting components from temporal data

SQL allows you to extract specific components from temporal data, such as the year, month, day, hour, or minute. The **EXTRACT()** function is a versatile tool for this purpose. For instance, to list all rentals by the year they occurred, you can use the following code:

```
SELECT
rental_id,
EXTRACT(YEAR FROM rental_date) AS rental_year
FROM rental;
```

This query adds a column showing the year of each rental, enabling you to analyze data by period. Similarly, you can extract other components, such as the month or day, to create more granular analyses.

In addition to **EXTRACT()**, SQL provides other functions like **YEAR()**, **MONTH()**, and **DAY()** for databases that support them. For example, to retrieve rentals made in December, you can use the following code:

```
SELECT
rental_id,
rental_date
FROM rental
```

```
WHERE MONTH(rental_date) = 12;
```

These functions simplify querying temporal data for specific periods.

Manipulating temporal data

Temporal data manipulation often involves adding or subtracting time intervals to calculate new dates or filter records. The **DATE_ADD()** and **DATE_SUB()** functions are commonly used for this purpose. For instance, to retrieve all rentals made in the last 30 days, you can use the following code:

```
SELECT
rental_id,
rental_date
FROM rental
WHERE rental_date >= DATE_SUB(CURRENT_DATE, INTERVAL 30 DAY);
```

This query calculates a dynamic date 30 days before the current date and filters rentals based on this range. Similarly, **DATE_ADD()** allows you to calculate future dates. For example, to predict due dates for rentals based on a seven-day rental period, you can use the following code:

```
SELECT
rental_id,
rental_date,
DATE_ADD(rental_date, INTERVAL 7 DAY) AS due_date
FROM rental;
```

This query generates a new column showing the due date for each rental, ensuring that all calculations are handled within the query.

Calculating date and time differences

SQL supports interval calculations to determine the difference between two temporal values. The **DATEDIFF()** function calculates the number of days between two dates. For example, to find how many days have passed since each rental was made, you can use the following code:

```
SELECT
rental_id,
rental_date,
DATEDIFF(CURRENT_DATE, rental_date) AS days_since_rental
FROM rental;
```

This query calculates each rental's time in days, providing insights into transaction histories. For more granular differences, such as hours or minutes, use the **TIMESTAMPDIFF()** function; you can use the following code:

```
SELECT
rental_id,
rental_date,
TIMESTAMPDIFF(HOUR, rental_date, NOW()) AS hours_since_rental
FROM rental;
```

This allows for precise interval calculations and is instrumental in tracking active rentals or measuring processing times.

Formatting temporal data

SQL provides tools for formatting temporal data into readable or customized formats. The **DATE_FORMAT()** function allows you to display dates in various styles. For example, to format rental dates as Month Day, Year, you can use the following code:

```
SELECT
rental_id,
DATE_FORMAT(rental_date, '%M %d, %Y') AS formatted_date
FROM rental;
```

This query converts the **rental_date** column into a more user-friendly format, improving the readability of reports. Similarly, **TIME_FORMAT()** can format time values for display:

```
SELECT
rental_id,
TIME_FORMAT(rental_date, '%h:%i %p') AS formatted_time
FROM rental;
```

This reformats the time portion of **rental_date** into a 12-hour clock with minutes and an AM or PM indicator.

Working with time zones

SQL provides functions to handle conversions and adjustments for applications that span multiple time zones. The **CONVERT_TZ()** function converts temporal values between time zones. For instance, to convert rental dates from UTC to a local time zone, you can use the following code:

```
SELECT
rental_id,
rental_date,
CONVERT_TZ(rental_date, 'UTC', 'America/New_York') AS local_rental_date
FROM rental;
```

This ensures that temporal data aligns with the correct regional time zone, an essential consideration for global applications.

Using temporal data in conditional logic

Conditional logic with temporal data enables you to create dynamic queries based on time-based conditions. For example, to classify rentals as **recent** *or* **old** based on whether they occurred within the last 90 days, you can use the following code:

```
SELECT rental_id, rental_date,
      CASE
            WHEN rental_date >= DATE_SUB(CURRENT_DATE, INTERVAL 90 DAY) THEN
'Recent'
            ELSE 'Old'
      END AS rental_status
FROM rental;
```

This query adds a new column that categorizes rentals based on their recency, providing actionable insights for decision-making.

Combining temporal functions for advanced queries

Advanced queries often combine multiple temporal functions to address complex scenarios. For example, to generate a report showing the total number of rentals per month in the current year, you can use the following code:

```
SELECT EXTRACT(MONTH FROM rental_date) AS rental_month,
      COUNT(*) AS total_rentals
FROM rental
WHERE EXTRACT(YEAR FROM rental_date) = YEAR(CURRENT_DATE)
GROUP BY rental_month
ORDER BY rental_month;
```

This query uses **EXTRACT()** and **GROUP BY** to aggregate rental data by month, offering a clear view of monthly activity trends. Combining temporal functions in this way allows you to answer detailed business questions efficiently.

Mastering temporal data manipulation equips you to handle a wide range of time-based scenarios in SQL, enabling precise analysis and reporting.

Converting between data types and pitfalls

Data type conversions in SQL are fundamental, enabling you to transform data from one type to another to meet the requirements of queries, calculations, or reporting. While converting data types expands the flexibility of SQL queries, improper or unplanned conversions can lead to performance issues, data loss, or unexpected results. Understanding how to perform data type conversions and avoid common pitfalls is essential for effective database management.

Implicit and explicit data type conversions

SQL supports two types of data type conversions: implicit and explicit. Implicit conversions occur automatically when the database engine determines that one data type needs to be converted to match another. For example, if you compare a numeric column with a string value, the database may implicitly convert the string to a number:

```
SELECT *
FROM rental
WHERE rental_id = '5';
```

In this query, the string '5' is implicitly converted to a numeric type to match the **rental_id** column's data type. While implicit conversions simplify query writing, relying on them can lead to inefficiencies or unexpected behavior, mainly when working with large datasets.

Explicit conversions, on the other hand, are performed using SQL functions like **CAST()** or **CONVERT()**. For example, to convert a numeric column to a string explicitly, you can use the following code:

```
SELECT CAST(rental_id AS CHAR) AS rental_id_string
FROM rental;
```

This approach makes the conversion process explicit, providing greater data type and format control.

Common data type conversions

SQL supports a variety of conversions between data types, including numeric, string, and temporal transformations. One common use case is converting numeric values to strings for formatting or concatenation. For example, refer to the following code:

```
SELECT
CONCAT('Rental ID: ', CAST(rental_id AS CHAR)) AS rental_message
FROM rental;
```

This query converts the **rental_id** column to a string and concatenates it with text, creating a custom message for each rental.

Another frequent conversion is transforming string data into numeric or date formats for calculations or comparisons. For instance, if a date is stored as a string, you can convert it to a **DATE** type:

```
SELECT
rental_id
FROM rental
WHERE rental_date = CAST('2005-05-25' AS DATE);
```

This ensures that the comparison is performed accurately and efficiently by treating both values as temporal data.

Pitfalls of data type conversions

Data type conversions can introduce several pitfalls, including performance degradation, data truncation, and incorrect results. One common issue arises from converting large datasets without proper indexing. For example, if you convert a string column to a number in a **WHERE** clause, the database may be unable to use an index on the original column, resulting in a full table scan. Refer to the following code:

```
SELECT *
FROM rental
WHERE CAST(rental_id AS CHAR) = '5';
```

This query forces the database to evaluate every row, even if the **rental_id** column is indexed. To avoid this, convert constants or parameters instead of columns whenever possible.

Data truncation is another common pitfall, especially when converting strings to fixed-length types or numeric values with limited precision. For instance, to convert a floating-point number to an integer that discards the fractional part, you can use the following code:

```
SELECT CAST(10.75 AS INT) AS truncated_value;
```

The result is 10, which may not align with the intended calculation. Being mindful of the constraints of the target data type helps prevent unintended data loss.

Dealing with NULL values

Converting columns that contain NULL values can lead to unexpected behavior if not handled explicitly. For example, converting a NULL value to a numeric or string type typically results in a NULL output, which may affect calculations or query logic. To handle NULL values, use the **COALESCE()** function to provide a default value:

```
SELECT
COALESCE(CAST(rental_rate AS CHAR), 'N/A') AS rental_rate_string
FROM rental;
```

In this query, **COALESCE()** ensures that NULL values in the **rental_rate** column are replaced with 'N/A', preventing string concatenation or reporting issues.

Best practices for data type conversions

Adhering to best practices ensures accurate and efficient data type conversions. First, always verify the compatibility of the source and target data types. For example, converting a large string to a numeric type may fail if the string contains non-numeric characters. To prevent errors, validate the input data using functions like **ISNUMERIC()** (in SQL Server) or similar database-specific checks.

Second, avoid unnecessary conversions. Additional conversions add overhead without improving functionality if the source and target columns share compatible data types. For example, if a **rental_id** column is already numeric, avoid casting it to a different numeric type unless required for a specific use case.

Finally, be cautious when performing conversions in production environments with large datasets. Test queries on smaller datasets first to evaluate performance and identify potential issues. For example, if a column frequently requires conversions, consider modifying the table schema to store the data in the desired type directly. Refer to the following code:

```
ALTER TABLE rental
MODIFY rental_date DATE;
```

This eliminates the need for repetitive query conversions, improving performance and maintainability. When modifying the table schema, keep in mind different SQL database engines. For example, the above code works in most SQL database engines; however, in SQLite 3, you would need to create a new schema with the modified column, copy the data from the old table to the new table, and once verified, drop the old table and rename the new table.

Combining data type conversions with other functions

Data type conversions often work with other SQL functions to achieve specific goals. For instance, to format a rental rate as a currency string, you can use the following code:

```
SELECT CONCAT('$', FORMAT(rental_rate, 2)) AS formatted_rate
FROM rental;
```

In this query, the **FORMAT()** function ensures that the numeric value is displayed with two decimal places, and the **CONCAT()** function adds the dollar sign. Combining conversions with other functions enables more sophisticated data manipulation and presentation.

Another example involves converting strings to dates and calculating intervals:

```
SELECT rental_id,
    DATEDIFF(CURRENT_DATE, CAST(rental_date AS DATE)) AS days_since_
rental
FROM rental;
```

This query converts the **rental_date** string to a **DATE** type, allowing the **DATEDIFF()** function to calculate the number of days since each rental.

Conclusion

This chapter provides essential techniques for generating, manipulating, and converting data types in SQL, equipping you to handle diverse datasets effectively. We began by exploring string data operations, including functions for concatenation, case transformation, trimming, and pattern matching. These tools enable us to clean and format text data for better readability and analysis. We also learned advanced techniques like using regular expressions to extract and manipulate complex patterns in string data.

We also looked at numeric data, teaching us how to perform arithmetic operations, handle precision, and manage signed values. These skills are crucial for financial calculations, statistical analysis, or any scenario requiring accurate numerical data handling. Temporal data operations were also covered, including generating and manipulating dates and times. These techniques allow us to handle dynamic time-based queries, such as filtering records by date ranges or calculating time differences.

Finally, we looked at data type conversions, mastering data transformation between formats. Here, we learned to avoid common pitfalls and ensure that conversions maintain data integrity. Combining these skills allows you to confidently manage and prepare data for analysis, making this chapter an essential foundation for working with complex datasets.

In the next chapter, we will focus on advanced SQL techniques, including window functions, **common table expressions (CTEs)**, and recursive queries. We will also learn about transactions and concurrency control, which ensures data consistency in multi-user environments. These concepts will enable us to write more powerful and efficient queries, handle complex data transformations, and manage large datasets effectively. By integrating these advanced SQL techniques, you will enhance your ability to optimize database performance and execute sophisticated analytical queries.

Exercises

In these exercises, you will explore generating, manipulating, and converting data types in SQL. Working with the Sakila sample database will give you practical experience in enhancing query efficiency and applying best practices to real-world scenarios.

Generation and manipulation of string data

In this exercise, you will practice generating and manipulating string data using SQLite functions such as concatenation, length, and substring:

- At the **sqlite>** prompt, combine the **first_name** and **last_name** columns from the customer table into a single **full_name** column, separated by a space. Refer to the following code:

```
SELECT first_name || ' ' || last_name AS full_name
FROM customer;
```

- At the **sqlite>** prompt, retrieve the first five characters of the title column from the film table:

```
SELECT SUBSTR(title, 1, 5) AS short_title
FROM film;
```

- At the **sqlite>** prompt, count the number of characters in the address column from the address table:

```
SELECT address, LENGTH(address) AS address_length
FROM address;
```

Arithmetic functions and handling with numeric data

In this exercise, you will use arithmetic functions to manipulate numeric data, such as calculating totals, rounding, and percentages:

- At the **sqlite>** prompt, calculate the total rental cost for each film by multiplying **rental_rate** by **rental_duration** from the film table. Refer to the following code:

```
SELECT
title,
rental_rate,
rental_duration,
rental_rate * rental_duration
AS total_cost
FROM film;
```

- At the **sqlite>** prompt, round the total cost of rentals to two decimal places:

```
SELECT
title,
ROUND(rental_rate * rental_duration, 2) AS rounded_total_cost
FROM film;
```

- At the **sqlite>** prompt, calculate the percentage of films with a **rental_rate** greater than 3.99:

```
SELECT (COUNT(*) * 100.0 / (SELECT COUNT(*) FROM film)) AS percentage
FROM film

WHERE rental_rate > 3.99;
```

Generation and manipulation of temporal data

In this exercise, you will work with temporal data, such as generating dates, calculating intervals, and formatting dates:

- At the **sqlite>** prompt, generate the current date for all rentals from the rental table:

```
SELECT
rental_id,
```

```
DATE('now') AS current_date
FROM rental;
```

- At the **sqlite>** prompt, calculate the difference in days between the **return_date** and **rental_date** for each rental:

```
SELECT
rental_id,
JULIANDAY(return_date) - JULIANDAY(rental_date) AS days_rented
FROM rental;
```

- At the **sqlite>** prompt, format the **rental_date** column to display only the year and month:

```
SELECT
rental_id,
STRFTIME('%Y-%m', rental_date) AS rental_year_month
FROM rental;
```

Converting between data types and pitfalls

In this exercise, you will explore data type conversions and learn how to avoid common pitfalls:

- At the **sqlite>** prompt, convert the **rental_rate** column from the film table to a string and concatenate it with the title:

```
SELECT title || ' (Rate: ' || CAST(rental_rate AS TEXT) || ')' AS
film_info
FROM film;
```

- At the **sqlite>** prompt, attempt to convert a text column to a number and handle the error gracefully:

```
SELECT CASE
WHEN typeof(address_id)='integer' THEN CAST(address_id AS INTEGER)
ELSE NULL
END AS address_as_integer
FROM address;
```

- At the **sqlite>** prompt, identify rows in the payment table where the amount column contains non-numeric data due to an invalid conversion:

```
SELECT payment_id, amount
FROM payment
WHERE typeof(amount) != 'real';
```

Join our Discord space

Join our Discord workspace for latest updates, offers, tech happenings around the world, new releases, and sessions with the authors:

https://discord.bpbonline.com

CHAPTER 11
Advanced SQL Techniques

Introduction

In this chapter, you will explore advanced SQL techniques that enhance your ability to handle complex data management and analysis tasks. You will begin by learning about window functions, which enable sophisticated calculations across sets of rows while retaining granular data. Next, you will explore **common table expressions** (**CTEs**) and recursive queries, powerful tools for simplifying and structuring complex queries, especially those involving hierarchical data. The chapter also covers transaction and concurrency control, providing insights into maintaining data consistency and managing simultaneous access in multi-user environments. These advanced techniques will equip you with the skills to solve intricate data challenges and optimize database operations effectively.

Structure

This chapter covers the following topics:

- Windows functions
- Common table expressions
- Recursive queries
- Transaction and concurrency control

Objectives

By the end of this chapter, you will have a comprehensive understanding of advanced SQL techniques essential for managing complex data operations. You will learn how to use window functions to perform detailed calculations over specific sets of rows, enabling advanced analytical queries. You will gain proficiency in implementing CTEs to simplify complex questions and structure your SQL code effectively. Additionally, you will explore recursive queries, which are invaluable for navigating hierarchical data and self-referential relationships. You will also understand the principles of transaction and concurrency control, ensuring data integrity and efficient multi-user database management. These skills will empower you to handle sophisticated SQL challenges with confidence and precision.

Windows functions

Window functions in SQL are potent tools for performing calculations across a defined set of rows related to the current row. Unlike aggregate functions, which collapse results into a single value, window functions allow you to retain individual rows while performing operations like ranking, running totals, and moving averages. These functions are essential for advanced data analysis and are widely used in complex reporting scenarios.

Understanding window functions

Window functions operate over a **window** of rows defined by the **OVER()** clause. The window specifies the set of rows used for the calculation, which can include all rows in a query or a subset defined by partitions. For example, to calculate the total revenue for all rentals in the Sakila database, you can use the **SUM()** function as a window function:

```
SELECT rental_id, customer_id,
SUM(rental_rate) OVER () AS total_revenue
FROM rental;
```

This query calculates the total revenue for all rentals while retaining each row in the result set. The **OVER()** clause defines the calculation's scope, including all table rows.

Partitioning with window functions

Partitioning allows you to break the data into subsets for separate calculations. For instance, if you want to calculate the total revenue generated by each customer, you can partition the data by **customer_id**. Refer to the following code:

```
SELECT customer_id, rental_id,
SUM(rental_rate) OVER (PARTITION BY customer_id) AS customer_revenue
FROM rental;
```

This query calculates the total revenue for each customer by restricting the window to rows with the same **customer_id**. Partitioning helps analyze grouped data without aggregating the results into a single row per group.

Using ranking functions

SQL provides several ranking functions, including **RANK()**, **DENSE_RANK()**, and **ROW_NUMBER()**, to assign ranks or numbers to rows within a partition. These functions are invaluable for identifying top performers or organizing data for analysis.

For example, to rank films in the film table by rental rate within each category, you can use the following code:

```
SELECT category_id, title, rental_rate,
RANK() OVER (PARTITION BY category_id ORDER BY rental_rate DESC) AS rank
FROM film;
```

This query assigns a rank to each film within its category based on the rental rate. The **ORDER BY** clause determines the ranking order, and ties receive the same rank, with subsequent ranks skipped. If you need consecutive ranks without skipping, use **DENSE_RANK()** instead.

Calculating running totals and averages

Window functions are ideal for calculating running totals and averages, providing cumulative metrics that update as new rows are processed. For instance, to calculate a running total of revenue for each customer, you can use the following code:

```
SELECT customer_id, rental_id, rental_rate,
SUM(rental_rate) OVER (PARTITION BY customer_id ORDER BY rental_date) AS
running_total
FROM rental;
```

This query calculates the cumulative revenue for each customer, sorted by **rental_date**. The **ORDER BY** clause within the **OVER()** statement ensures that the running total updates are in chronological order.

Similarly, you can calculate moving averages by combining the **AVG()** function with a specific window frame. For example, to calculate a three-row moving average of rental rates. You can use the following code:

```
SELECT rental_id, rental_rate,
AVG(rental_rate) OVER (ORDER BY rental_date ROWS 2 PRECEDING) AS moving_avg
FROM rental;
```

The **ROWS 2 PRECEDING** clause defines a window frame that includes the current and two preceding rows, ensuring that the moving average updates dynamically as new rows are included.

Lag and lead functions

The **LAG()** and **LEAD()** functions provide access to values from previous or subsequent rows within the same result set. These functions help calculate differences between rows or compare values across time.

For example, to calculate the difference in rental rates between consecutive rentals, you can use the following code:

```
SELECT rental_id, rental_rate,
LAG(rental_rate) OVER (ORDER BY rental_date) AS prev_rental_rate,
rental_rate - LAG(rental_rate) OVER (ORDER BY rental_date) AS rate_
difference
FROM rental;
```

This query retrieves the rental rate of the previous row and calculates the difference, allowing you to analyze trends or identify anomalies.

Combining window functions

You can combine multiple window functions in a query to perform advanced analyses. For instance, to calculate a customer's rank, running total, and average rental rate simultaneously, you can use the following code:

```
SELECT customer_id, rental_id, rental_rate,
RANK() OVER (PARTITION BY customer_id ORDER BY rental_rate DESC) AS rank,
SUM(rental_rate) OVER (PARTITION BY customer_id) AS total_revenue,
AVG(rental_rate) OVER (PARTITION BY customer_id) AS avg_rate
FROM rental;
```

This query generates a comprehensive view of each customer's rental data, providing insights into their ranking, spending habits, and average rental rate. Combining window functions in this way creates powerful and flexible reporting capabilities.

Best practices for using window functions

Always thoughtfully define partitions and frames when using window functions to ensure accurate and meaningful results. Over-partitioning or failing to use partitions, when necessary, can lead to incorrect calculations or excessive resource usage. Additionally, consider the performance implications of using window functions with large datasets, as they can be computationally expensive. Indexing columns used in the **PARTITION BY** or **ORDER BY** clauses can help improve performance.

Mastering window functions enhances your ability to analyze data dynamically, making them an essential tool for advanced SQL applications.

Common table expressions

CTEs are a powerful SQL feature that simplifies complex queries by allowing you to define temporary, named result sets. These result sets can be referenced within a query, making it easier to structure, organize, and debug SQL code. CTEs improve readability and maintainability, especially when dealing with nested queries or repeated calculations.

Defining and using CTEs

A CTE is defined using the **WITH** keyword, followed by the name of the CTE and the query that generates its result set. For example, to calculate the total revenue generated by each film, you can define a CTE called **FilmRevenue**, and you can use the following code:

```
WITH FilmRevenue AS (
SELECT film_id, SUM(amount) AS total_revenue
FROM payment
GROUP BY film_id
)
SELECT f.title, fr.total_revenue
FROM FilmRevenue fr
JOIN film f ON fr.film_id = f.film_id;
```

Let us understand this example in detail:

- The **FilmRevenue** CTE calculates the total revenue for each film and simplifies the main query by eliminating the need to repeat this logic.

- The CTE acts as a temporary table that is available only for the duration of the query.

Benefits of CTEs

CTEs offer several advantages over traditional subqueries or temporary tables. First, they improve query readability by separating complex logic into distinct, named sections. This modular approach makes it easier to understand and debug SQL code. Second, CTEs are reusable within the same query, allowing you to reference them multiple times without duplicating code.

For example, you can use a CTE to calculate film popularity and reference it in multiple aggregations:

```
WITH FilmPopularity AS (
SELECT film_id, COUNT(*) AS rental_count
FROM rental
GROUP BY film_id
)
```

```
SELECT f.title, fp.rental_count
FROM FilmPopularity fp
JOIN film f ON fp.film_id = f.film_id
ORDER BY fp.rental_count DESC;
```

This query calculates rental counts for each film and uses the **FilmPopularity** CTE to display the results and sort them by popularity.

Recursive CTEs

Recursive CTEs extend the functionality of standard CTEs by allowing a query to reference itself. This is particularly useful for working with hierarchical data, such as organizational charts or category trees. A recursive CTE consists of two parts: an anchor query, which defines the base result set, and a recursive query, which references the CTE to build successive rows.

For example, to find all the employees under a specific manager in a hierarchical employee table, you can use the following code:

```
WITH RECURSIVE EmployeeHierarchy AS (
SELECT employee_id, manager_id, first_name, last_name
FROM employee
WHERE manager_id IS NULL -- Start with the top-level manager
UNION ALL
SELECT e.employee_id, e.manager_id, e.first_name, e.last_name
FROM employee e
JOIN EmployeeHierarchy eh ON e.manager_id = eh.employee_id
)
SELECT *
FROM EmployeeHierarchy;
```

Let us understand this example in detail:

- In this query, the anchor query retrieves the top-level manager, and the recursive query iteratively retrieves employees reporting to the current level.
- Recursive CTEs are invaluable for navigating hierarchical relationships without requiring complex loops or additional queries.

CTEs for complex calculations

CTEs excel at breaking down complex calculations into manageable steps. For example, to calculate the average rental duration and identify films with above-average durations, you can use the following code:

```
WITH AverageDuration AS (
SELECT AVG(DATEDIFF(return_date, rental_date)) AS avg_duration
FROM rental
),
LongRentals AS (
SELECT f.title, DATEDIFF(r.return_date, r.rental_date) AS rental_duration
FROM rental r
JOIN film f ON r.inventory_id = f.inventory_id
WHERE DATEDIFF(r.return_date, r.rental_date) > (SELECT avg_duration FROM
AverageDuration)
)
SELECT *
FROM LongRentals;
```

Let us understand this example in detail:

- This query uses two CTEs: **AverageDuration** calculates the average rental duration, and **LongRentals** identifies films exceeding this average.
- Using CTEs clarifies the logic and avoids nesting queries within **WHERE** clauses.

Chaining multiple CTEs

CTEs can be chained together to build a series of intermediate result sets, each refining the data further. For example, to calculate the total revenue for each customer and rank them by spending, you can use the following code:

```
WITH CustomerRevenue AS (
SELECT customer_id, SUM(amount) AS total_revenue
FROM payment
GROUP BY customer_id
),
RankedCustomers AS (
SELECT customer_id, total_revenue,
RANK() OVER (ORDER BY total_revenue DESC) AS rank
FROM CustomerRevenue
)
SELECT *
FROM RankedCustomers
WHERE rank <= 10;
```

Let us understand this example in detail:

- In this query, the **CustomerRevenue** CTE calculates each customer's total revenue, and the **RankedCustomers** CTE ranks them.
- Chaining CTEs allows you to build upon earlier results incrementally, keeping each step clear and focused.

Limitations and considerations

While CTEs offer many benefits, they are not always the most efficient solution for performance-critical queries. Unlike temporary tables, CTEs are recalculated each time they are referenced within the query. Compared to materialized intermediate tables, this can result in slower performance for complex or heavily used CTEs.

To mitigate performance issues, use CTEs for logical clarity and development, but consider alternative approaches, such as indexing or temporary tables, for production environments with significant data volumes.

CTEs in reporting

CTEs are particularly useful in generating detailed reports by organizing query logic into comprehensible steps. For instance, to create a report summarizing rental activity by month and customer, you can use the following code:

```
WITH MonthlyActivity AS (
SELECT customer_id,
EXTRACT(YEAR FROM rental_date) AS rental_year,
EXTRACT(MONTH FROM rental_date) AS rental_month,
COUNT(*) AS rental_count
FROM rental
GROUP BY customer_id, rental_year, rental_month
),
CustomerSummary AS (
SELECT customer_id, rental_year, rental_month, rental_count,
RANK() OVER (PARTITION BY rental_year, rental_month ORDER BY rental_count
DESC) AS rank
FROM MonthlyActivity
)
SELECT *
FROM CustomerSummary
WHERE rank <= 5;
```

This query uses multiple CTEs to break down and organize the report logic, resulting in a clear and concise SQL structure that can be easily maintained or modified.

CTEs empower you to simplify complex SQL queries, making them easier to read, maintain, and extend. For hierarchical data, iterative calculations, or detailed reporting, mastering CTEs is essential for advanced SQL proficiency.

Recursive queries

Recursive queries are an advanced feature of SQL that efficiently retrieves and processes hierarchical or self-referential data. They are handy for traversing parent-child relationships, such as organizational charts, file systems, or category trees. Recursive queries rely on CTEs with the **RECURSIVE** keyword to define iterative logic, enabling you to query data structures that would otherwise require multiple steps or complex joins.

Understanding recursive queries

Recursive queries are structured in two parts: an anchor query and a recursive query. The anchor query defines the base result set, typically representing the top level of the hierarchy. The recursive query references the CTE itself, iteratively expanding the result set to include related rows. This process continues until no additional rows meet the recursive condition.

For example, consider a hypothetical employee's table with the following structure:

employee_id	first_name	manager_id
1	Alice	NULL
2	Bob	1
3	Carol	1
4	Penelope	2
5	Sophia	2
6	Jennifer	1
7	Monica	1

Table 11.1: A hypothetical employee table to demonstrate recursive queries

A recursive query can be used to retrieve all employees under a specific manager, such as Alice. Refer to the following example:

```
WITH RECURSIVE EmployeeHierarchy AS (
-- Anchor query: Start with the top-level manager
SELECT employee_id, first_name, manager_id
FROM employee
WHERE manager_id IS NULL
```

```
UNION ALL
-- Recursive query: Retrieve employees reporting to the current level
SELECT e.employee_id, e.first_name, e.manager_id
FROM employee e
JOIN EmployeeHierarchy eh ON e.manager_id = eh.employee_id
)
SELECT *
FROM EmployeeHierarchy;
```

Let us understand this example in detail:

- In this query, the anchor query retrieves the top-level manager (Alice), and the recursive query iteratively retrieves all employees reporting to her directly or indirectly.

- The **UNION ALL** operator combines the anchor and recursive results, creating a complete hierarchy.

Practical use cases for recursive queries

Recursive queries are invaluable for a wide range of applications, including the following:

- **Organizational hierarchies**: Navigating employee-manager relationships or reporting structures.

- **Bill of materials**: Analyzing product components and subcomponents in manufacturing.

- **Category trees**: Exploring nested categories in e-commerce or content management systems.

- **Network graphs**: Identifying connections in social networks or communication systems.

- **Pathfinding**: Calculating routes or dependencies in logistics or software workflows.

Each use case involves a hierarchical or interconnected structure, making recursive queries a natural fit.

Controlling recursion depth

To prevent infinite loops or overly large result sets, it is essential to control the recursion depth. SQL provides tools like the **WITH MAXRECURSION** option (in SQL Server) or manual constraints in the recursive query. For example, to limit the recursion depth to three levels in the employee hierarchy, you can use the following code:

```
WITH RECURSIVE EmployeeHierarchy AS (
```

```
SELECT employee_id, first_name, manager_id, 1 AS level
FROM employee
WHERE manager_id IS NULL
UNION ALL
SELECT e.employee_id, e.first_name, e.manager_id, eh.level + 1
FROM employee e
JOIN EmployeeHierarchy eh ON e.manager_id = eh.employee_id
WHERE eh.level < 3
)
SELECT *
FROM EmployeeHierarchy;
```

Let us understand this example in detail:

- In this query, a level column tracks the recursion depth, and the **WHERE** clause ensures that only three levels are processed.

- This approach prevents excessive recursion and maintains query efficiency.

Working with cyclic data

Cyclic data, where relationships form loops, can challenge recursive queries. For example, when an employee is erroneously listed as their manager, the query may enter an infinite loop. To handle such cases, include conditions to detect and exclude cycles. Using a **PATH** column to track visited nodes is a common solution. Refer to the following code:

```
WITH RECURSIVE EmployeeHierarchy AS (
SELECT employee_id, first_name, manager_id, CAST(employee_id AS CHAR) AS
path
FROM employee
WHERE manager_id IS NULL
UNION ALL
SELECT e.employee_id, e.first_name, e.manager_id, CONCAT(eh.path, '->',
e.employee_id)
FROM employee e
JOIN EmployeeHierarchy eh ON e.manager_id = eh.employee_id
WHERE NOT FIND_IN_SET(e.employee_id, eh.path)
)
SELECT *
FROM EmployeeHierarchy;
```

In this query, the path column tracks the sequence of visited nodes, and the **WHERE** clause ensures that no node is revisited, effectively breaking cycles.

Performance considerations

Recursive queries can be resource-intensive, especially with deep hierarchies or large datasets. To optimize performance, consider the following strategies:

- **Indexing:** Ensure that columns used in joins, such as **manager_id**, are indexed to speed up recursive lookups.

- **Filtering:** Use **WHERE** clauses in the anchor and recursive queries to limit the scope of the recursion.

- **Incremental output:** Return only the necessary columns to reduce the size of intermediate results.

For instance, for indexing the **manager_id** column in the employee table, you can use the following command:

```
CREATE INDEX idx_manager_id ON employee (manager_id);
```

This improves the efficiency of the recursive query by enabling faster lookups for each iteration.

Advanced applications

Recursive queries can be combined with other SQL features to perform advanced analyses. For example, to calculate the total number of employees reporting to each manager (directly or indirectly):

```
WITH RECURSIVE EmployeeHierarchy AS (
SELECT employee_id, manager_id, 1 AS depth
FROM employee
WHERE manager_id IS NULL
UNION ALL
SELECT e.employee_id, e.manager_id, eh.depth + 1
FROM employee e
JOIN EmployeeHierarchy eh ON e.manager_id = eh.employee_id
)
SELECT manager_id, COUNT(*) AS total_employees
FROM EmployeeHierarchy
GROUP BY manager_id;
```

Let us understand this example in detail:

- This query calculates hierarchical employee counts by recursively building the employee hierarchy and grouping the results by **manager_id**.

- Such applications demonstrate the versatility of recursive queries in solving real-world problems.

Transaction and concurrency control

Transactions and concurrency control are foundational concepts in SQL that ensure data integrity, consistency, and reliability in multi-user database environments. A transaction represents a sequence of SQL operations performed as a single, logical unit of work. Concurrency control mechanisms manage simultaneous database access by multiple users or applications, preventing conflicts and maintaining data consistency.

Understanding transactions

A transaction is a series of operations that must all succeed or fail as a single unit. SQL provides commands to define the start, commit, and rollback of transactions. For example, a transaction in the Sakila database might involve adding a new rental, updating the inventory, and logging the payment. If any step fails, the entire transaction must roll back to ensure the database remains consistent.

Here is a simple transaction example:

```
BEGIN TRANSACTION;
INSERT INTO rental (rental_date, inventory_id, customer_id, staff_id)
VALUES ('2024-12-01', 1, 2, 1);
UPDATE inventory
SET quantity = quantity - 1
WHERE inventory_id = 1;
COMMIT;
```

Let us understand this example in detail:

- In this example, the transaction ensures that the rental insertion and the inventory update occur together.
- If an error occurs during the update, a **ROLLBACK** command reverts the database to its previous state:
  ```
  ROLLBACK;
  ```

This approach prevents partial updates that could lead to data inconsistencies.

ACID properties of transactions

The **atomicity, consistency, isolation, and durability (ACID)** properties define the reliability of transactions. Let us look at them in detail:

- **Atomicity:** Ensures that all operations within a transaction are treated as a single unit. If any operation fails, the entire transaction fails.
- **Consistency:** Guarantees that a transaction transitions the database from one valid state to another, adhering to defined rules and constraints.

- **Isolation:** Prevents transactions from interfering with each other, even when executed concurrently.
- **Durability:** Ensures that its changes are permanent once a transaction is committed, even in a system failure.

These properties form the backbone of transaction management and protect the database from corruption or inconsistent states.

Concurrency issues and their solutions

In multi-user environments, concurrent access to the database can lead to conflicts, such as the ones listed here:

- **Dirty reads:** Occurs when a transaction reads uncommitted changes from another transaction.
- **Non-repeatable reads:** This happens when a transaction reads the same row twice and sees different data due to another transaction's updates.
- **Phantom reads:** Arise when new rows are added or removed by another transaction, changing the results of a repeated query.

SQL addresses these issues using isolation levels, which define how a transaction is isolated from other transactions. The four standard isolation levels are as follows:

- **Read uncommitted:** Allows transactions to read uncommitted changes, leading to potential dirty reads.
- **Read committed:** Prevents dirty reads by ensuring that only committed data is visible.
- **Repeatable read:** Prevents dirty and non-repeatable reads by ensuring the same data remains visible during a transaction.
- **Serializable:** The highest isolation level, preventing dirty reads, non-repeatable reads, and phantom reads by fully isolating transactions.

To set an isolation level in SQL, use the following code:

```
SET TRANSACTION ISOLATION LEVEL REPEATABLE READ;
BEGIN TRANSACTION;
SELECT * FROM rental
WHERE rental_date = '2024-12-01';
COMMIT;
```

This query ensures that the data read remains consistent throughout the transaction.

Locking mechanisms

Locks are a critical part of concurrency control, preventing multiple transactions from accessing the same resource simultaneously in a conflicting manner. SQL uses various types of locks. Let us look at the types of locks in detail:

- **Shared locks:** Allow multiple transactions to read the same data but prevent modifications.

- **Exclusive locks:** Prevent all access (read and write) to the locked data by other transactions.

- **Intent locks:** Indicate a transaction's intention to acquire a specific lock type on a resource.

For example, when updating a record in the inventory table, SQL automatically applies an exclusive lock to ensure that other transactions cannot modify the same record until the current transaction completes. Refer to the following code:

```
BEGIN TRANSACTION;
UPDATE inventory
SET quantity = quantity - 1
WHERE inventory_id = 1;
COMMIT;
```

Proper lock management is essential to avoid issues like deadlocks, where two or more transactions wait indefinitely for each other to release resources.

Deadlocks and their resolution

Deadlocks occur when two or more transactions hold locks on resources that the other transactions need, creating a circular dependency. For instance, look at the following example:

- Transaction A locks inventory_id = 1 and waits for inventory_id = 2.
- Transaction B locks inventory_id = 2 and waits for inventory_id = 1.

Neither transaction can proceed, resulting in a deadlock. SQL resolves deadlocks by identifying and terminating one of the conflicting transactions. As a best practice, always access resources consistently to minimize the risk of deadlocks.

Optimistic versus pessimistic concurrency control

SQL supports two main concurrency control strategies:

- **Optimistic concurrency control:** Assumes that conflicts are rare and allows transactions to proceed without locks. Conflicts are detected during the commit phase, and transactions may be retried if conflicts occur.

- **Pessimistic concurrency control:** This approach applies locks during transactions to prevent conflicts. While this approach reduces the chance of conflicts, it can lead to decreased performance due to locking overhead.

  For example, optimistic control might involve checking a timestamp before updating a record:

```
UPDATE rental
SET rental_rate = rental_rate * 1.1
WHERE rental_id = 1 AND last_updated = '2024-12-01 10:00:00';
```

If another transaction has updated the record since the timestamp, the update fails, ensuring data integrity.

Savepoints and partial rollbacks

Savepoints provide additional control within a transaction, allowing you to roll back only a portion of the transaction if needed. For example:

```
BEGIN TRANSACTION;
INSERT INTO rental (rental_date, inventory_id, customer_id, staff_id)
VALUES ('2024-12-01', 1, 2, 1);
SAVEPOINT after_rental;
UPDATE inventory
SET quantity = quantity - 1
WHERE inventory_id = 1;
ROLLBACK TO after_rental;
COMMIT;
```

In this example, the transaction returns to the **SAVEPOINT** without affecting the earlier **INSERT** operation, providing flexibility in handling errors.

Best practices for transaction and concurrency control

To ensure efficient and reliable transactions, follow these best practices:

- Keep transactions short to minimize the time locks are held.
- Use appropriate isolation levels based on the application's requirements.
- Regularly monitor for and resolve deadlocks.
- Test transactions in multi-user environments to identify potential conflicts.
- Leverage indexing and efficient query design to reduce contention.

Mastering transaction and concurrency control ensures that databases remain consistent, reliable, and performant, even in high-demand environments. These principles are essential for effectively managing data integrity in multi-user systems.

Conclusion

This chapter explored advanced SQL techniques that empower us to manage and analyze complex data with precision and efficiency, hence gaining insights into window functions and learning how to calculate running totals, rankings, and moving averages while retaining the detailed granularity of data. Mastering CTEs enhanced our ability to write clear and modular queries, simplifying even the most intricate logic. Recursive queries help expand our skillset further by enabling us to navigate and analyze hierarchical data structures such as organizational charts or category trees.

The chapter also gave us a deep understanding of transaction and concurrency control. You learned how to manage simultaneous database operations effectively, maintain data integrity, and handle conflicts in multi-user environments. By exploring isolation levels, locking mechanisms, and strategies for resolving deadlocks, we developed the tools necessary to ensure reliable and consistent database performance.

These advanced SQL techniques provide the foundation for solving real-world challenges, enabling us to build robust, scalable, and efficient database solutions. Whether optimizing queries, analyzing hierarchical data, or managing concurrent access, these tools will elevate your SQL expertise professionally.

In the next chapter, we will shift our focus to working with different SQL databases. You will explore the features and differences between popular SQL database systems, such as MySQL, PostgreSQL, and SQLite. We will also cover choosing the right database for your projects based on specific requirements and performance needs. Additionally, we will learn how to connect to and interact with various SQL databases, ensuring that we can apply our skills across different platforms.

Points to remember

As we wrap up this chapter, it is important to consolidate the advanced SQL concepts and techniques introduced in this section. These tools expand your capabilities for handling complex queries, managing data hierarchies, and ensuring reliable database operations. The techniques covered—window functions, CTEs, recursive queries, and transaction management—equip you to solve real-world challenges in both analytical and multiuser environments. By understanding these concepts and applying best practices, you can ensure data consistency, optimize performance, and maintain the integrity of your database, even under demanding conditions.

Here are the key takeaways from this chapter:

- Window functions perform calculations across a specific set of rows while retaining individual row details, making them ideal for advanced analytics such as running totals, rankings, and moving averages.

- CTEs improve query readability by structuring complex logic into manageable, reusable components using the WITH clause.

- Recursive queries enable efficient traversal of hierarchical or self-referential data structures, combining an anchor query with recursive logic to build results iteratively.

- Transactions ensure data consistency and reliability by grouping multiple operations into a single unit that either fully succeeds or fully rolls back in case of failure.

- The ACID properties: atomicity, consistency, isolation, and durability, are critical for ensuring reliable transaction processing.

- Concurrency control mechanisms like isolation levels and locks prevent issues such as dirty, non-repeatable, and phantom reads in multi-user environments.

- Deadlocks occur when two or more transactions are waiting for each other to release resources, requiring resolution strategies such as resource ordering or timeout policies.

- Savepoints allow partial rollbacks within transactions, providing greater control over error handling.

- Optimizing queries with advanced techniques such as window functions and efficient transaction management helps maintain performance and scalability in complex database systems.

Join our Discord space

Join our Discord workspace for latest updates, offers, tech happenings around the world, new releases, and sessions with the authors:

https://discord.bpbonline.com

CHAPTER 12

Working with Different SQL Databases

Introduction

In this chapter, we will explore the diverse landscape of **Structured Query Language** (**SQL**) database systems, gaining a deeper understanding of their unique features and capabilities. We will start with an overview of popular SQL databases, examining how their architectures and functionalities differ. The chapter is a guide for identifying the database that best suits project requirements, whether that involves prioritizing scalability, performance, or specific use cases. Additionally, we will learn how to connect to and interact with SQL databases, ensuring seamless integration with your applications. By the end, readers will be equipped to make informed decisions and effectively work with various SQL database systems.

Structure

This chapter covers the following topics:

- Overview of SQL database systems
- Database-specific features and differences
- Choosing the right database for your project
- Connecting to SQL databases

Objectives

By the end of this chapter, readers will have a comprehensive understanding of the diverse SQL database systems and their unique characteristics. They will learn to identify the strengths and use cases of different database systems, helping them choose the right database for specific projects or requirements. Readers will explore database-specific features, such as performance optimizations, scalability options, and supported data types, enabling them to leverage the full potential of the chosen system. Additionally, they will gain practical knowledge of connecting to SQL databases from various applications, ensuring seamless integration and efficient interaction. These insights will equip them with the skills to select, configure, and work effectively with SQL databases in real-world scenarios.

Overview of SQL database systems

SQL database systems are the backbone of modern data storage, management, and retrieval, providing structured environments for organizing information. These systems adhere to the principles of relational databases, using SQL to interact with data stored in tables. Each SQL database system offers unique features, performance optimizations, and use cases, making understanding their differences and strengths essential.

Relational database management systems

Relational database management systems (RDBMS) form the foundation of SQL databases. These systems store data in tables with rows and columns, supporting relationships between tables through keys. Popular RDBMSs include MySQL, PostgreSQL, Microsoft SQL Server, and Oracle database. Each system adheres to SQL standards while incorporating proprietary features to extend functionality.

For example, MySQL is widely used for web applications due to its speed, reliability, and ease of use. It supports scalability, making it a favorite for WordPress and e-commerce websites. On the other hand, PostgreSQL emphasizes standards compliance and advanced features, including support for JSON data types and full-text search, making it ideal for complex, high-precision applications.

MySQL

MySQL is one of the most popular open-source RDBMS platforms. It offers high performance, strong community support, and flexibility for various use cases. MySQL suits web applications and environments requiring quick deployments and low overhead. Key features include the following:

- Support for large datasets and concurrent users.
- Wide compatibility with programming languages and frameworks.
- Optimized read-heavy workloads for reporting and analytics.

Hence, the simplicity and scalability SQL offers make it a top choice for small-sized to medium-sized application developers.

PostgreSQL

PostgreSQL stands out for its rich feature set and adherence to SQL standards. Known as the *world's most advanced open-source database*, it supports complex queries, advanced indexing, and sophisticated data types. Developers favor PostgreSQL for applications requiring high precision and advanced functionality, such as geospatial analysis and scientific computing. Key features include the following:

- Support for custom functions and stored procedures in multiple languages.

- Extensive indexing options, including GiST and GIN indexes.

- Compatibility with relational and non-relational data types.

PostgreSQL is ideal for high-precision workloads and applications demanding robust data integrity.

Microsoft SQL Server

Microsoft SQL Server is a proprietary RDBMS tailored for enterprise environments. Its tight integration with the Microsoft ecosystem makes it an excellent choice for businesses relying on Windows-based applications. Key features include the following:

- Comprehensive support for business intelligence tools like SQL **Server Analysis Services** (**SSAS**) and **Reporting Services** (**SSRS**).

- Advanced security features, including **Transparent Data Encryption** (**TDE**).

- High availability options are available through Always On availability groups.

SQL Server's enterprise-grade functionality ensures it can handle demanding workloads with ease.

SQLite

SQLite is a serverless, self-contained RDBMS that is lightweight and easy to deploy. It is an excellent choice for small-scale applications, embedded systems, and environments with minimal administrative overhead. Key characteristics include the following:

- Zero-configuration setup, requiring no separate server installation.

- Portability with a single-file database format.

- Suitable for mobile apps, IoT devices, and prototyping.

SQLite prioritizes simplicity and is often used for projects where speed and minimalism are critical.

Oracle database

Oracle database is a robust, enterprise-grade RDBMS known for its scalability and support for mission-critical applications. It offers extensive tools for performance tuning, data warehousing, and cloud integration. Key features include the following:

- Partitioning and clustering capabilities for large datasets.
- In-memory data processing for faster analytics.
- Support for hybrid cloud environments.

Oracle database is preferred in finance, healthcare, and telecommunications industries, where reliability and scalability are paramount.

Choosing the right SQL database system

The choice of an SQL database system depends on project requirements, scalability needs, and specific features. For example, developers working on lightweight, single-user applications might choose SQLite for its simplicity. Conversely, teams managing enterprise-scale workloads could opt for Microsoft SQL Server or Oracle database for their advanced features and robust performance.

In cloud environments, databases like Amazon Aurora (compatible with MySQL and PostgreSQL) and Google Cloud SQL provide managed services, reducing administrative overhead while offering scalability and reliability.

Understanding the nuances of each SQL database system allows developers and administrators to select the best solution for their specific needs, ensuring efficient and reliable data management.

Database-specific features and differences

SQL database systems share a common foundation in relational data management, offering distinct features and optimizations tailored to different use cases. Understanding these differences allows you to choose the proper database for specific requirements and fully utilize its capabilities.

Speed and simplicity in MySQL

MySQL prioritizes performance and simplicity, making it an ideal choice for web applications and read-heavy workloads. It is widely adopted for dynamic websites like e-commerce platforms and content management systems. Key features of MySQL include the following:

- **Replication**: MySQL supports master-slave replication, enabling data redundancy and improving read performance by distributing queries across replicas.

- **Storage engines:** MySQL allows developers to select storage engines, such as InnoDB for transactional support or MyISAM for read-heavy operations.

- **Ease of use**: MySQL offers user-friendly configuration and compatibility with popular programming languages, reducing setup and development time.

While MySQL excels in performance and ease of use, it may lack some advanced features in other systems, such as full compliance with SQL standards.

Advanced features and standards compliance in PostgreSQL

PostgreSQL is known for its adherence to SQL standards and extensive feature set, including advanced data types and indexing options. This makes it suitable for complex applications like data science projects or geospatial analysis. Key PostgreSQL features include the following:

- **Custom data types:** PostgreSQL supports JSON, XML, and array data types, enabling hybrid relational and non-relational workflows.

- **Advanced indexing:** PostgreSQL optimizes query performance for a wide range of use cases, with support for GiST, GIN, and BRIN indexes.

- **Transactional integrity**: PostgreSQL enforces strict ACID compliance, ensuring reliable data handling even in multi-user environments.

- **Full-text search:** Its built-in search capabilities enable efficient text analysis and retrieval without requiring external tools.

PostgreSQL's versatility and focus on precision make it a go-to database for developers who need both performance and advanced functionality.

Lightweight and self-contained in SQLite

SQLite is a serverless database system designed for simplicity and portability. Its compact architecture makes it popular for embedded systems, mobile apps, and lightweight projects. Notable features include the following:

- **Single-file database:** SQLite stores an entire database in a single file, simplifying backups and portability.

- **Zero configuration:** It requires no setup or management, reducing administrative overhead.

- **In-memory mode:** SQLite supports in-memory databases that erase data after use for temporary operations or fast prototyping.

While SQLite's minimalism is its strength, it lacks built-in multi-user capabilities and advanced features required for large-scale enterprise applications.

Microsoft SQL Server enterprise integration

Microsoft SQL Server is designed for enterprise environments, offering seamless integration with the Microsoft ecosystem. It supports a range of business intelligence tools and high availability options, making it ideal for large-scale applications. Key features include the following:

- **Integration with Microsoft tools:** SQL Server integrates with Power BI, Excel, and Azure services, enhancing its utility in data analysis and cloud solutions.

- **Advanced security:** Features like **Transparent Data Encryption (TDE)** and role-based access control ensure secure data handling.

- **High availability**: SQL Server supports Always On availability groups for failover clustering and disaster recovery.

While SQL Server excels in enterprise settings, its licensing costs can be a limiting factor for smaller organizations.

Scalability and reliability in Oracle database

Oracle database is an enterprise-grade solution known for its scalability and high availability. It is designed to handle mission-critical workloads in industries such as finance and healthcare. Notable features include the following:

- **Partitioning:** Oracle supports horizontal partitioning, allowing developers to divide large datasets into manageable segments for improved performance.

- **Advanced analytics:** Built-in machine learning algorithms and predictive analytics tools enable data-driven decision-making.

- **Hybrid cloud support:** Oracle provides robust options for deploying databases in on-premises, cloud, or hybrid environments.

Oracle database's comprehensive feature set makes it a leader in high-stakes applications, though its complexity and cost can be barriers for smaller teams.

Key differences between SQL databases

When comparing SQL database systems, several factors distinguish them:

- **Performance and scalability:** MySQL excels in simplicity and speed for read-heavy workloads, while PostgreSQL and Oracle provide advanced features for complex queries and large datasets.

- **Standards compliance:** PostgreSQL adheres to SQL standards, offering precision and advanced functionality. MySQL and SQL Server introduce proprietary extensions that may diverge from the standard.

- **Deployment models:** SQLite's serverless architecture contrasts with the managed services offered by cloud-based databases like Amazon Aurora or Google Cloud SQL.

- **Security:** SQL Server and Oracle prioritize robust security features like encryption and fine-grained access control.

- **Cost**: MySQL and PostgreSQL are open-source and cost-effective, while Oracle and SQL Server involve licensing fees, reflecting their enterprise-grade features.

Choosing the right database

Selecting a database depends on your project's requirements. SQLite offers simplicity and ease of use for small-scale applications or prototyping. MySQL's speed and flexibility make it an excellent choice for dynamic web applications. Developers handling complex analytics or hybrid workloads often prefer PostgreSQL for its precision and advanced tools. SQL Server and Oracle database stand out for their robust performance and integration capabilities in enterprise scenarios requiring scalability.

Understanding each database system's specific features and trade-offs enables you to make informed decisions, ensuring optimal application performance and efficiency.

Choosing the right database for your project

Selecting the correct database for a project is a critical decision influencing the application's performance, scalability, and maintainability. Each SQL database system offers unique strengths and features tailored to specific use cases. By understanding your project's requirements and the capabilities of various databases, you can ensure a reliable and efficient implementation.

Assessing project requirements

The first step in choosing a database is understanding the project's specific requirements. Key factors to consider include the following:

- **Data volume:** Determine the size of the dataset the database will manage. Large-scale applications may require databases like PostgreSQL or Oracle database, designed to handle significant volumes of data efficiently.

- **Performance needs:** Evaluate whether the application demands high-speed read operations, complex analytics, or frequent updates. MySQL is well-suited for read-heavy workloads, while PostgreSQL excels in complex querying and transactional accuracy.

- **Scalability:** Projects anticipating growth should choose a horizontal or vertical scaling database. For instance, MySQL supports replication for scaling reads, and Oracle database offers clustering for high availability.

- **Data complexity:** Consider the data's type and structure. PostgreSQL's support for advanced data types, such as JSON and arrays, makes it ideal for hybrid datasets.

- **Budget constraints:** Open-source databases like MySQL and PostgreSQL provide cost-effective solutions, while proprietary systems like Oracle and Microsoft SQL Server may involve licensing costs.

Defining these requirements helps narrow the options to databases that align with the project's objectives.

Use case scenarios

Selecting the right database hinges on the application's specific requirements. Consider the following examples:

- **Web applications:** MySQL's speed and simplicity make it a preferred choice for dynamic websites or content management systems. It integrates seamlessly with popular web technologies like PHP and Python, enabling rapid development.

- **Data analytics:** Applications requiring in-depth analysis and reporting benefit from PostgreSQL's advanced indexing and full-text search capabilities. Its ability to handle complex queries with precision is valuable for data scientists and analysts.

- **Enterprise systems**: Oracle database and Microsoft SQL Server are tailored for large-scale enterprise applications. Their advanced security, high availability, and integration with business intelligence tools make them ideal for mission-critical systems.

- **Mobile and IoT applications:** SQLite is a lightweight, serverless database that suits embedded systems, mobile apps, and **Internet of Things** (**IoT**) devices. Its small footprint and zero-configuration setup simplify deployment.

Understanding the project's primary use case ensures the database's features align with the application's functionality.

Evaluating performance and scalability

Performance and scalability are key considerations for database selection. Some databases are optimized for specific workloads. Let us look at them in detail:

- **MySQL:** Known for its speed in handling read-heavy workloads, MySQL is an excellent choice for real-time applications like online marketplaces or social platforms.

- **PostgreSQL:** Its advanced query optimization and support for parallel processing make it suitable for analytics-driven environments.

- **SQL Server**: It offers enterprise-grade performance with features like in-memory processing and column store indexes, enhancing performance for **online analytical processing** (**OLAP**) workloads.

For projects requiring horizontal scalability, cloud-based solutions such as Amazon Aurora or Google Cloud SQL offer managed database services that provide auto-scaling and replication features.

Considering database management and maintenance

Database management plays a significant role in operational efficiency. Consider the level of administrative effort required:

- **Ease of use:** MySQL's straightforward setup and maintenance make it accessible for developers with basic database knowledge.

- **Automation features:** Managed databases like Azure SQL Database reduce administrative overhead by automating backups, updates, and scaling.

- **Customization options**: PostgreSQL allows extensive customization through extensions and configuration settings, making it suitable for specialized projects.

Choosing a database that aligns with your team's expertise and resource availability ensures smooth deployment and long-term management.

Security and compliance

Security is paramount, especially in applications handling sensitive data. Databases like SQL Server and Oracle database prioritize robust security features:

- **Encryption:** SQL Server and Oracle offer TDE to secure data at rest.

- **Access control:** Role-based access control and fine-grained permissions ensure that only authorized users can access critical data.

- **Compliance:** Enterprise databases often include tools to meet compliance standards like GDPR or HIPAA, making them suitable for industries like healthcare and finance.

Open-source databases still offer basic encryption and authentication features for applications requiring less stringent security measures.

Evaluating ecosystem and integration

A database's ecosystem and compatibility with tools and technologies influence its suitability for a project. For example:

- MySQL integrates seamlessly with popular web frameworks and hosting providers.

- PostgreSQL supports integrations with data science tools like R and Python's pandas library.

- SQL Server offers tight integration with Microsoft products, including Azure services, Excel, and Power BI.

Ensure that the chosen database supports the programming languages, frameworks, and third-party tools your project relies on.

Testing and prototyping

Before committing to a database, test it with a prototype of your application. Evaluate performance under simulated workloads, validate compatibility with application components, and assess scalability options. For example, developers can use benchmarking tools like pgbench for PostgreSQL or sysbench for MySQL to measure query performance and transaction handling.

Prototyping helps identify potential bottlenecks and ensures the database can handle the demands of the production environment. It also provides an opportunity to fine-tune configurations for optimal performance.

Future-proofing your database choice

Selecting a database with future scalability and compatibility in mind is essential for long-term success. Consider how the database will adapt to changes in data volume, workload, or application requirements. Cloud-based databases, such as Amazon RDS or Microsoft Azure SQL Database, offer flexibility for evolving needs, including seamless migration, automated scaling, and support for hybrid deployments.

Choosing the right database is not just about meeting current requirements but about preparing for future growth and ensuring the database remains a reliable foundation for your application.

Connecting to SQL databases

Connecting to SQL databases is critical in integrating database functionality with applications. Establishing this connection enables developers to execute queries, retrieve data, and interact with the database seamlessly. SQL database connections can be established using various programming languages, frameworks, and tools, each suited to different application environments. Mastering this process ensures secure and efficient communication between the application and the database.

Understanding connection basics

To connect to an SQL database, you typically need the following details:

- **Hostname:** The server address where the database is hosted. This is often a local host, while remote databases may use an IP address or domain name.

- **Port:** The communication port for the database service. Standard defaults include 3306 for MySQL, 5432 for PostgreSQL, and 1433 for Microsoft SQL Server.

- **Database name:** The name of the specific database you want to connect to within the server.

- **Username and password:** Authentication credentials are required to access the database.

- **Driver or library:** Software that enables the application to communicate with the database, such as psycopg2 for PostgreSQL in Python or the JDBC driver for Java.

You can connect with these details using appropriate tools or programming interfaces.

Connecting to MySQL

To connect to a MySQL database, you can use a variety of programming languages and tools. For example, in Python, the **mysql-connector** library allows you to establish connections. Refer to the following code:

```
import mysql.connector
connection = mysql.connector.connect(
host="localhost",
user="root",
password="password",
database="sakila"
)
cursor = connection.cursor()
cursor.execute("SELECT * FROM film LIMIT 10")
for row in cursor.fetchall():
print(row)
connection.close()
```

This code demonstrates a simple connection to the Sakila sample database, followed by a query to retrieve the first ten rows from the film table.

In PHP, the mysqli extension provides similar functionality:

```
$connection = new mysqli("localhost", "root", "password", "sakila");
if ($connection->connect_error) {
die("Connection failed: " . $connection->connect_error);
}
$result = $connection->query("SELECT * FROM film LIMIT 10");
while ($row = $result->fetch_assoc()) {
```

```
echo $row['title'] . "\n";
}
$connection->close();
```

These examples highlight the versatility of MySQL connections across different programming environments.

Connecting to PostgreSQL

PostgreSQL connections are equally flexible, supporting many libraries and tools. In Python, the **psycopg2** library is commonly used. Refer to the following code:

```
import psycopg2
connection = psycopg2.connect(
host="localhost",
user="postgres",
password="password",
database="sakila"
)
cursor = connection.cursor()
cursor.execute("SELECT * FROM film LIMIT 10")
for row in cursor.fetchall():
print(row)
connection.close()
```

PostgreSQL also supports advanced features, such as connection pooling with libraries like **pgbouncer**, which optimizes resource usage by reusing connections.

For Java applications, the JDBC driver enables PostgreSQL connectivity. Refer to the following code:

```
import java.sql.Connection;
import java.sql.DriverManager;
import java.sql.ResultSet;
import java.sql.Statement;
public class PostgreSQLConnection {
public static void main(String[] args) {
try {
Connection connection = DriverManager.getConnection(
"jdbc:postgresql://localhost:5432/sakila", "postgres", "password");
Statement statement = connection.createStatement();
```

```
ResultSet resultSet = statement.executeQuery("SELECT * FROM film LIMIT 10");
while (resultSet.next()) {
System.out.println(resultSet.getString("title"));
}
connection.close();
} catch (Exception e) {
e.printStackTrace();
    }
  }
}
```

These examples showcase PostgreSQL's adaptability to various development needs.

Connecting to Microsoft SQL Server

Microsoft SQL Server integrates seamlessly with applications in the Microsoft ecosystem. In C#, the ADO.NET framework simplifies connections:

```
using System;
using System.Data.SqlClient;
class Program {
static void Main() {
string connectionString = "Server=localhost;Database=sakila;User
Id=sa;Password=your_password;";
using (SqlConnection connection = new SqlConnection(connectionString)) {
connection.Open();
SqlCommand command = new SqlCommand("SELECT TOP 10 * FROM film",
connection);
SqlDataReader reader = command.ExecuteReader();
while (reader.Read()) {
Console.WriteLine(reader["title"]);
      }
    }
  }
}
```

This example highlights SQL Server's compatibility with .NET applications, making it an ideal choice for enterprise projects built within the Microsoft ecosystem.

Best practices for secure connections

When connecting to SQL databases, prioritize security to protect sensitive data and maintain system integrity:

- **Use environment variables:** Store credentials, such as usernames and passwords, in environment variables instead of hardcoding them in your application. For example, refer to the following code:

```
import os
import mysql.connector
connection = mysql.connector.connect(
host=os.getenv("DB_HOST"),
user=os.getenv("DB_USER"),
password=os.getenv("DB_PASSWORD"),
database="sakila"
)
```

- **Enable encryption:** Use **Secure Sockets Layer/Transport Layer Security (SSL/ TLS)** encryption for secure communication between your application and the database server. Most databases support SSL connections, which can be enabled through configuration settings or connection parameters.

- **Restrict IP access:** To limit exposure to the Internet, configure your database to accept connections only from trusted IP addresses or use **virtual private networks (VPNs)**.

- **Connection pooling:** Implement connection pooling to manage resources efficiently. Pooling reuses connections for multiple queries, reducing the overhead of establishing new connections.

- **Regularly update drivers:** Keep database drivers and libraries up-to-date to address security vulnerabilities and ensure compatibility with the latest database features.

Troubleshooting connection issues

When establishing database connections, common issues include incorrect credentials, network configurations, or firewall restrictions. Use diagnostic tools like ping to test server accessibility and database logs to identify specific errors. For example, MySQL's ERROR 1045 often indicates authentication issues, while PostgreSQL's FATAL: no pg_hba.conf entry points to a misconfigured client authentication file.

By following these best practices and leveraging the right tools, you can establish efficient, secure, and reliable connections to SQL databases, ensuring seamless integration with your applications.

Conclusion

This chapter explored the diverse world of SQL database systems, gaining valuable insights into their unique characteristics and capabilities. You learned how databases such as MySQL, PostgreSQL, Microsoft SQL Server, and SQLite offer distinct features and use cases, allowing you to make informed decisions based on project requirements. The chapter highlighted the importance of aligning database selection with performance needs, scalability, and specific application goals, ensuring the best fit for your projects.

We also examined database-specific functionalities, understanding how features like indexing strategies, partitioning, and optimization techniques can vary across systems. This knowledge equips us to take full advantage of each database's tools and capabilities. Additionally, the chapter covered the practical aspects of connecting to SQL databases, ensuring we can establish reliable and efficient integrations with applications.

By mastering these concepts, individuals can confidently choose, configure, and interact with SQL databases. Whether an individual is working with small-scale applications or large enterprise systems, their ability to leverage the strengths of various SQL databases will enhance their development and data management expertise.

In the next chapter, we will focus on database security, a critical aspect of managing SQL databases. We will explore the principles and practices of securing data, including access control, encryption, and protecting against common vulnerabilities like SQL injection attacks. The chapter will also cover strategies for auditing, monitoring, and ensuring compliance with data protection regulations.

Points to remember

Here are some key takeaways from this chapter:

- SQL databases like MySQL, PostgreSQL, SQLite, and SQL Server each offer unique strengths and use cases tailored to different scenarios.
- MySQL excels in speed and simplicity, making it ideal for web applications and read-heavy workloads.
- PostgreSQL supports advanced features, such as custom data types and full-text search, making it suitable for complex analytical tasks.
- SQLite is lightweight and serverless, perfect for embedded systems, mobile applications, and prototyping.
- SQL Server and Oracle database provide enterprise-grade features, including robust security, scalability, and business intelligence tools.
- Selecting the correct database involves evaluating project requirements such as scalability, performance, and cost.

- Secure database connections rely on best practices, such as using environment variables, enabling encryption, and restricting IP access.

- Testing and prototyping database choices in a controlled environment ensures compatibility and optimal performance.

- Cloud-based databases like Amazon Aurora and Google Cloud SQL offer scalability and ease of management for dynamic applications.

Join our Discord space

Join our Discord workspace for latest updates, offers, tech happenings around the world, new releases, and sessions with the authors:

https://discord.bpbonline.com

CHAPTER 13
Security Considerations in SQL

Introduction

In this chapter, readers will explore the essential practices and techniques for securing SQL databases and ensuring the integrity and confidentiality of data. They will learn about access control and permissions, which establish who can view or modify specific data, and encryption methods to protect sensitive information. The chapter guides readers through identifying and mitigating common vulnerabilities, such as SQL injection attacks, and implementing robust auditing and monitoring processes to track database activity. Additionally, readers will look into strategies for backup and recovery to safeguard against data loss, along with compliance measures to meet regulatory standards. Mastering these security practices will give them the tools to protect databases in dynamic and high-risk environments.

Structure

This chapter covers the following topics:

- Introduction to database security
- Access control and permissions
- Data encryption
- Preventing SQL injection attacks

- Auditing and monitoring
- Backup and recovery
- Compliance and data protection

Objectives

By the end of this chapter, readers will understand the critical principles and practices for securing SQL databases in various environments. They will learn how to implement access control mechanisms to manage user permissions and ensure that only authorized individuals can access or modify data. Hence, they will gain the skills to encrypt sensitive information, protecting it from unauthorized access in transit and at rest. Additionally, readers will explore techniques to prevent SQL injection attacks and other common vulnerabilities, safeguarding databases from malicious exploitation. The chapter will also equip them with auditing and monitoring database activity strategies to detect potential security threats and ensure compliance with industry regulations. Finally, readers will understand the importance of robust backup and recovery plans, enabling you to protect your data from accidental loss or system failures. These objectives will empower you to build secure, resilient, compliant database systems.

Introduction to database security

Database security is critical to modern data management, ensuring that information stored in SQL databases remains protected from unauthorized access, corruption, or theft. As organizations increasingly rely on data-driven processes, safeguarding databases cannot be overstated. Effective security measures protect sensitive information, maintain trust, support compliance with regulations, and reduce the risk of costly breaches.

Importance of database security

SQL databases are central to many applications, storing everything from customer data to financial records and operational insights. This central role makes them a prime target for malicious actors. Security breaches can lead to severe consequences, including data theft, financial losses, reputational damage, and legal penalties. Protecting a database is not just about locking it away—it is about enabling secure access for legitimate users while preventing unauthorized access.

For example, a retail organization using the Sakila sample database may store customer rental histories and payment details. Attackers could exploit this data without robust security measures, leading to identity theft or financial fraud. Database security measures ensure this information is only accessible to authorized users under predefined conditions.

Core principles of database security

Adequate database security relies on several foundational principles, such as:

- **Confidentiality:** Only authorized individuals or systems can access sensitive data. Techniques such as encryption and access controls play a key role in maintaining confidentiality.

- **Integrity:** Protecting data from unauthorized modifications or corruption. This principle ensures that information remains accurate and trustworthy over time.

- **Availability:** Ensuring the database and data are accessible to authorized users whenever needed. High-availability solutions and **disaster recovery plans** (**DRPs**) help maintain availability even during failures.

By adhering to these principles, organizations create a balanced approach to database security that meets operational and regulatory requirements.

Common threats to SQL databases

Understanding potential threats is the first step toward securing a database. Common threats include the following:

- **Unauthorized access:** Attackers may attempt to gain unauthorized access to a database using stolen credentials or exploit weak authentication mechanisms.

- **SQL injection attacks:** These occur when attackers manipulate SQL queries through unvalidated user inputs, potentially exposing or altering sensitive data.

- **Insider threats**: Employees or contractors with access to the database may misuse their privileges, intentionally or accidentally, leading to data breaches.

- **Data leakage:** Sensitive information can be unintentionally exposed through misconfigured permissions, backups, or logs.

- **Denial of Service (DoS) attacks**: Attackers may target database servers with excessive traffic or resource requests, making them unavailable to legitimate users.

Addressing these threats requires a layered security approach, combining preventive, detective, and corrective measures.

Building a strong security foundation

The first step in securing an SQL database is establishing robust authentication and authorization mechanisms. Authentication ensures only verified users can access the system, while authorization defines the actions those users can perform. For instance, **role-based access control** (**RBAC**) allows administrators to assign specific permissions to roles, ensuring users only access data and functions necessary for their jobs.

Encryption is another essential element of database security. Encrypting data at rest and in transit protects it from unauthorized access, even if the physical storage media or communication channels are compromised. For example, enabling **Secure Socket Layer** and **Transport Layer Security (SSL/TLS)** for database connections ensures secure communication between the client and server.

Regulatory compliance and security

Many industries are subject to data protection regulations that mandate specific security measures. For instance, the **General Data Protection Regulation (GDPR)** requires organizations handling *European Union* citizens' data to implement stringent privacy and security practices. Similarly, the **Health Insurance Portability and Accountability Act (HIPAA)** in the *United States* sets standards for securing healthcare data.

Compliance with these regulations often requires implementing access controls, encryption, and regular security audits. Failing to comply can result in significant fines and reputational harm, emphasizing the need for robust database security strategies.

Integrating security into the development lifecycle

Security should not be an afterthought. It must be integrated into every stage of the database and application development life cycle. Secure coding practices like input validation and parameterized queries help prevent vulnerabilities like SQL injection. Regular security testing, including penetration testing and vulnerability assessments, ensures that potential weaknesses are identified and addressed before they can be exploited.

Maintaining a clear separation between development, testing, and production environments minimizes the risk of accidental data exposure. For instance, using anonymized or synthetic data in non-production environments protects sensitive information.

Role of monitoring and auditing

Continuous monitoring and auditing are essential components of database security. Monitoring tools track database activity in real time, providing alerts for suspicious behavior, such as repeated login failures or unauthorized data access. Auditing records detailed logs of database operations, creating a trail that can be analyzed to investigate incidents or ensure compliance.

For example, enabling database auditing in a system like SQL Server allows administrators to track changes to critical tables or detect anomalous query patterns. This visibility helps organizations respond quickly to potential threats and maintain accountability.

Developing a security mindset

Securing an SQL database requires more than technical tools—it requires a proactive mindset focused on identifying and mitigating risks. Regular training for database administrators, developers, and other stakeholders ensures everyone understands their role in protecting data. By fostering a security culture, organizations can build resilient systems capable of withstanding evolving threats.

Access control and permissions

Access control and permissions form the cornerstone of database security, ensuring that only authorized users can access, modify, or manage data. Organizations can prevent unauthorized access and protect sensitive information from internal and external threats by implementing robust access control mechanisms. Access control is a multi-layered process that involves authentication, authorization, and fine-grained permission settings.

Authentication and verifying user identity

Authentication is the first step in securing database access. It verifies the identity of users or systems attempting to connect to the database. Common authentication methods include the following:

- **Username and password:** This is the most basic form of authentication, requiring users to provide valid credentials. Strong password policies, such as requiring a mix of characters and regular updates, enhance security.

- **Multi-factor authentication (MFA):** MFA adds an extra layer of security by requiring users to verify their identity through multiple means, such as a password and a one-time code sent to their device.

- **Certificate-based authentication:** This method uses digital certificates to authenticate users or applications, ensuring a secure connection.

- **Integrated authentication:** Systems like Windows Authentication allow users to log in using their network credentials, reducing the need for separate database credentials.

For example, in a PostgreSQL database, enabling certificate-based authentication ensures that only verified users or applications with valid certificates can connect.

Authorization and defining user roles

Once authenticated, users need appropriate permissions to perform specific actions. Authorization involves assigning roles and defining permissions to control what users can access and modify within the database. Roles simplify permission management by grouping users with similar access needs. Common authorization methods include the following:

- **Role-based access control (RBAC)**: This approach assigns roles to users based on their responsibilities. For example:
  - o **Database administrators (DBAs)** have full control over the database, including configuration and maintenance.
  - o Developers may have permission to create or modify schemas and write queries.
  - o Analysts typically have read-only access to specific tables for reporting purposes.

In MySQL, roles can be created and managed using commands, such as:

```
CREATE ROLE analyst;
GRANT SELECT ON sakila.* TO analyst;
GRANT analyst TO 'user1'@'localhost';
```

This example creates an analyst role with read-only access to all tables in a MySQL database and assigns it to a specific user.

Now, let us look at granular permissions. Modern databases allow fine-grained control over access, ensuring users can only perform specific actions on specific resources. For instance, a few examples will include the following:

- Granting **SELECT** permissions on a table for a reporting user.
- Allowing **INSERT** or **UPDATE** operations only on specific columns within a table.
- Denying access to sensitive information, such as customer payment details.

In SQL Server, you can grant column-specific permissions using the following code:

```
GRANT SELECT (first_name, last_name) ON customer TO reporting_user;
```

This command allows the **reporting_user** to view only the **first_name** and **last_name** columns in the customer table.

Implementing the principle of least privilege

The principle of least privilege ensures that users and applications receive only the minimum permissions required to perform their tasks. This reduces the risk of accidental or intentional misuse of database access. A few examples might be:

- A customer service representative should only have access to customer contact information, not financial records.
- An application should only have permission to execute stored procedures rather than direct access to tables.

Organizations can maintain strict control over database access by regularly reviewing and adjusting permissions.

Auditing access and permissions

Auditing access and permissions provides visibility into who is accessing the database and their actions. Logs can help detect unauthorized access attempts, monitor compliance with access policies, and identify potential security threats.

For example, enabling logging in PostgreSQL to capture all login attempts and queries provides a detailed audit trail:

```
ALTER SYSTEM SET log_connections = 'on';
ALTER SYSTEM SET log_disconnections = 'on';
ALTER SYSTEM SET log_statement = 'all';
```

Analyzing these logs helps administrators ensure access policies are followed and identify anomalous behavior.

Dynamic access control

Dynamic access control adjusts permissions based on contextual factors such as time, location, or device. For instance:

- A user may only access the database during business hours.
- Certain permissions may be restricted when accessed from an unrecognized device or IP address.

These policies add an extra layer of protection, especially for remote or distributed work environments. Some databases, like Oracle, offer features like **Virtual Private Database (VPD)** to implement dynamic access control.

Challenges and best practices

Managing access control and permissions effectively requires careful planning and regular updates. Common challenges include the following:

- **Overprovisioning:** Granting excessive permissions to users or roles can lead to security vulnerabilities.
- **Complexity:** Managing permissions across large databases or multiple systems can become cumbersome without clear policies.
- **Inconsistent policies:** Varying access control rules between environments like development and production can create loopholes.

To address these challenges, follow these best practices:

- Use roles to simplify permission management and avoid assigning permissions directly to users.

- Regularly review and update access policies to reflect changes in user roles or database structure.

- Automate permission management using tools or scripts to ensure consistency across environments.

- Implement periodic audits to verify compliance with access control policies.

Integrating access control with application logic

Access control should extend beyond the database to the application layer. For instance, an e-commerce platform using the Sakila sample database might restrict customer service representatives from viewing customer profiles, while administrators can manage customer accounts. Combining application-level restrictions with database permissions creates a comprehensive security model.

By effectively managing access control and permissions, organizations can safeguard their SQL databases against unauthorized access and ensure that data remains secure and accessible to those who need it. This proactive approach is essential for maintaining database integrity and trustworthiness.

Data encryption

Data encryption is fundamental to database security, ensuring that sensitive information remains protected even if accessed by unauthorized parties. Encryption converts plaintext data into an unreadable format, known as ciphertext, which can only be decrypted using a specific key. This process safeguards data at rest and in transit, reducing the risk of breaches and ensuring compliance with regulatory requirements.

Understanding encryption basics

Encryption operates through cryptographic algorithms that encode data using a key. Common encryption algorithms include **Advanced Encryption Standard (AES)**, **Rivest-Shamir-Adleman (RSA)**, and **Triple Data Encryption Standard (3DES)**. These algorithms vary in complexity and use cases, but all aim to make intercepted data unreadable without the correct decryption key.

For example, the Sakila sample database may store customer payment details encrypted using AES-256. Even if an attacker gains access to the database, the encrypted data will remain secure unless the decryption key is compromised.

Encrypting data at rest

Data at rest refers to information stored on physical or virtual devices, such as database files, backups, or logs. Encrypting data at rest ensures that the data remains protected even if storage media is stolen or accessed without authorization. Refer to the following list:

- **Transparent Data Encryption (TDE):** Many database systems, including Microsoft SQL Server, Oracle database, and PostgreSQL, support TDE. This feature automatically encrypts data stored in the database files without requiring application-level changes. For example, enabling TDE in SQL Server involves the following code:

```
CREATE MASTER KEY ENCRYPTION BY PASSWORD = 'your_password';
CREATE CERTIFICATE TDECert WITH SUBJECT = 'TDE Certificate';
CREATE DATABASE ENCRYPTION KEY
    WITH ALGORITHM = AES_256
    ENCRYPTION BY SERVER CERTIFICATE TDECert;
ALTER DATABASE [your_database] SET ENCRYPTION ON;
```

This setup ensures that all data stored in the database is encrypted transparently.

- **Column-level encryption**: For more granular control, specific columns containing sensitive information, such as credit card numbers or social security numbers, can be encrypted. MySQL, for instance, allows column-level encryption using functions like **AES_ENCRYPT**:

```
INSERT INTO customer (name, credit_card)
VALUES ('John Doe', AES_ENCRYPT('4111111111111111', 'encryption_
key'));
```

When retrieving the data, the **AES_DECRYPT** function is used:

```
SELECT AES_DECRYPT(credit_card, 'encryption_key') AS decrypted_card
FROM customer;
```

- **Encrypted backups:** Backups should also be encrypted to prevent data exposure during storage or transfer. Tools like mysqldump for MySQL and pg_dump for PostgreSQL offer options for encrypting backup files, ensuring they remain secure even when stored externally.

Encrypting data in transit

Data in transit refers to information transmitted between a database and its clients or applications. Encrypting this data prevents interception and unauthorized access during transmission.

Using SSL and TLS protocols encrypts client communication between clients and the database. Most database systems support SSL/TLS encryption. For example, MySQL and PostgreSQL handle encryption differently as it relates to their specific database engine:

- **MySQL**: Enable SSL by configuring the server with a certificate and key. Refer to the following code:

```
[mysqld]
```

```
ssl-ca=/path/to/ca-cert.pem
ssl-cert=/path/to/server-cert.pem
```
```
ssl-key=/path/to/server-key.pem
```
On the client side, use the --ssl-ca option to specify the CA certificate when connecting.

- **PostgreSQL:** Enable SSL by modifying the **postgresql.conf** file. Refer to the following code:

```
ssl = on
```
```
ssl_cert_file = '/path/to/server-cert.pem'
```
```
ssl_key_file = '/path/to/server-key.pem'
```
When connecting, use the sslmode=require parameter.

- **Encrypted connections in cloud databases**: Managed cloud databases, such as Amazon RDS or Google Cloud SQL, provide built-in support for encrypted connections. These platforms often offer one-click options to enforce SSL/TLS, simplifying the configuration process.

Key management

Effective encryption relies on secure key management. Keys should be stored securely and accessed only by authorized processes or individuals. Key management strategies include the following:

- **Hardware Security Modules (HSMs):** Physical devices designed to securely generate, store, and manage encryption keys.

- **Key Management Services (KMS):** Cloud-based solutions, such as AWS Key Management Service or Azure Key Vault, provide secure key storage and rotation mechanisms.

- **Key rotation policies:** Regularly rotating encryption keys reduces the risk of compromise. For example, a key to encrypt customer data can be rotated every 90 days, with re-encryption processes ensuring continuity.

Compliance and regulatory requirements

Encryption is often a legal requirement for protecting sensitive data. Regulations such as GDPR, HIPAA, and PCI DSS mandate encryption for certain types of information, including personal data, healthcare records, and payment details. Non-compliance can result in severe penalties, emphasizing the importance of implementing encryption in a comprehensive security strategy.

Encryption overheads and performance

While encryption enhances security, it can introduce performance overhead. Encrypted queries take slightly longer to execute, and encrypted backups require more time to create and restore. To minimize these impacts, you can:

- Use hardware acceleration for encryption algorithms, such as Intel AES-NI.
- Optimize database queries and indexing to reduce the performance cost of encryption.
- Encrypt only the data that requires protection, avoiding unnecessary overhead.

For example, encrypting only the sensitive columns in a customer table, rather than the entire database, balances security with performance.

Best practices for data encryption

Implementing data encryption effectively requires adherence to the following best practices:

- **Encrypt sensitive data by default:** Always encrypt personal identifiers, financial records, and other critical information.
- **Combine encryption with access control:** Encryption complements access control by ensuring that the data remains unreadable even if unauthorized access occurs.
- **Regularly update and patch systems:** Ensure the database system and encryption libraries are updated to address vulnerabilities.
- **Test encryption implementations:** Periodically test decryption processes and key recovery mechanisms to validate reliability.

By following these practices, you can create a robust encryption framework that protects your data from unauthorized access while maintaining operational efficiency.

Preventing SQL injection attacks

SQL injection attacks are one of database management's most common and potentially devastating security vulnerabilities. These attacks exploit weaknesses in input validation by injecting malicious SQL code into queries, allowing attackers to manipulate database operations. Preventing SQL injection is critical for maintaining the security and integrity of your database systems.

Understanding SQL injection

SQL injection occurs when unvalidated user input is incorporated directly into a query. For example, consider a vulnerable query in a web application:

```
SELECT * FROM customer WHERE email = 'user_input';
```

If an attacker enters `' OR 1=1 --`, the query becomes the following:

```
SELECT * FROM customer WHERE email = '' OR 1=1 --';
```

This query bypasses authentication, returning all records from the customer table. SQL injection can lead to unauthorized data access, data modification, or even complete system compromise.

Parameterized queries

Parameterized queries are one of the most effective defences against SQL injection. They separate query structure from data, ensuring user input is treated as a value rather than executable code. Most programming languages and database drivers support parameterized queries.

For example, in Python with MySQL, you can use the following command:

```
cursor.execute("SELECT * FROM customer WHERE email = %s", (user_input,))
```

Alternatively, in PHP, using PDO, you can use the following code:

```
$stmt = $pdo->prepare("SELECT * FROM customer WHERE email = :email");
$stmt->execute(['email' => $user_input]);
```

These approaches safely handle user input, preventing malicious code from altering the query structure.

Stored procedures

Stored procedures can also mitigate SQL injection risks. By pre-compiling SQL statements and avoiding direct user input incorporation, they provide an additional layer of security. For instance, in SQL Server, you can use the following code:

```
CREATE PROCEDURE GetCustomerByEmail @Email NVARCHAR(255)
AS
BEGIN
    SELECT * FROM customer WHERE email = @Email;
END;
```

Calling the procedure from an application ensures the query structure remains fixed:

```
EXEC GetCustomerByEmail @Email = 'user_input';
```

Stored procedures are particularly useful in enterprise environments where query logic is centralized.

Input validation

Validating user input before using it in queries reduces the likelihood of SQL injection. Input validation ensures data conforms to expected formats, such as email addresses or numeric IDs.

For example, in Python, you can use the following code:

```
import re
if not re.match(r'^[a-zA-Z0-9._%+-]+@[a-zA-Z0-9.-]+\.[a-zA-Z]{2,}$', user_
input):
    raise ValueError("Invalid email format")
```

Rejecting input not meeting validation criteria prevents attackers from injecting malicious payloads.

Escaping special characters

While less effective than parameterized queries or stored procedures, escaping special characters is a supplementary measure. Escaping ensures that characters like single quotes do not break query syntax. For example, in MySQL, you can use the following command:

```
SELECT * FROM customer WHERE email = 'O\'Reilly';
```

It is recommended that libraries or database drivers handle escaping automatically. However, this method alone cannot prevent SQL injection, as it may fail against sophisticated attacks.

Least privilege principle

Restricting database permissions limits the damage that SQL injection can cause. Applications should connect to the database using accounts with minimal privileges, ensuring they can only perform necessary operations. For instance:

- A web application that retrieves customer records should use a read-only database account.

- Separate accounts should handle administrative tasks, such as schema changes or backups.

In MySQL, you can create a read-only user with the following code:

```
CREATE USER 'readonly_user'@'localhost' IDENTIFIED BY 'secure_password';
GRANT SELECT ON sakila.* TO 'readonly_user'@'localhost';
```

This approach ensures that the attacker cannot execute destructive commands like **DROP TABLE**, even if an SQL injection occurs.

Using web application firewalls

Web application firewalls (**WAFs**) monitor and filter HTTP traffic, blocking SQL injection attempts before they reach the database. WAFs use rule-based systems to detect malicious patterns, such as query structures with unexpected keywords or excessive use of special characters.

For instance, a WAF can block requests containing **UNION SELECT** or **DROP TABLE**. Integrating a WAF with your application provides an additional security layer, especially for public-facing systems.

Logging and monitoring

Monitoring database queries and application logs can help detect and respond to SQL injection attempts. Suspicious activities, such as queries with excessive or unexpected parameters, may indicate an attack in progress. Enabling query logging in your database system provides valuable insights.

In MySQL, enable the general log to capture all queries using the following code:

```
SET GLOBAL general_log = 'ON';
SET GLOBAL general_log_file = '/var/log/mysql/general.log';
```

Use tools like PostgreSQL's **log_statement** to log specific query types.

Analyzing these logs helps identify patterns and refine security measures.

Testing for vulnerabilities

Regular testing helps identify SQL injection vulnerabilities in your application. Tools like SQLmap automate detecting and exploiting injection flaws, allowing developers to address issues proactively. Conducting security assessments during development and after deployments ensures ongoing protection.

For example, run SQLmap against a test environment, using the following command:

```
sqlmap -u "http://example.com?email=user_input" -dbs
```

This test identifies vulnerabilities and recommends fixes, enabling teams to close security gaps before exploiting them.

Educating developers

Security awareness is crucial for preventing SQL injection. Developers should be trained to write secure code, use parameterized queries, and follow best practices. Regular training sessions, code reviews, and access to up-to-date documentation help reinforce these principles.

For example, providing developers with a secure coding checklist ensures project consistency. Encouraging adherence to industry standards, such as **Open Web Application Security Project's (OWASP)** guidelines, strengthens your organization's overall security posture.

Combining measures for maximum security

No single measure can fully protect against SQL injection. A comprehensive strategy combines parameterized queries, stored procedures, input validation, access controls, and monitoring. By layering these defences, you reduce the likelihood of successful attacks and minimize their impact.

Preventing SQL injection requires a proactive approach, combining technical safeguards with secure coding practices. When implemented consistently, these measures protect your databases and maintain the trust of users and stakeholders.

Auditing and monitoring

Auditing and monitoring are critical components of database security, enabling organizations to track activities, detect anomalies, and maintain accountability within SQL databases. These practices provide visibility into databases' access and use, ensuring policy compliance, detecting potential threats, and identifying unauthorized activities. Administrators can safeguard data integrity and confidentiality by proactively auditing and monitoring databases while responding quickly to security incidents.

Understanding database auditing

Database auditing involves recording and reviewing activities performed within the database. Audit logs capture details about operations, such as queries executed, data accessed, and user logins, providing a chronological record of events.

Common objectives of database auditing include:

- **Detecting unauthorized access:** Audit logs help identify attempts to access data without proper permissions.

- **Compliance:** Regulatory frameworks like GDPR, HIPAA, and PCI DSS often require organizations to maintain detailed audit trails.

- **Incident investigation:** In the event of a security breach, audit logs provide crucial information for forensic analysis.

For example, enabling auditing in PostgreSQL can be achieved using the pgAudit extension:

```
CREATE EXTENSION pgaudit;
ALTER SYSTEM SET pgaudit.log = 'ddl, read, write';
SELECT pg_reload_conf();
```

This configuration logs **Data Definition Language** (DDL) operations, reads queries, and writes transactions, giving administrators visibility into critical database actions.

Types of auditing

Let us look at the types of auditing in further detail:

- **Statement auditing:** This type of auditing tracks SQL statements executed in the database, such as **SELECT**, **INSERT**, **UPDATE**, and **DELETE**. It is useful for understanding query patterns and monitoring sensitive data access.

- **Object auditing**: Monitors access to specific database objects, such as tables, views, or stored procedures. For instance, auditing access to the payment table in the Sakila sample database ensures visibility into financial transactions.

- **Privilege auditing:** Records instances where users exercise specific privileges, such as granting permissions or creating new database users.

- **Login and logout auditing:** This process captures details about user authentication, including successful and failed login attempts. This information helps identify brute-force attacks or unauthorized access attempts.

  In MySQL, login auditing can be enabled using the audit log plugin:

  ```
  INSTALL PLUGIN audit_log SONAME 'audit_log.so';

  SET GLOBAL audit_log_policy = 'ALL';
  ```

These logs provide valuable insights into user behavior and potential security threats.

Monitoring database activities

Monitoring complements auditing by providing real-time insights into database activities. While auditing focuses on recording events for later review, monitoring tools actively track ongoing operations, enabling immediate detection and response to suspicious activities. Let us understand this in further detail:

- **Performance monitoring**: Ensures that the database operates efficiently and identifies queries causing performance bottlenecks. Tools like PostgreSQL's **pg_stat_activity** and MySQL's **SHOW PROCESSLIST** command display active queries and resource usage.

- **Anomaly detection:** Monitoring tools can identify unusual patterns, such as repeated failed login attempts or an unexpected surge in data queries. For instance, a sudden increase in **DELETE** statements might indicate malicious activity.

- **Alerting:** Database monitoring systems can trigger alerts based on predefined thresholds or rules. For example, setting an alert for more than ten failed login attempts in a minute can help administrators respond to potential brute-force attacks.

Using built-in database features

Most modern SQL databases provide built-in auditing and monitoring capabilities, such as:

- **SQL Server:** Use SQL Server Audit to track events. For example, creating an audit to monitor **SELECT** statements on the customer table:

```
CREATE SERVER AUDIT Audit_Sample
TO FILE (FILEPATH = 'C:\AuditLogs\');
CREATE DATABASE AUDIT SPECIFICATION Audit_Spec
FOR SERVER AUDIT Audit_Sample
ADD (SELECT ON OBJECT::customer BY public);
ALTER SERVER AUDIT Audit_Sample WITH (STATE = ON);
```

- **Oracle database:** Enable unified auditing to capture various database activities.

- **MySQL:** Configure the general and slow query logs for auditing query activities and performance monitoring.

Third-party and open-source tools

In addition to built-in features, third-party and open-source tools enhance auditing and monitoring capabilities. Examples include the following:

- **AWS CloudTrail:** Logs API calls and database activity in cloud environments like Amazon RDS.

- **pgAudit:** Provides detailed logging for PostgreSQL databases.

- **Datadog and New Relic:** Offer comprehensive database monitoring, including performance metrics, query analysis, and anomaly detection.

These tools integrate seamlessly with SQL databases, providing administrators with advanced insights and analytics.

Storing and managing audit logs

Effective log management ensures that audit records are accessible, secure, and tamper-proof. Best practices include the following:

- **Centralized storage:** Store audit logs in a central repository for easier analysis and management. Forwarding logs to a **Security Information and Event Management** (**SIEM**) system enhances threat detection and correlation across multiple systems.

- **Log rotation**: Configure log rotation to prevent storage issues. Most databases allow automatic log rotation based on file size or time intervals.

- **Encryption:** Encrypt audit logs to protect their integrity and confidentiality. Enabling SSL/TLS in MySQL ensures the secure transmission of audit logs to external systems.

Compliance and reporting

Audit logs play a critical role in meeting regulatory requirements. Reports generated from audit logs demonstrate compliance with standards like GDPR, HIPAA, or PCI DSS. These reports should include the following:

- A summary of database activities.

- Details of access to sensitive data.

- Logs of privilege changes or administrative actions.

Automating report generation streamlines compliance processes and reduces manual effort.

Proactive monitoring strategies

To maximize the effectiveness of monitoring, adopt proactive strategies:

- **Baseline behavior**: Establish a baseline of regular database activity to identify deviations. For example, if a typical activity includes 50 queries per hour, a sudden spike to 500 queries may indicate an attack.

- **Real-time dashboards:** Use dashboards to visualize database performance, query execution times, and resource usage.

- **Role-specific alerts:** Tailor alerts to specific roles or actions. For example, alert administrators to privilege escalations or failed login attempts.

By combining auditing and monitoring with these proactive strategies, organizations can maintain robust database security, detect threats early, and ensure data integrity.

Backup and recovery

Backup and recovery are essential components of database management. They ensure data availability and resilience in the face of failures, cyberattacks, or disasters. Implementing a robust backup and recovery strategy minimizes downtime and data loss, protecting an organization's critical assets and enabling quick service restoration.

Understanding backup types

There are several types of database backups, each serving specific purposes and recovery scenarios. Let us look at them in detail:

- **Full backup:** A complete copy of the database, capturing all data and metadata. Full backups provide a comprehensive restore point but can be time-consuming and require significant storage.

- **Incremental backup:** This type of backup captures only the changes made since the last backup, reducing storage requirements and backup time. However, restoring from incremental backups may take longer as multiple backup files must be combined.

- **Differential backup**: Records changes since the last full backup, offering a balance between full and incremental backups regarding speed and storage efficiency.
- **Logical backup:** Extracts database objects like tables, schemas, and data into a readable format. It is often used for migrations or testing. Tools like mysqldump for MySQL or pg_dump for PostgreSQL generate logical backups.
- **Snapshot**: Captures a point-in-time image of the database's storage, typically used in virtualized or cloud environments. Snapshots are fast but may not offer the same level of detail as traditional backups.

The following table provides a detailed comparison of the various backup types, highlighting their characteristics, advantages, disadvantages, and ideal use cases to help determine the most suitable option for your database needs:

Backup type	Description	Advantages	Disadvantages	Use case
Full backup	A complete copy of the entire database, including all data and metadata.	Comprehensive restore point; easy to restore.	Time-consuming; requires significant storage.	Initial setup, periodic backups for critical systems.
Incremental backup	Captures only the changes made since the last backup (full or incremental).	Efficient in terms of storage and backup time.	Slower restore as multiple backups must be combined.	Frequent backups for dynamic systems with frequent changes.
Differential backup	Captures changes made since the last full backup.	Faster restore than incremental, balanced storage.	Larger size over time compared to incremental.	Systems with moderate changes, paired with periodic full backups.
Logical backup	Extracts database objects into a readable format like SQL scripts or files.	Ideal for migrations and testing, highly portable.	Not as fast or comprehensive as full backups.	Migrating between systems, creating test environments.
Snapshot	Captures a point-in-time image of the database storage.	Very fast to create, minimal performance impact.	Storage-intensive, not detailed for granular recovery.	Virtualized environments, disaster recovery for rapid restoration.

Table 13.1: Comparison of different database backup types

This table highlights each backup type's key features, benefits, and limitations to help select the most appropriate strategy for specific database requirements.

Creating a backup strategy

An effective backup strategy involves defining key parameters to ensure backups meet organizational needs, such as:

- **Backup frequency:** Determine how often backups should occur based on the database's update frequency and criticality. For example:
    - ○ **High-transaction systems**: Perform hourly incremental backups with nightly full backups.
    - ○ **Low-change databases:** Perform weekly full backups with daily differentials.
- **Retention period:** Define how long backups are stored to meet operational and regulatory requirements. For instance, financial data may require retention for several years.
- **Storage location:** Store backups in secure, geographically diverse locations. Combining on-premises and cloud storage enhances redundancy.
- **Encryption:** Encrypt backups to protect data confidentiality, especially for sensitive information. For example, in PostgreSQL, you can encrypt backups using tools like pg_dump with OpenSSL:

```
pg_dump your_database | openssl aes-256-cbc -e -out backup.sql.enc
```

Automating backups

Automating backups ensures consistency and reduces administrative overhead. Most databases offer tools for scheduling automated backups, such as:

- **MySQL:** Use the `mysqlbackup` tool to automate backup tasks. For example:

```
mysqlbackup --user=root --password=your_password \
--backup-dir=/backups/full --backup-image=full_backup.mbi backup-to-image
```

- **PostgreSQL:** Automate backups using cron jobs and pg_dump:

```
0 2 * * * pg_dump -U postgres -F c your_database > /backups/db_backup_$(date +\%F).dump
```

- **Cloud databases:** Managed services like Amazon RDS and Azure SQL Database provide built-in automated backup options, simplifying backup configuration.

Testing backup integrity

A backup is only as good as its ability to restore data. Regularly testing backups ensures that files are intact and can be used in real recovery scenarios. Testing involves the following:

- Restoring backups to a test environment to verify data consistency and completeness.
- Checking logs for errors during the backup process.
- Performing checksum validations to detect data corruption.
- For example, in SQL Server, you can restore a backup to a secondary server and run queries to validate data integrity:

```
RESTORE DATABASE TestDB
FROM DISK = 'C:\Backups\TestDB.bak'
WITH MOVE 'TestDB_Data' TO 'C:\Data\TestDB.mdf',
MOVE 'TestDB_Log' TO 'C:\Logs\TestDB.ldf';
```

Understanding recovery models

Every database engine has its own unique way of backing up data. The following sub-sections provide an expanded explanation of recovery models for common database engines, outlining how they manage backup and recovery processes to meet different operational requirements.

Microsoft SQL Server

SQL Server offers three primary recovery models: Full, Simple, and Bulk-Logged, which dictate how transaction logs are maintained and used during recovery. Refer to the following table:

Recovery model	Description	Use cases
Full	Logs every transaction, allowing for **point-in-time recovery** (**PITR**). Requires regular transaction log backups.	Critical systems requiring minimal data loss, such as financial systems or e-commerce platforms.
Simple	Automatically truncates transaction logs after each checkpoint, reducing storage needs but limiting recovery options.	Non-critical systems where occasional data loss is acceptable, such as development environments.
Bulk-Logged	Temporarily minimizes log space usage during bulk operations like BULK INSERT. Logs are not point-in-time.	Databases with heavy bulk imports, where high performance is prioritized over fine-grained recovery.

Table 13.2: SQL Server Recovery Models

An example of how to change a SQL Server's database recovery mode would be the following:

```
ALTER DATABASE [YourDatabase] SET RECOVERY FULL;
```

MySQL

MySQL's recovery capabilities depend on its storage engine, with InnoDB being the most commonly used due to its ACID compliance and advanced recovery features. Refer to the following table:

Feature	Description	Use cases
Binary log	Logs all changes to the database, enabling PITR and replication.	Systems requiring replication or granular recovery options, such as high-availability setups.
Redo log	Maintains a record of changes for crash recovery, ensuring data consistency after unexpected failures.	Any production system using InnoDB for transactional integrity.
Undo log	Tracks uncommitted transactions, allowing rollback and maintaining isolation levels.	Scenarios requiring strict transactional consistency, such as banking systems.

Table 13.3: MySQL recovery capabilities

An example of how to add **log_bin** to MySQL database engine through its **conf** file:

```
[mysqld]
log_bin=/var/log/mysql/mysql-bin.log
```

PostgreSQL

PostgreSQL supports robust recovery through its **Write-Ahead Logging** (**WAL**) and PITR features. Refer to the following table:

Recovery method	Description	Use cases
Write-Ahead Logging (WAL)	Ensures data durability by logging changes before applying them to the database files.	Systems requiring ACID compliance and data durability.
Point-in-time recovery (PITR)	Allows restoring the database to a specific moment by replaying WAL archives.	Critical systems needing minimal downtime and precise recovery options.

Base backups	Provides a snapshot of the database, used in conjunction with WAL for comprehensive recovery.	General-purpose systems where a combination of base and incremental backups is sufficient.

Table 13.4: Recovery methods in PostgreSQL

An example on how to add archive mode to PostgreSQL via its configuration file:

```
archive_mode = on
archive_command = 'cp %p /path/to/archive/%f'
```

Oracle database

Oracle provides highly granular recovery options through its **ARCHIVELOG** and **NOARCHIVELOG** modes, along with features like Flashback Technology. Refer to the following table:

Recovery feature	Description	Use cases
ARCHIVELOG mode	Logs all transactions and archives them for PITR.	Critical applications requiring detailed recovery options, such as ERP systems.
NOARCHIVELOG mode	Does not archive logs, offering limited recovery options.	Non-production environments or systems where data loss is acceptable.
Flashback Technology	Enables rolling back the database or individual tables to a previous state without full restores.	Scenarios requiring quick fixes to logical errors or accidental data changes.

Table 13.5: Recovery features in Oracle database

An example of how to enable **ARCHIVELOG** mode in Oracle is as follows:

```
SHUTDOWN IMMEDIATE;
STARTUP MOUNT;
ALTER DATABASE ARCHIVELOG;
ALTER DATABASE OPEN;
```

SQLite

SQLite is a serverless database engine, and its recovery options are more straightforward compared to server-based systems. Refer to the following table:

Feature	Description	Use cases
Rollback Journal	Ensures atomic transactions by storing rollback data during transactions.	Small-scale applications where transactional integrity is required, such as mobile apps.
Write-Ahead Logging (WAL)	Provides better performance and crash recovery by appending changes to a log file.	Applications needing high read concurrency, such as embedded systems.
Backups	Backups are taken by copying the database file while ensuring no active writes occur.	Lightweight systems needing basic backup mechanisms.

Table 13.6: Recovery options in SQLite

An example of how to switch SQLite to WAL mode is given as follows:

```
PRAGMA journal_mode=WAL;
```

Summary of recovery models by database engine

This comprehensive view highlights each database engine's unique recovery options, allowing administrators to select the most appropriate method for their specific needs. Refer to the following table:

Database engine	Recovery models and features	Best use cases
SQL Server	Full, Simple, Bulk-Logged	High-criticality systems for Full, development or testing for Simple, and bulk operations for Bulk-Logged.
MySQL	Binary Log, Redo Log, Undo Log	Granular recovery and replication for Binary Log; transactional integrity for Redo and Undo Logs.
PostgreSQL	WAL, PITR, Base Backups	Critical systems requiring precise recovery and ACID compliance.
Oracle	ARCHIVELOG, NOARCHIVELOG, Flashback	Enterprise applications need comprehensive recovery options for ARCHIVELOG and Flashback.
SQLite	Rollback Journal, WAL	Lightweight, embedded systems need basic transaction and recovery capabilities.

Table 13.7: Summary of recovery features in database management systems

Point-in-time recovery

PITR restores a database to a specific moment, allowing administrators to undo accidental changes or recover from malicious activity. This process relies on transaction logs to replay or roll back changes. For example, in PostgreSQL, you can use continuous archiving with PITR:

Enable WAL archiving, using the following code:

```
wal_level = replica
archive_mode = on
archive_command = 'cp %p /archive/%f'
```

Restore the database and replay logs to a specific point:

```
pg_restore -D /data/your_database -X restore_target_time="2024-12-01 12:00:00"
```

Handling ransomware and disasters

Quick recovery minimizes downtime and data loss in ransomware attacks or disasters. Maintain isolated backups that cannot be accessed or encrypted by malicious actors. To prevent modifications to backup files, use immutable storage options, such as AWS S3 with Object Lock.

DRPs outline steps for restoring services, including the following:

- Identifying the failure's scope and selecting the appropriate backup.
- Prioritizing the restoration of critical systems.
- Communicating progress to stakeholders.

Versioning and archiving

Database versioning involves maintaining multiple backup versions, allowing rollback to previous states. Archiving old backups ensures compliance with regulations requiring long-term data retention. Tools like Amazon Glacier or Azure Blob Storage provide cost-effective solutions for archiving rarely accessed backups.

Best practices for backup and recovery

Best practices for backup and recovery are listed as follows:

- **Implement redundancy**: Store backups in multiple locations to protect against single points of failure.
- **Use incremental strategies**: Combine full, incremental, and differential backups to balance speed and storage efficiency.
- **Encrypt and protect backups**: Ensure backup files are encrypted and stored in secure environments.
- **Test regularly**: Verify that backups can be restored without errors to avoid surprises during critical recovery scenarios.

Backup and recovery processes are vital for ensuring database resilience and maintaining business continuity in the face of unexpected events. Proper planning and execution of these strategies provide peace of mind and protect valuable organizational data.

Compliance and data protection

Compliance and data protection are essential to database security, ensuring that legal, regulatory, and ethical standards handle sensitive information. As organizations collect and store increasing amounts of data, the need for robust data protection strategies has grown. Compliance with regulations like GDPR, HIPAA, and PCI DSS not only protects the rights of individuals but also shields organizations from legal and financial consequences.

Understanding compliance requirements

Regulatory frameworks establish rules for how organizations must handle specific types of data. These regulations vary by industry and jurisdiction but often share common goals, such as safeguarding personal information, maintaining data accuracy, and preventing unauthorized access. Let us look at them in detail:

- **General Data Protection Regulation (GDPR):** Applicable to organizations handling data from European Union residents, GDPR requires robust data protection measures and grants rights to individuals over their data. Key provisions include:

    o   Ensuring data accuracy and security.

    o   Allowing individuals to access, correct, or delete their data.

    o   Reporting data breaches within 72 hours.

- **Health Insurance Portability and Accountability Act (HIPAA):** Focused on protecting health information in the *United States,* HIPAA mandates encryption, access controls, and audit logs for systems handling patient data.

- **Payment Card Industry Data Security Standard (PCI DSS):** Relevant for organizations handling payment card information, PCI DSS requires strong encryption, secure storage, and regular security assessments.

Organizations must identify which regulations apply to their operations and ensure their databases meet compliance standards.

Implementing data protection policies

Data protection begins with clear policies that define how sensitive information is stored, accessed, and shared. Policies should address the following:

- **Data classification:** Categorize data based on sensitivity levels. For example:
    - **Public data**: Non-sensitive information accessible to anyone.
    - **Confidential data:** Internal information restricted to authorized personnel.
    - **Sensitive data: Personally identifiable information (PII)** or financial details requiring the highest level of protection.
- **Access control:** Enforce the principle of least privilege, ensuring users only access the data necessary for their roles. Use RBAC to streamline permission management.
- **Data minimization:** Collect and retain only the data necessary for specific purposes. For instance, avoid storing sensitive customer data like credit card numbers if not required.
- **Retention and disposal:** Define retention periods for different data types and establish secure disposal methods for outdated or unnecessary information.

Encryption for data protection

Encryption plays a vital role in safeguarding data at rest and in transit. Compliance regulations often mandate encryption for sensitive information to ensure it remains protected even if intercepted or accessed without authorization. Different types of data protection include:

- **Data at rest**: Use full-disk or column-level encryption for sensitive database fields. For example:
    - Encrypt PII in the customer table using AES-256 encryption.
    - Secure backup files with password protection and encryption tools.
- **Data in transit**: Use SSL/TLS to encrypt communication between clients and databases, preventing eavesdropping or tampering. Configure database systems to require encrypted connections by default.

Auditing and monitoring for compliance

Regular auditing and monitoring are critical for demonstrating compliance and identifying potential violations. Audit logs record database activities, including access, modifications, and deletions. These logs should include the following:

- **User activity**: Track who accessed the database and their actions.
- **Data changes**: Record modifications to sensitive data, such as updates to the payment table in the Sakila sample database.
- **Access attempts**: Log successful and failed login attempts to identify unauthorized access.

For example, enabling auditing in MySQL with the Audit Log Plugin ensures comprehensive tracking of database activities. Refer to the following code:

```
INSTALL PLUGIN audit_log SONAME 'audit_log.so';
SET GLOBAL audit_log_policy = 'ALL';
```

These logs should be reviewed regularly to detect anomalies and ensure adherence to compliance policies.

Incident response and breach management

Compliance regulations often require organizations to have an incident response plan for managing data breaches. Key components of an effective plan include the following:

- **Detection:** Implement monitoring tools to identify breaches promptly. For instance, detecting a sudden spike in database queries may indicate unauthorized activity.

- **Containments:** Immediately isolate affected systems to prevent further damage. This may involve revoking user credentials or disconnecting compromised servers.

- **Notification:** Comply with regulatory reporting requirements, such as GDPR's 72-hour breach notification rule, by informing authorities and affected individuals.

- **Remediation:** Address vulnerabilities that led to the breach and implement additional safeguards to prevent recurrence.

Data anonymization and pseudonymization

Anonymization and pseudonymization techniques can protect sensitive information while maintaining its utility for analysis or testing, which is essential for complying with privacy regulations. Let us compare them:

- **Anonymization**: Irreversibly remove identifying details from data, ensuring individuals cannot be identified. For example, replace customer names with generic IDs.

- **Pseudonymization**: Replace identifying details with pseudonyms that can be reversed using a secure key. This approach balances privacy with the need for traceability.

Using these techniques in non-production environments, such as development or testing, reduces the risk of exposing sensitive data.

Training and awareness

Training and awareness should include the following points:

- Familiarize teams with relevant laws and standards.

- Ensuring compliance and data protection requires ongoing education for DBAs, developers, and end-users. Training should cover:

  o **Best practices:** Teach secure coding practices, proper handling of sensitive data, and incident response procedures.

   o **Regular updates:** Keep staff informed about changes to regulations and emerging threats.

- By fostering a culture of security awareness, organizations can minimize human errors that may lead to compliance violations.

Regular assessments and audits

Conducting regular assessments ensures that compliance measures remain effective and up to date. These assessments should include:

- **Vulnerability scans**: Identify weaknesses in database configurations or access controls.

- **Penetration testing:** Simulate attacks to evaluate the resilience of security measures.

- **Compliance audits:** Verify that policies and practices align with regulatory requirements.

Automating assessments using tools like AWS Audit Manager or third-party compliance platforms streamlines this process and reduces manual effort.

Maintaining an incident-free environment

Organizations can ensure their SQL databases remain secure and compliant by combining robust policies, technical safeguards, and regular training. Compliance and data protection are ongoing processes that require vigilance, adaptability, and a proactive approach to address evolving threats and regulations.

Conclusion

This chapter explored the foundational and advanced techniques required to secure SQL databases effectively. We gained insights into implementing access control mechanisms to ensure only authorized users can access or modify sensitive data. The chapter covered encryption techniques for protecting data in transit and, at rest, safeguarding it against unauthorized access. We also learned how to prevent SQL injection attacks, a common and potentially devastating vulnerability, using parameterized queries and other best practices. Furthermore, we looked into auditing and monitoring strategies to detect and respond to suspicious database activity. We examined the importance of maintaining robust backup and recovery systems to ensure data resilience. These skills are critical for creating secure and compliant database systems that withstand evolving threats.

In the next chapter, we will shift our focus to practical applications of SQL through hands-on projects. We will learn to apply the concepts and techniques covered throughout this book to real-world scenarios, such as designing data models, building complex queries, and optimizing database performance. This chapter will bridge theory and practice, giving us the confidence to tackle SQL challenges in professional environments.

Points to remember

Securing SQL databases is a fundamental responsibility for DBAs and developers. This chapter highlighted the essential techniques and best practices for protecting data from unauthorized access, vulnerabilities, and potential loss. By applying these principles, you can build robust systems that ensure data confidentiality, integrity, and compliance with regulatory standards. Here are the key points to remember from this chapter:

- **Access control and permissions**: Implement RBAC to restrict user permissions and minimize unauthorized access.

- **Data encryption**: Use encryption methods to protect sensitive data both in transit and at rest, ensuring it remains secure even if intercepted.

- **Preventing SQL injection**: Mitigate SQL injection attacks by using parameterized queries and validating all user inputs.

- **Auditing and monitoring**: Track database activity using auditing tools to detect unauthorized access or suspicious actions.

- **Backup and recovery:** Establish regular backup routines and test recovery plans to protect against data loss and ensure business continuity.

- **Compliance and data protection:** Adhere to industry regulations like GDPR, HIPAA, or CCPA to meet legal requirements and protect sensitive information.

- **Least privilege principle:** Grant users the minimum level of access necessary for their role to reduce potential vulnerabilities.

- **Regular updates**: Keep database systems and security patches up to date to mitigate newly discovered vulnerabilities.

Join our Discord space

Join our Discord workspace for latest updates, offers, tech happenings around the world, new releases, and sessions with the authors:

https://discord.bpbonline.com

CHAPTER 14
Practical SQL Projects

Introduction

In this chapter, readers will apply the SQL concepts and techniques learned throughout the book to practical projects. These hands-on exercises range from building a **customer relationship management (CRM)** database to analyzing sales data, creating a blog platform, visualizing data, and automating reports.

Additionally, the projects leverage the Sakila sample database to design customer feedback and rating systems and generate detailed rental data reports. Each project provides step-by-step guidance, offering a real-world context to enhance problem-solving skills and reinforce key database management principles. By the end of this chapter, readers will have gained valuable experience in designing, querying, and optimizing databases for diverse applications.

Structure

This chapter covers the following topics:

- Project one, building a simple CRM database
- Project two, analyzing sales data
- Project three, creating a blog platform
- Project four, data visualization with SQL

- Project five, automating data reports
- Project six, creating a customer feedback system
- Project seven, creating a customer rating system
- Project eight, creating rental data reports

Objectives

By the end of this chapter, readers will be able to apply SQL knowledge to real-world scenarios by completing a series of practical projects. They will learn how to design and implement databases for specific use cases, such as building a CRM system, creating a blog platform, and developing data visualization tools.

Readers will gain experience in querying data for analysis, automating report generation, and integrating SQL workflows with external tools like Python. Through projects using the Sakila sample database, they will design feedback and rating systems, analyze rental trends, and generate detailed reports. These objectives aim to equip readers with hands-on experience solving database challenges, enhancing their SQL proficiency, and problem-solving capabilities.

Project one, building a simple CRM database

A CRM database is a critical tool for businesses to manage and streamline customer interactions, track sales leads, and maintain valuable relationships. This project focuses on creating a simple CRM database using SQLite 3. You will design and implement a relational database schema, populate it with sample data, and query it to extract actionable insights. This hands-on project allows us to apply the SQL concepts we have learned in a real-world scenario, emphasizing database design, data manipulation, and querying techniques.

Use case and scenario

Let us imagine you are a database consultant for a small marketing agency. The agency needs a CRM system to manage customer information and track interactions such as emails, phone calls, and meetings. The goal is to create a lightweight, efficient database that helps the agency organize customer data, monitor client interactions, and generate insights for improved customer engagement strategies. By designing this CRM database, you will help the agency enhance operational efficiency, foster better client relationships, and identify potential business opportunities.

Through this project, you will build a practical CRM system that supports standard business functions like recording new customer information, logging interactions, and generating reports. This project's step-by-step guide ensures you can follow along seamlessly, learning how to structure, populate, and query a relational database to address real-world business challenges.

Step 1: Set up SQLite 3

Before starting, ensure SQLite 3 is installed and set up on your system. Refer to *Chapter 1, Introduction to SQL, Setting up your SQL environment,* for detailed instructions on installing SQLite 3. Use the SQLite 3 command-line tool to create and manage your database.

Follow these steps to set up SQLite 3:

1. Open a terminal or command prompt.

2. Create a new database file called **crm.db**:

   ```
   sqlite3 crm.db
   ```

3. Enter the SQLite shell to begin executing SQL commands.

Step 2: Create the database structure

Design and create tables for your CRM database. You will need tables to store customer information and their interactions. Use concepts from *Chapter 8, Managing Database Objects, Creating and modifying tables,* to define the structure.

Follow these steps to create the database structure:

1. Create a **customers** table to store customer details:

   ```
   CREATE TABLE customers (
       customer_id INTEGER PRIMARY KEY AUTOINCREMENT,
       first_name TEXT NOT NULL,
       last_name TEXT NOT NULL,
       email TEXT UNIQUE NOT NULL,
       phone TEXT,
       created_at DATETIME DEFAULT CURRENT_TIMESTAMP
   );
   ```

2. Create an interactions table to track customer interactions:

   ```
   CREATE TABLE interactions (
       interaction_id INTEGER PRIMARY KEY AUTOINCREMENT,
       customer_id INTEGER NOT NULL,
       interaction_date DATETIME NOT NULL,
       interaction_type TEXT NOT NULL,
       notes TEXT,
       FOREIGN KEY (customer_id) REFERENCES customers(customer_id)
   );
   ```

Step 3: Insert sample data

Populate your tables with sample data to work with. Use techniques from *Chapter 6, Modifying Data, Inserting data with INSERT INTO.*

Follow these steps to insert sample data:

1. Insert sample customers into the customers table:

```
INSERT INTO customers (first_name, last_name, email, phone)
VALUES
    ('John', 'Doe', 'john.doe@example.com', '123-456-7890'),
    ('Jane', 'Smith', 'jane.smith@example.com', '098-765-4321'),
    ('Alice', 'Johnson', 'alice.johnson@example.com', NULL);
```

2. Add interactions for these customers:

```
INSERT INTO interactions (customer_id, interaction_date,
interaction_type, notes)
VALUES
    (1, '2024-01-15', 'Phone Call', 'Discussed service options'),
    (2, '2024-01-20', 'Email', 'Sent follow-up details'),
    (1, '2024-01-25', 'Meeting', 'Reviewed contract terms');
```

Step 4: Query customer data

Retrieve and analyze data using **SELECT** statements. Apply techniques from *Chapter 3, Basic SQL Queries, Retrieving data in SQL.*

Follow these steps to query customer data:

1. View all customers in the database:

```
SELECT * FROM customers;
```

2. Find a customer by their email address:

```
SELECT first_name, last_name
FROM customers
WHERE email = 'john.doe@example.com';
```

3. List all interactions for a specific customer:

```
SELECT interaction_date, interaction_type, notes
FROM interactions
WHERE customer_id = 1
ORDER BY interaction_date;
```

Step 5: Update and manage data

Modify existing records using **UPDATE** and **DELETE** statements. Refer to the sections *Updating data with UPDATE* and *Deleting data with DELETE* in *Chapter 6, Modifying Data.*

Follow these steps to update and manage data:

1. Update a customer's phone number:

```
UPDATE customers
```

```
SET phone = '111-222-3333'
WHERE email = 'alice.johnson@example.com';
```

2. Remove an outdated interaction:

```
DELETE FROM interactions
WHERE interaction_id = 2;
```

Step 6: Analyze and summarize data

Use aggregate functions and grouping to analyze the data. Explore concepts from sections *Grouping data with GROUP BY* and *Aggregate functions* in *Chapter 5, Advanced Data Retrieval*.

Follow these steps to analyze and summarize data:

1. Count the number of interactions for each customer:

```
SELECT

c.first_name,

c.last_name,

COUNT(i.interaction_id) AS total_interactions
FROM customers c
JOIN interactions i

ON c.customer_id = i.customer_id
GROUP BY c.customer_id;
```

2. Find the most recent interaction for each customer:

```
SELECT

c.first_name,

c.last_name,

MAX(i.interaction_date) AS last_interaction
FROM customers c
JOIN interactions i

ON c.customer_id = i.customer_id
GROUP BY c.customer_id;
```

Step 7: Secure the database

Implement basic security measures to protect sensitive data. Use insights from *Chapter 13, Security Considerations in SQL*.

Follow these steps to secure the database:

1. Ensure unique constraints on sensitive fields like email:

```
CREATE UNIQUE INDEX idx_email ON customers(email);
```

2. Type `.exit` at the `sqlite>` command prompt. Now, back up the database for disaster recovery:

```
sqlite3 crm.db ".backup crm_backup.db"
```

By completing these steps, you will have created a fully functional CRM database, applied SQL concepts from multiple chapters, and gained practical experience in building a real-world database application.

Project two, analyzing sales data

Sales data analysis is essential for businesses to understand customer behavior, identify trends, and optimize revenue generation. In this project, you will create and analyze a sales data database using SQLite 3. The project includes designing a relational schema, populating it with sample data, and performing advanced queries to uncover meaningful insights. You will apply concepts from earlier chapters to build a database that provides actionable insights into sales performance and trends.

Use case and scenario

Imagine you are tasked with building a sales analytics tool for a small retail company. The company sells various products across categories like electronics, furniture, and appliances. They need a simple, effective database to track product sales, understand top-selling categories, and analyze seasonal trends. The database will also help the company identify customer purchasing patterns, enabling data-driven decisions for inventory management and marketing strategies.

By completing this project, you will design a sales data database capable of tracking transactions, calculating revenues, and highlighting key trends. This hands-on exercise will guide you through every process step, including creating the schema, populating data, and performing advanced SQL queries for analytics. Whether calculating total sales by product or detecting peak sales months, this project provides a practical foundation for leveraging SQL in data analysis scenarios.

Step 1: Set up SQLite 3 and create the database

Ensure SQLite 3 is installed and configured on your system. Refer to *Chapter 1, Introduction to SQL, Setting up your SQL environment,* for setup instructions.

Follow these steps to set up SQLite 3 and create the database:

1. Open a terminal or command prompt.
2. Create a new database file named **sales_data.db**:

```
sqlite3 sales_data.db
```

3. Enter the SQLite shell to begin working with the database.

Step 2: Design the database schema

Design tables to store sales, products, and customer information. Use principles from *Chapter 2, Understanding Databases,* and *Chapter 8, Managing Database Objects, Creating and modifying tables.*

Follow these steps to design the database schema:

1. Create a products table to store product details:

```
CREATE TABLE products (
    product_id INTEGER PRIMARY KEY AUTOINCREMENT,
    product_name TEXT NOT NULL,
    category TEXT NOT NULL,
    price REAL NOT NULL
);
```

2. Create a sales table to track transactions:

```
CREATE TABLE sales (
    sale_id INTEGER PRIMARY KEY AUTOINCREMENT,
    product_id INTEGER NOT NULL,
    quantity INTEGER NOT NULL,
    sale_date DATETIME NOT NULL,
    customer_name TEXT NOT NULL,
    FOREIGN KEY (product_id) REFERENCES products(product_id)
);
```

Step 3: Insert sample data

Populate the database with sample data for analysis. Apply techniques from *Chapter 6, Modifying Data, Inserting data with INSERT INTO.*

Follow these steps to insert sample data:

1. Add product information to the products table:

```
INSERT INTO products (product_name, category, price)
VALUES
    ('Laptop', 'Electronics', 1200.00),
    ('Headphones', 'Electronics', 150.00),
    ('Coffee Maker', 'Appliances', 80.00),
    ('Desk Chair', 'Furniture', 200.00);
```

2. Insert sales records into the sales table:

```
INSERT INTO sales (product_id, quantity, sale_date, customer_name)
VALUES
    (1, 2, '2024-01-10', 'John Doe'),
    (2, 1, '2024-01-11', 'Jane Smith'),
    (3, 3, '2024-01-12', 'Alice Johnson'),
    (4, 1, '2024-01-13', 'Tom Brown');
```

Step 4: Query basic sales data

Retrieve and explore sales data using **SELECT** statements. Refer to *Chapter 3, Basic SQL Queries, Retrieving data in SQL.*

Follow these steps to query basic sales data:

1. View all sales records:

```
SELECT * FROM sales;
```

2. Join sales and products tables to view sales with product details:

```
SELECT
s.sale_date,
s.customer_name,
p.product_name,
s.quantity,
p.price
FROM
sales s
JOIN products p
ON s.product_id = p.product_id;
```

Step 5: Analyze sales trends

Perform analysis to uncover trends and insights. Use concepts from *Chapter 5, Advanced Data Retrieval,* and *Chapter 9, SQL Performance Optimization.*

Follow these steps to analyze sales trends:

1. Calculate total sales revenue for each product:

```
SELECT
        p.product_name,
        SUM(s.quantity * p.price) AS total_revenue
FROM sales s
JOIN products p
        ON s.product_id = p.product_id
GROUP BY p.product_id
ORDER BY total_revenue DESC;
```

2. Find the top-selling product category:

```
SELECT
p.category,
SUM(s.quantity) AS total_quantity
```

```
FROM sales s
JOIN products p ON s.product_id = p.product_id
GROUP BY p.category
ORDER BY total_quantity DESC;
```

Step 6: Identify seasonal patterns

Analyze sales data over time to detect seasonal patterns. Apply techniques from *Chapter 5, Advanced Data Retrieval, Grouping data with GROUP BY.*

Follow these steps to identify seasonal patterns:

1. Group sales by month:

```
SELECT
        strftime('%Y-%m', s.sale_date) AS month,
        SUM(s.quantity * p.price) AS monthly_revenue
FROM sales s
JOIN products p ON s.product_id = p.product_id
GROUP BY month
ORDER BY month;
```

2. Identify peak months for sales:

```
SELECT
strftime('%Y-%m', sale_date) AS month,
COUNT(*) AS total_sales
FROM sales
GROUP BY month
ORDER BY total_sales DESC
LIMIT 1;
```

Step 7: Optimize and secure the database

Apply security measures and performance optimizations. Use insights from *Chapter 8, Managing Database Objects,* and *Chapter 13, Security Considerations in SQL.*

Follow these steps to optimize and secure the database:

1. Create indexes to speed up queries:

```
CREATE INDEX idx_product_id ON sales(product_id);
CREATE INDEX idx_sale_date ON sales(sale_date);
```

2. Back up the database:

```
sqlite3 sales_data.db ".backup sales_data_backup.db"
```

Step 8: Visualize data

Export data for visualization using external tools.

Follow these steps to visualize data:

1. Open a terminal or command prompt.
2. Open the database file named **sales_data.db**:

    ```
    sqlite3 sales_data.db
    ```
3. Enter the SQLite shell to begin working with the database.
4. Turn headers, change mode to csv, and create an output file called **sales_ analysis.csv**.

    ```
    .headers on
    .mode csv
    .output sales_analysis.csv
    ```
5. Run the SQL query to ouput to the **csv**:

    ```
    SELECT p.product_name, SUM(s.quantity * p.price) AS total_revenue
    FROM sales s
    JOIN products p ON s.product_id = p.product_id
    GROUP BY p.product_id;
    ```
6. Output the SQL query results to the **sales_analysis.csv** file:

    ```
    .output
    ```
7. Type **.exit** at the **sqlite>** command prompt.
8. Open the **sales_analysis.csv** file to review the results.

By following these steps, you will create and analyze a sales data database, apply SQL techniques from multiple chapters, and gain experience in solving real-world analytical challenges.

Project three, creating a blog platform

A blog platform is fundamental for individuals and businesses to share knowledge, express creativity, and engage with their audience. In this project, you will design and implement a simple blog platform using SQLite 3. This platform will allow authors to create blog posts, readers to leave comments, and administrators to manage content. By following a step-by-step guide, you will build a relational database that supports essential blogging functionalities, applying SQL techniques from earlier chapters to create a robust and efficient system.

Use case and scenario

Imagine you are a freelance developer hired by a small media startup that needs a lightweight blogging platform to publish articles and engage with readers. The startup wants a database to manage its content, including authors, blog posts, and reader comments. It also needs tools to analyze blog performance, such as identifying the most popular posts and tracking author contributions. Your task is to create a scalable database backend for this platform, enabling the startup to organize content, interact with its audience, and make data-driven decisions to enhance its reach.

This project will teach you how to structure and populate a blog database, perform advanced queries to retrieve and analyze content, and apply SQL concepts in a real-world scenario. By completing this project, you will gain practical experience in building a blogging system that meets the needs of modern content creators and their audiences.

Step 1: Set up SQLite 3 and create the database

Ensure SQLite 3 is installed and configured on your system. Refer to *Chapter 1, Introduction to SQL, Setting up your SQL environment,* for setup instructions.

Follow these steps to set up SQLite 3 and create the database:

1. Open a terminal or command prompt.
2. Create a new database file named **blog_platform.db**:

    ```
    sqlite3 blog_platform.db
    ```
3. Enter the SQLite shell to begin working with the database.

Step 2: Design the database schema

Design tables to manage authors, blog posts, and comments. Use principles from *Chapter 2, Understanding Databases,* and *Chapter 8, Managing Database Objects, Creating and modifying tables.*

Follow these steps to design the database schema:

1. Create an authors table to store author information:

    ```
    CREATE TABLE authors (
        author_id INTEGER PRIMARY KEY AUTOINCREMENT,
        name TEXT NOT NULL,
        email TEXT UNIQUE NOT NULL,
        bio TEXT
    );
    ```
2. Create a posts table to store blog posts:

    ```
    CREATE TABLE posts (
        post_id INTEGER PRIMARY KEY AUTOINCREMENT,
        author_id INTEGER NOT NULL,
        title TEXT NOT NULL,
        content TEXT NOT NULL,
        published_date DATETIME DEFAULT CURRENT_TIMESTAMP,
    ```

```
        FOREIGN KEY (author_id) REFERENCES authors(author_id)
);
```

3. Create a comments table to store comments on blog posts:

```
CREATE TABLE comments (
comment_id INTEGER PRIMARY KEY AUTOINCREMENT,
post_id INTEGER NOT NULL,
commenter_name TEXT NOT NULL,
comment_text TEXT NOT NULL,
commented_date DATETIME DEFAULT CURRENT_TIMESTAMP,
FOREIGN KEY (post_id) REFERENCES posts(post_id)
);
```

Step 3: Insert sample data

Populate the database with sample data for blog authors, posts, and comments. Use techniques from *Chapter 6, Modifying Data, Inserting data with INSERT INTO.*

Follow these steps to insert sample data:

1. Add sample authors to the authors table:

```
INSERT INTO authors (name, email, bio)
VALUES
    ('John Doe', 'john.doe@example.com', 'Tech enthusiast and
blogger'),
    ('Jane Smith', 'jane.smith@example.com', 'Writer and digital
marketer');
```

2. Add sample blog posts to the posts table:

```
INSERT INTO posts (author_id, title, content)

VALUES

(1, 'Introduction to SQLite', 'SQLite is a lightweight database
system...'),

(2, 'Marketing Strategies for 2024', 'The key to successful marketing
is...');
```

3. Add sample comments to the comments table:

```
INSERT INTO comments (post_id, commenter_name, comment_text)
VALUES
    (1, 'Alice', 'Great introduction to SQLite!'),
    (1, 'Tom', 'I found this post very helpful. Thanks!'),
    (2, 'Sarah', 'I will try these strategies for my campaigns.');
```

Step 4: Query blog data

Retrieve and explore blog data using **SELECT** statements. Refer to *Chapter 3, Basic SQL Queries, Retrieving data in SQL.*

Follow these steps to query blog data:

1. View all blog posts along with their authors:

```
SELECT
p.title,
p.content,
a.name AS author,
p.published_date
FROM posts p
JOIN authors a ON p.author_id = a.author_id;
```

2. Retrieve all comments for a specific blog post:

```
SELECT c.commenter_name, c.comment_text, c.commented_date
FROM comments c
WHERE c.post_id = 1;
```

Step 5: Update blog content

Modify existing blog data using **UPDATE**. Refer to *Chapter 6, Modifying Data, Updating data with UPDATE.*

Follow these steps to update blog content:

1. Update the title of a blog post:

```
UPDATE posts
SET title = 'Getting Started with SQLite'
WHERE post_id = 1;
```

2. Update an author's bio:

```
UPDATE authors
SET bio = 'Experienced tech blogger'
WHERE email = 'john.doe@example.com';
```

Step 6: Delete blog content

Remove outdated data using **DELETE**. Refer to *Chapter 6, Modifying Data, Deleting data with DELETE.*

Follow these steps to delete blog content:

1. Delete a comment:

```
DELETE FROM comments
WHERE comment_id = 2;
```

2. Delete a blog post and its associated comments:

```
DELETE FROM comments
WHERE post_id = 1;
DELETE FROM posts
WHERE post_id = 1;
```

Step 7: Analyze blog performance

Perform analysis to understand blog performance. Use aggregate functions in sections *Grouping data with GROUP BY* and *Aggregate functions* from *Chapter 5, Advanced Data Retrieval*.

Follow these steps to analyze blog performance:

1. Count the number of posts by each author:

```
SELECT a.name, COUNT(p.post_id) AS post_count
FROM authors a
JOIN posts p ON a.author_id = p.author_id
GROUP BY a.author_id;
```

2. Find the most commented blog post:

```
SELECT p.title, COUNT(c.comment_id) AS comment_count
FROM posts p
JOIN comments c ON p.post_id = c.post_id
GROUP BY p.post_id
ORDER BY comment_count DESC
LIMIT 1;
```

Step 8: Optimize and secure the database

Apply optimizations and security measures to enhance database performance. Use techniques from *Chapter 8, Managing Database Objects, Improving queries with indexes,* and *Chapter 13, Security Considerations in SQL, Introduction to database security*.

Follow these steps to optimize and secure the database:

1. Create indexes to speed up queries:

```
CREATE INDEX idx_author_id ON posts(author_id);
CREATE INDEX idx_post_id ON comments(post_id);
```

2. Back up the database:

```
sqlite3 blog_platform.db ".backup blog_platform_backup.db"
```

Through this step-by-step guide, you will design and implement a functional blog platform, integrating multiple SQL concepts to create and manage a real-world application. This project demonstrates the power of SQL for organizing and analyzing data in a practical context.

Project four, data visualization with SQL

Data visualization transforms raw data into insightful and actionable information, making it easier to identify trends, uncover patterns, and communicate findings effectively. In this project, you will use SQLite 3 to design a sales database, extract meaningful data with SQL queries, and create visual representations using Python's Matplotlib library. This project integrates SQL with data visualization techniques to build a comprehensive analytics workflow.

Use case and scenario

Imagine you are working for a regional retail chain that wants to understand its sales performance across different regions and product categories. The company uses you to create visual dashboards highlighting revenue distribution, monthly trends, and product popularity. These visualizations will help management decide on inventory planning, marketing strategies, and regional expansion.

The database you design will store transaction details, including regions, products, and sales data. You will query the data to calculate revenue, track performance over time, and identify key insights. This project enables you to communicate findings effectively through visualizations like bar charts and line graphs, bridging the gap between data analysis and decision-making. Completing this project will give you practical experience integrating SQL queries with data visualization tools to deliver impactful results.

Step 1: Set up SQLite 3 and the environment

Ensure SQLite 3 is installed and configured. Refer to *Chapter 1, Introduction to SQL, Setting up your SQL environment,* for installation steps. Additionally, install Python and Matplotlib for visualization.

Follow these steps to set up SQLite 3 and the environment:

1. Install Python and Matplotlib:
    ```
    pip install matplotlib==3.10.0
    pip install pandas==2.2.3
    ```

2. Create a new SQLite database named **visualization_project.db**:
    ```
    sqlite3 visualization_project.db
    ```

Step 2: Design the database schema

Define the schema for storing sales data. This dataset will be used for visualization. Apply concepts from *Chapter 2, Understanding Databases,* and *Chapter 8, Managing Database Objects, Creating and modifying tables.*

Follow this step to design the database schema:

1. Create a sales table to store sales transactions:

```
CREATE TABLE sales (
    sale_id INTEGER PRIMARY KEY AUTOINCREMENT,
    region TEXT NOT NULL,
    product TEXT NOT NULL,
    quantity INTEGER NOT NULL,
    price REAL NOT NULL,
    sale_date DATETIME NOT NULL
);
```

Step 3: Populate the database

Insert sample sales data to simulate real-world transactions. Use techniques from *Chapter 6, Modifying Data, Inserting data with INSERT INTO.*

Follow this step to populate the database:

1. Add sample records to the sales table:

```
INSERT INTO sales (region, product, quantity, price, sale_date)
VALUES
('North', 'Laptop', 10, 1200.00, '2024-01-10'),
('South', 'Tablet', 15, 500.00, '2024-01-11'),
('East', 'Smartphone', 20, 800.00, '2024-01-12'),
('West', 'Headphones', 25, 150.00, '2024-01-13'),
('North', 'Tablet', 12, 300.00, '2024-02-14'),
('South', 'Laptop', 8, 2000.00, '2024-02-15'),
('North', 'Laptop', 10, 1500.00, '2024-02-10'),
('South', 'Tablet', 15, 400.00, '2024-03-11'),
('East', 'Smartphone', 20, 1300.00, '2024-03-12'),
('West', 'Headphones', 25, 750.00, '2024-03-13');
```

Step 4: Query data for visualization

Extract and organize data for visualization using SQL queries. Refer to *Chapter 3, Basic SQL Queries,* and *Chapter 5, Advanced Data Retrieval, Grouping data with GROUP BY.*

Follow these steps to query data for visualization:

1. Calculate total revenue by region:

```
SELECT region, SUM(quantity * price) AS total_revenue
FROM sales
GROUP BY region;
```

2. Calculate total sales by product:

```
SELECT product, SUM(quantity) AS total_sales
FROM sales
GROUP BY product;
```

3. Aggregate monthly revenue:

```
SELECT strftime('%Y-%m', sale_date) AS month, SUM(quantity * price)
AS monthly_revenue
FROM sales
GROUP BY month
ORDER BY month;
```

Step 5: Export data for visualization

Export query results into a format suitable for visualization. Use the SQLite shell to create CSV files. Refer to *Chapter 14, Practical SQL Projects, Project five, automating data reports,* for exporting data.

Follow these steps to export data for visualization:

1. Turn headers, change mode to csv, and create an output file called **regional_revenue.csv** to export regional revenue data:

```
.headers on
.mode csv
.output regional_revenue.csv
```

2. Run the SQL query to ouput to the csv:

```
SELECT region, SUM(quantity * price) AS total_revenue
FROM sales
GROUP BY region;
```

3. Output the SQL query results to the **regional_revenue.csv** file

```
.output
```

4. Follow the same steps (*Steps 1 to 3*), replacing the SQL query with the following one to get monthly revenue and the file name (**monthly_revenue.csv**):

```
SELECT strftime('%Y-%m', sale_date) AS month, SUM(quantity * price)
AS monthly_revenue
FROM sales
GROUP BY month
ORDER BY month;
```

Step 6: Visualize data using Python and Matplotlib

Leverage Matplotlib to create graphs and charts for the exported data.

Follow these steps to visualize data using Python and Matplotlib:

1. Type in **.exit**, to exit out of the **sqlite** command.

2. Type in **python** to enter the Python command shell.

3. Copy the following python code into a file called **projectfour.py**:

```
import pandas as pd
import matplotlib.pyplot as plt
# Load data
regional_revenue = pd.read_csv('regional_revenue.csv')
monthly_revenue = pd.read_csv('monthly_revenue.csv')

revenue'], color='blue')

plt.title('Total Revenue by Region')

plt.xlabel('Region')

plt.ylabel('Revenue')

plt.show()
```

4. Run the python code with the following command: **python projectfour.py**. Refer to the following figure for a better understanding:

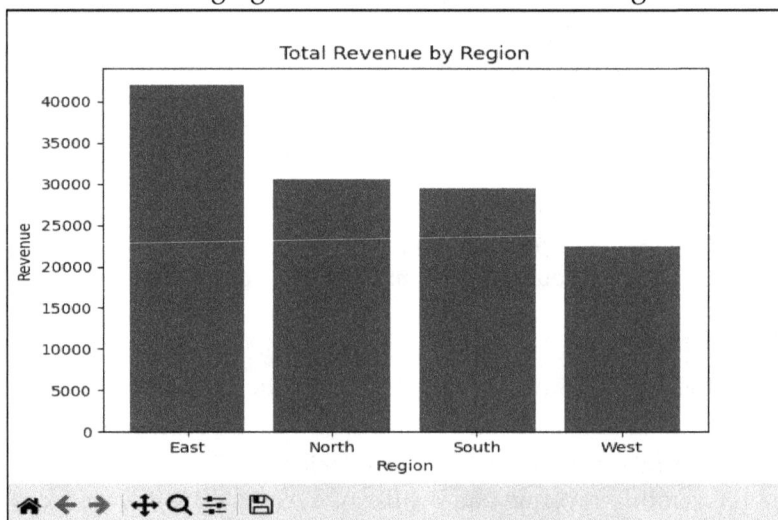

Figure 14.1: Screenshot of regional revenue using Python and SQLite

5. Just as you did in *Step 4*, add additional python code to create a line chart, shown in *Figure 14.2*, for monthly revenue. Run the python file again to execute the code as you did in *Step 4*:

```
plt.plot(monthly_revenue['month'],monthly_revenue['monthly_
revenue'], marker='o')
plt.title('Monthly Revenue Trends')
plt.xlabel('Month')
plt.ylabel('Revenue')
plt.xticks(rotation=45)
```

```
plt.show()
```

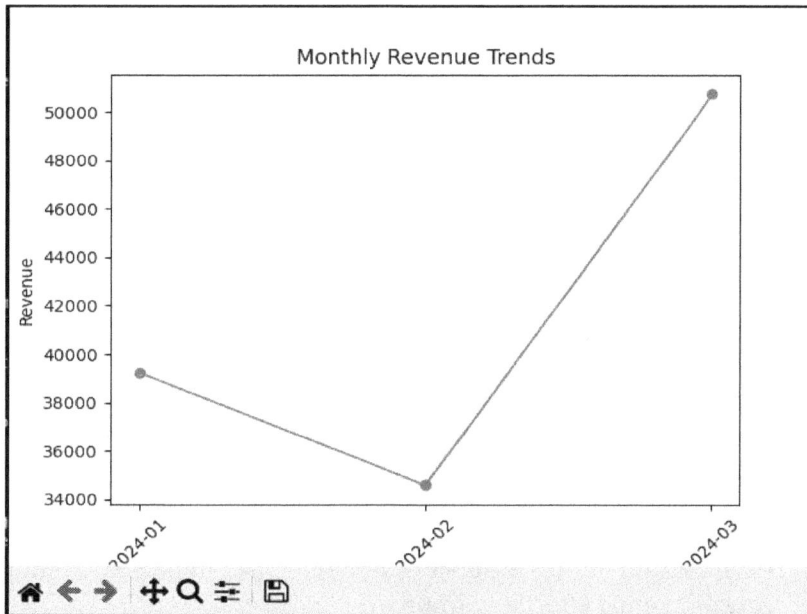

Figure 14.2: *Screenshot of monthly revenue trends using Python and SQLite*

Step 7: Interpret and present results

Summarize the insights gained from the visualizations. Use techniques from *Chapter 5, Advanced Data Retrieval,* to refine queries if needed. Follow these steps:

1. The bar chart shows the region with the highest revenue.

2. Observe revenue trends over time and highlight peak months using the line chart.

3. Add more sales data for different months to review more data trends.

By completing this project, you will have created and visualized sales data using SQLite 3 and Python. This hands-on experience will enhance your ability to use SQL for real-world data visualization and analysis scenarios.

Project five, automating data reports

Automating data reports is critical for businesses that rely on timely and accurate insights to make informed decisions. This project focuses on creating a system to automate the generation and distribution of sales reports using SQLite 3 and Python. Following a step-by-step guide, you will design a database, develop SQL queries, and create automated workflows to generate reports in formats suitable for sharing with stakeholders. This project showcases how automation reduces manual effort, improves efficiency, and ensures consistency in reporting.

Use case and scenario

Let us assume you work for a regional retail chain that manages sales across multiple locations. The management team needs daily and weekly sales reports to evaluate performance across regions and products. These reports include total revenue by region, monthly trends, and top-selling products. Generating these reports involves manual effort, which is time-consuming and prone to errors. Your task is to build an automated system that extracts sales data, processes it, and creates shareable Excel reports.

This automated reporting system will save time, reduce errors, and ensure stakeholders can access updated reports immediately. By completing this project, you will gain practical experience integrating SQL and Python for automation, preparing you to address real-world business challenges with efficient data-driven solutions.

Automating data reports is essential for streamlining workflows and ensuring the timely delivery of critical insights. In this project, you will create a system to automate sales data reporting using SQLite 3 and Python. The process will involve designing a database, generating SQL queries for data extraction, and automating report creation and distribution. This hands-on guide references earlier chapters to help you build a practical solution that reduces manual effort and improves efficiency.

Step 1: Set up SQLite 3 and Python

Ensure SQLite 3 and Python are installed and configured on your system. Refer to *Chapter 1, Introduction to SQL, Setting up your SQL environment,* for installation instructions.

Follow these steps to set up SQLite 3 and Python:

1. Install SQLite 3 and Python.

2. Install additional Python libraries for automation:

    ```
    pip install pandas==2.2.3
    pip install openpyxl==3.1.5
    ```

3. Create a new SQLite database named **automated_reports.db**:

    ```
    sqlite3 automated_reports.db
    ```

Step 2: Design the database schema

Create tables to store sales data. Use principles from *Chapter 2, Understanding Databases,* and *Chapter 8, Modifying Database Objects.*

Follow these steps to design the database schema:

1. Define the sales table:

    ```
    CREATE TABLE sales (
        sale_id INTEGER PRIMARY KEY AUTOINCREMENT,
        region TEXT NOT NULL,
    ```

```
    product TEXT NOT NULL,
    quantity INTEGER NOT NULL,
    price REAL NOT NULL,
    sale_date DATETIME NOT NULL
);
```

Step 3: Populate the database

Add sample data to the sales table to simulate real-world transactions. Refer to *Chapter 6, Modifying Data, Inserting data with INSERT INTO.*

Follow these steps to populate the database:

1. Insert sample sales records:

```
INSERT INTO sales (region, product, quantity, price, sale_date)
VALUES
('North', 'Laptop', 10, 1200.00, '2024-01-10'),
('South', 'Tablet', 15, 500.00, '2024-01-11'),
('East', 'Smartphone', 20, 800.00, '2024-01-12'),
('West', 'Headphones', 25, 150.00, '2024-01-13'),
('North', 'Tablet', 12, 300.00, '2024-02-14'),
('South', 'Laptop', 8, 2000.00, '2024-02-15'),
('North', 'Laptop', 10, 1500.00, '2024-02-10'),
('South', 'Tablet', 15, 400.00, '2024-03-11'),
('East', 'Smartphone', 20, 1300.00, '2024-03-12'),
('West', 'Headphones', 25, 750.00, '2024-03-13');
```

Step 4: Write SQL queries for reports

Develop SQL queries to extract data for your reports. Refer to *Chapter 5, Advanced Data Retrieval, Grouping data with GROUP BY,* and *Chapter 9, SQL Performance Optimization.*

Follow these steps to write SQL queries for reports:

1. Calculate total revenue by region:

```
SELECT
region,
SUM(quantity * price) AS total_revenue
FROM sales
GROUP BY region;
```

2. Generate a monthly revenue report:

```
SELECT
strftime('%Y-%m', sale_date) AS month, SUM(quantity * price) AS
```

```
monthly_revenue
FROM sales
GROUP BY month
ORDER BY month;
```

Step 5: Automate report generation using Python

Use Python to execute SQL queries, generate reports, and save them in an Excel file.

Follow these steps to automate report generation using Python:

1. Type in **.exit**, to exit out of the **sqlite** command.

2. Create a file called **projectfive.py.**

3. Copy and past the following code to Connect to the SQLite database and execute queries:

```python
import sqlite3
import pandas as pd
# Connect to the database
conn = sqlite3.connect('automated_reports.db')

# Query total revenue by region
query1 = "SELECT region, SUM(quantity * price) AS total_revenue FROM sales GROUP BY region"
regional_revenue = pd.read_sql_query(query1, conn)

# Query monthly revenue
query2 = "SELECT strftime('%Y-%m', sale_date) AS month, SUM(quantity * price) AS monthly_revenue FROM sales GROUP BY month ORDER BY month"
monthly_revenue = pd.read_sql_query(query2, conn)

# Write data to Excel
with pd.ExcelWriter('sales_report.xlsx', engine='openpyxl') as writer:
    regional_revenue.to_excel(writer,sheet_name='RegionalRevenue')
    monthly_revenue.to_excel(writer,sheet_name='Monthly Revenue')
print("Reports generated and saved as 'sales_report.xlsx'.")
```

4. Type in python projectfive.py to enter the Python command shell and execute the file.

By completing this project, you will create an automated data reporting system that integrates SQL with Python, reducing manual effort and ensuring the timely delivery of critical insights. This practical solution demonstrates the power of automation in enhancing productivity and accuracy in data-driven environments.

In the next few projects, we will focus on the Sakila sample database. Based on the sample database, we will create customer feedback and rating systems and run data reports. These projects will demonstrate how to work in existing databases using SQL.

Project six, creating a customer feedback system

Customer feedback provides valuable insights into preferences and areas for improvement. In this project, you will design and implement a **customer_feedback** table in the Sakila sample database to capture and analyze customer opinions on films. Integrating this feedback system into the existing database will enable meaningful data analysis and reporting, offering insights to enhance customer satisfaction and improve inventory decisions.

Use case and scenario

The Sakila Film Store is a popular rental service offering diverse films. The management wants to gather detailed customer feedback about the movies they rent to identify preference trends, assess the popularity of different genres, and evaluate customer satisfaction. This feedback will help the store make data-driven decisions to curate its film inventory and improve customer engagement.

Imagine the Sakila Film Store hires you to design a customer feedback system. The feedback will include comments about rented films, which can later be analyzed to identify the most-loved films, common criticisms, and suggestions for improvement. You will add a **customer_feedback** table to the Sakila sample database, populate it with sample data, and create queries to extract meaningful insights. Through this project, you will explore the practical application of relational database design and analysis in enhancing customer satisfaction and operational efficiency.

Step 1: Set up SQLite 3 and the Sakila sample database

Ensure your system correctly installs and configures SQLite 3 and the Sakila sample satabase. Refer to *Chapter 1, Introduction to SQL, Setting up your SQL environment,* for setup instructions.

Follow this step to set up SQLite 3 and the Sakila sample database:

1. Open the SQLite 3 command-line interface and connect to the Sakila sample database:

```
sqlite3 sqlite-sakila.db
```

Step 2: Design the customer feedback table

Create a new table called **customer_feedback** to store feedback data. Use concepts from *Chapter 2, Understanding Databases,* and *Chapter 8, Modifying Database Objects.*

Follow this step to design the customer feedback table:

1. Define the **customer_feedback** table structure:

```
CREATE TABLE customer_feedback (
feedback_id INTEGER PRIMARY KEY AUTOINCREMENT,
customer_id INTEGER NOT NULL,
film_id INTEGER NOT NULL,
feedback_text TEXT NOT NULL,
feedback_date DATETIME DEFAULT CURRENT_TIMESTAMP,
FOREIGN KEY (customer_id) REFERENCES customer(customer_id),
FOREIGN KEY (film_id) REFERENCES film(film_id)
);
```

Step 3: Populate the customer feedback table

Insert sample feedback data into the **customer_feedback** table. Use techniques from *Chapter 6, Modifying Data, Inserting data with INSERT INTO.*

Follow this step to populate the customer feedback table:

1. Add sample feedback records:

```
INSERT INTO customer_feedback (customer_id, film_id, feedback_text)
VALUES
    (1, 10, 'Amazing film with a captivating storyline.'),
    (2, 15, 'Good visuals but the plot was predictable.'),
    (3, 20, 'Not my taste, but others might enjoy it.'),
    (4, 5, 'One of the best performances I have seen.');
```

Step 4: Query customer feedback

Retrieve and analyze customer feedback using SQL queries. Apply skills from *Chapter 3, Basic SQL Queries, Retrieving data with SELECT,* and *Chapter 5, Advanced Data Retrieval.*

Follow these steps to query customer feedback:

1. View all feedback with customer and film details:

```
SELECT
cf.feedback_id,
c.first_name,
c.last_name,
```

```
f.title,

cf.feedback_text,

cf.feedback_date

FROM customer_feedback cf
JOIN customer c ON cf.customer_id = c.customer_id
JOIN film f ON cf.film_id = f.film_id;
```

2. Find feedback for a specific film:

```
SELECT

c.first_name,

c.last_name,

cf.feedback_text
FROM

customer_feedback cf
JOIN customer c ON cf.customer_id = c.customer_id
WHERE cf.film_id = 10;
```

Step 5: Analyze trends in feedback

Use aggregate functions and grouping to analyze feedback trends. Refer to sections *Grouping data with GROUP BY* and *Aggregate functions* in *Chapter 5, Advanced Data Retrieval*.

Follow these steps to analyze trends in feedback:

1. Count the number of feedback entries for each film:

```
SELECT

f.title,

COUNT(cf.feedback_id) AS feedback_count
FROM customer_feedback cf
JOIN film f ON cf.film_id = f.film_id
GROUP BY f.film_id
ORDER BY feedback_count DESC;
```

2. Identify customers providing the most feedback:

```
SELECT

c.first_name,

c.last_name,

COUNT(cf.feedback_id) AS total_feedback
FROM customer_feedback cf
JOIN customer c ON cf.customer_id = c.customer_id
GROUP BY cf.customer_id
ORDER BY total_feedback DESC;
```

Step 6: Secure the feedback data

Ensure the data is secure and optimized for performance. Refer to *Chapter 8, Managing Database Objects,* and *Chapter 13, Security Considerations in SQL.*

Follow these steps to secure the feedback data:

1. Create an index on **customer_id** and **film_id** to improve query performance:

```
CREATE INDEX idx_customer_id ON customer_feedback(customer_id);
CREATE INDEX idx_film_id ON customer_feedback(film_id);
```

2. Type in **.exit** at the **sqlite>** command prompt. Now, back up the database for disaster recovery:

```
sqlite3 sakila.db ".backup sakila_backup.db"
```

Step 7: Generate reports from feedback data

Use SQL queries to create summary reports. Refer to *Chapter 9, SQL Performance Optimization,* for advanced query techniques.

Follow these steps to generate reports from feedback data:

1. Identify films with the highest number of positive feedback entries:

```
SELECT
f.title,
COUNT(cf.feedback_id) AS positive_feedback
FROM customer_feedback cf
JOIN film f ON cf.film_id = f.film_id
WHERE cf.feedback_text LIKE '%amazing%' OR cf.feedback_text LIKE
'%best%'
GROUP BY cf.film_id
ORDER BY positive_feedback DESC;
```

2. Generate a report summarizing feedback trends by film category:

```
SELECT
c.name AS category,
COUNT(cf.feedback_id) AS total_feedback
FROM customer_feedback cf
JOIN film f ON cf.film_id = f.film_id
JOIN film_category fc ON f.film_id = fc.film_id
JOIN category c ON fc.category_id = c.category_id
GROUP BY c.name
ORDER BY total_feedback DESC;
```

By completing this project, you will gain hands-on experience in designing and extending databases, managing relational data, and querying for actionable insights. This project demonstrates the power of SQL for capturing and analyzing customer feedback to drive business improvements.

Project seven, creating a customer rating system

Ratings provide a structured way for businesses to gauge customer preferences and assess the popularity of their products. In this project, you will create and implement a **film_ratings** table in the Sakila sample database to store and analyze customer ratings for films. This project will walk you through designing the table, populating it with sample data, and querying it to uncover trends and actionable insights.

Use case and scenario

The Sakila Film Store wants to implement a star-based rating system to evaluate films. Customers will rate movies they have rented, and the store will use this data to determine the most popular titles, identify underperforming films, and refine its inventory. This system will also enable the store to create personalized recommendations and understand overall customer satisfaction trends.

Imagine you have been asked to design and implement a rating system for the Sakila Film Store. This system will allow customers to assign a rating of one to five stars to films they have rented. The store management will use the data to analyze film performance by genre, identify high-performing titles, and recognize trends in customer preferences. Through this project, you will integrate the **film_ratings** table with the existing Sakila database and apply SQL queries to generate reports that provide valuable business insights.

Step 1: Set up SQLite 3 and the Sakila sample database

Ensure SQLite 3 and the Sakila sample database are installed and configured. Refer to *Chapter 1, Introduction to SQL*, for detailed instructions.

Follow this step to set up SQLite 3 and the Sakila sample database:

1. Open the SQLite 3 command-line interface and connect to the Sakila sample database:

```
sqlite3 sqlite-sakila.db
```

Step 2: Design the customer rating table

Create a **film_ratings** table to store customer ratings. Use concepts from *Chapter 2, Understanding Databases,* and *Chapter 8, Modifying Database Objects.*

Follow this step to the customer rating table:

1. Define the table structure:

```
CREATE TABLE film_ratings (
    rating_id INTEGER PRIMARY KEY AUTOINCREMENT,
    customer_id INTEGER NOT NULL,
    film_id INTEGER NOT NULL,
    rating INTEGER NOT NULL CHECK (rating BETWEEN 1 AND 5),
    rating_date DATETIME DEFAULT CURRENT_TIMESTAMP,
    FOREIGN KEY (customer_id) REFERENCES customer(customer_id),
    FOREIGN KEY (film_id) REFERENCES film(film_id)
);
```

Step 3: Populate the customer rating table

Add sample ratings to the **film_ratings** table. Use techniques from *Chapter 6, Modifying Data, Inserting data with INSERT INTO*.

Follow this step to populate the customer rating table:

1. Insert sample records:

```
INSERT INTO film_ratings (customer_id, film_id, rating)
VALUES
    (1, 10, 5),
    (2, 15, 4),
    (3, 8, 3),
    (4, 20, 5),
    (5, 5, 2);
```

Step 4: Query and analyze ratings

Retrieve and analyze ratings using SQL queries. Apply techniques from *Chapter 3, Basic SQL Queries, Retrieving data with SELECT*, and *Chapter 5, Advanced Data Retrieval, Grouping data with GROUP BY*.

Follow these steps to query and analyze ratings:

1. View all ratings with customer and film details:

```
SELECT
fr.rating_id,
c.first_name,
c.last_name,
f.title,
fr.rating,
fr.rating_date
FROM film_ratings fr
```

```
JOIN customer c ON fr.customer_id = c.customer_id
JOIN film f ON fr.film_id = f.film_id;
```

2. Find the average rating for each film:

```
SELECT
f.title, AVG(fr.rating) AS avg_rating
FROM film_ratings fr
JOIN film f ON fr.film_id = f.film_id
GROUP BY f.film_id
ORDER BY avg_rating DESC;
```

3. Identify the films with perfect ratings (five stars):

```
SELECT
f.title
FROM
film_ratings fr
JOIN film f ON fr.film_id = f.film_id
WHERE fr.rating = 5;
```

Step 5: Generate summary reports

Create summary reports using aggregate functions and grouping. For advanced query techniques, refer to *Chapter 5, Advanced Data Retrieval*.

Follow these steps to generate summary reports:

1. Calculate the total number of ratings per film:

```
SELECT
f.title,
COUNT(fr.rating) AS total_ratings
FROM film_ratings fr
JOIN film f ON fr.film_id = f.film_id
GROUP BY f.film_id
ORDER BY total_ratings DESC;
```

2. Analyze the distribution of ratings:

```
SELECT
fr.rating,
COUNT(fr.rating) AS frequency
FROM film_ratings fr
GROUP BY fr.rating
ORDER BY frequency DESC;
```

Step 6: Optimize and secure the ratings data

Enhance query performance and secure the database. Refer to *Chapter 8, Managing Database Objects,* and *Chapter 13, Security Considerations in SQL.*

Follow these steps to optimize and secure the ratings data:

1. Create indexes on **customer_id** and **film_id**:

```
CREATE INDEX idx_customer_id ON film_ratings(customer_id);
CREATE INDEX idx_film_id ON film_ratings(film_id);
```

2. Type in **.exit** at the **sqlite>** command prompt. Now, back up the database for disaster recovery:

```
sqlite3 sakila.db ".backup sakila_backup.db"
```

Step 7: Present and interpret results

Generate insights from the rating data. Use advanced techniques from *Chapter 9, SQL Performance Optimization.*

Follow these steps to present and interpret results:

1. Identify the most highly rated genres:

```
SELECT
c.name AS category,
AVG(fr.rating) AS avg_rating
FROM film_ratings fr
JOIN film f ON fr.film_id = f.film_id
JOIN film_category fc ON f.film_id = fc.film_id
JOIN category c ON fc.category_id = c.category_id
GROUP BY c.name
ORDER BY avg_rating DESC;
```

2. Find the top-rated films by genre:

```
SELECT
c.name AS category,
f.title,
AVG(fr.rating) AS avg_rating
FROM film_ratings fr
JOIN film f ON fr.film_id = f.film_id
JOIN film_category fc ON f.film_id = fc.film_id
JOIN category c ON fc.category_id = c.category_id
GROUP BY c.name, f.title
HAVING AVG(fr.rating) > 4
ORDER BY avg_rating DESC;
```

By completing this project, you will design and implement a rating system that integrates seamlessly with the Sakila sample database. You will gain hands-on experience managing relational data, creating meaningful reports, and generating actionable insights based on customer feedback.

Project eight, creating rental data reports

Rental data reports are essential for analyzing trends, understanding customer behavior, and optimizing business operations. In this project, you will generate detailed reports using the rental data from the Sakila sample database. Applying advanced SQL techniques will extract meaningful insights, such as identifying top-performing films, analyzing customer activity, and tracking monthly trends. This hands-on project will guide you through creating and executing SQL queries to deliver actionable data insights.

Use case and scenario

The Sakila Film Store management team relies on rental data to evaluate its operational performance and identify areas for improvement. They need detailed reports that include revenue summaries, rental trends by category, and customer activity analysis. These reports will help management make informed decisions about inventory management, marketing strategies, and customer engagement initiatives.

Imagine you are a database analyst for the Sakila Film Store. Management has tasked you with generating comprehensive rental data reports to provide insights into the business's performance. You will analyze trends such as peak rental periods, most rented films, and customer engagement levels. Additionally, you will create detailed revenue reports that break down earnings by film category and period. Completing this project will give you practical experience designing SQL queries to generate reports supporting data-driven decision-making.

Step 1: Set up SQLite 3 and the Sakila sample database

Ensure SQLite 3 and the Sakila sample database are installed and set up. Refer to *Chapter 1, Introduction to SQL, Setting up your SQL environment,* for setup instructions.

Follow this step to set up SQLite 3 and the Sakila sample database:

1. Open the SQLite 3 command-line interface and connect to the Sakila sample database:

```
sqlite3 sqlite-sakila.db
```

Step 2: Analyze rental revenue

Calculate rental revenue to understand overall earnings and revenue distribution. Use techniques from *Chapter 5, Advanced Data Retrieval, Grouping data with GROUP BY.*

Follow these steps to analyze rental revenue:

1. Calculate total revenue by film:

```
SELECT

f.title,

SUM(p.amount)AStotal_revenue
FROM payment p
JOIN rental r ON p.rental_id = r.rental_id
JOIN inventory i ON r.inventory_id = i.inventory_id
JOIN film f ON i.film_id = f.film_id
GROUP BY f.title
ORDER BY total_revenue DESC;
```

2. Calculate revenue by rental category:

```
SELECT c.name AS category, SUM(p.amount) AS total_revenue
FROM payment p
JOIN rental r ON p.rental_id = r.rental_id
JOIN inventory i ON r.inventory_id = i.inventory_id
JOIN film_category fc ON i.film_id = fc.film_id
JOIN category c ON fc.category_id = c.category_id
GROUP BY c.name
ORDER BY total_revenue DESC;
```

Step 3: Generate customer activity reports

Analyze customer activity to identify engagement trends. Refer to *Chapter 3, Basic SQL Queries,* and *Chapter 5, Advanced Data Retrieval.*

Follow these steps to generate customer activity reports:

1. Identify the top five most active customers by rentals:

```
SELECT

c.first_name,

c.last_name,

COUNT(r.rental_id) AS total_rentals
FROM rental r
JOIN customer c ON r.customer_id = c.customer_id
GROUP BY c.customer_id
ORDER BY total_rentals DESC
LIMIT 5;
```

2. Find customers who have rented films in a specific category:

```
SELECT

c.first_name,
```

```
            c.last_name, cat.name AS category
      FROM rental r
      JOIN inventory i ON r.inventory_id = i.inventory_id
      JOIN film_category fc ON i.film_id = fc.film_id
      JOIN category cat ON fc.category_id = cat.category_id
      JOIN customer c ON r.customer_id = c.customer_id
      WHERE cat.name = 'Action'
      GROUP BY c.customer_id;
```

Step 4: Analyze monthly rental trends

Use date functions to identify trends over time. Apply concepts from *Chapter 9, SQL Performance Optimization.*

Follow these steps to analyze monthly rental trends:

1. Calculate monthly rental volume:

    ```
    SELECT
    strftime('%Y-%m', r.rental_date) AS month,
    COUNT(r.rental_id) AS rental_count
    FROM rental r
    GROUP BY month
    ORDER BY month;
    ```

2. Identify the peak rental month:

    ```
    SELECT
    strftime('%Y-%m', r.rental_date) AS month,
    COUNT(r.rental_id) AS rental_count
    FROM rental r
    GROUP BY month
    ORDER BY rental_count DESC
    LIMIT 1;
    ```

Step 5: Generate inventory performance reports

Assess the performance of the store's inventory. Use techniques from *Chapter 8, Managing Database Objects.*

Follow these steps to generate inventory performance reports:

1. Find the most rented films:

    ```
    SELECT
    f.title,
    COUNT(r.rental_id) AS rental_count
    FROM rental r
    JOIN inventory i ON r.inventory_id = i.inventory_id
    ```

```
JOIN film f ON i.film_id = f.film_id
GROUP BY f.film_id
ORDER BY rental_count DESC
LIMIT 10;
```

2. Determine the performance of films by genre:

```
SELECT
c.name AS category,
COUNT(r.rental_id) AS rental_count
FROM rental r
JOIN inventory i ON r.inventory_id = i.inventory_id
JOIN film_category fc ON i.film_id = fc.film_id
JOIN category c ON fc.category_id = c.category_id
GROUP BY c.name
ORDER BY rental_count DESC;
```

Step 6: Create advanced reports

Combine data from multiple tables for comprehensive reports. Refer to *Chapter 11, Advanced SQL Techniques.*

Follow these steps to create advanced reports:

1. Generate a detailed revenue and rental report:

```
SELECT
c.name AS category,
f.title, COUNT(r.rental_id) AS rental_count,
SUM(p.amount) AS total_revenue
FROM payment p
JOIN rental r ON p.rental_id = r.rental_id
JOIN inventory i ON r.inventory_id = i.inventory_id
JOIN film_category fc ON i.film_id = fc.film_id
JOIN category c ON fc.category_id = c.category_id
JOIN film f ON i.film_id = f.film_id
GROUP BY c.name, f.title
ORDER BY total_revenue DESC;
```

2. Generate a report on late returns:

```
SELECT
c.first_name,
c.last_name,
f.title,
r.rental_date,
r.return_date,
julianday(r.return_date) - julianday(r.rental_date) AS days_rented
```

```
FROM rental r
JOIN customer c ON r.customer_id = c.customer_id
JOIN inventory i ON r.inventory_id = i.inventory_id
JOIN film f ON i.film_id = f.film_id
WHERE julianday(r.return_date) - julianday(r.rental_date) > 7
ORDER BY days_rented DESC;
```

Step 7: Present and interpret results

Use SQL queries to prepare visually appealing and actionable reports.

Follow these steps to present and interpret results:

1. Turn headers, change mode to csv, and create an output file called **rental_report.csv**:

   ```
   .headers on
   .mode csv
   .output rental_report.csv
   ```

2. Run the SQL query to output to the **csv**:

   ```
   SELECT
   c.name AS category,
   f.title,
   COUNT(r.rental_id) AS rental_count,
   SUM(p.amount) AS total_revenue
   FROM payment p
   JOIN rental r ON p.rental_id = r.rental_id
   JOIN inventory i ON r.inventory_id = i.inventory_id
   JOIN film_category fc ON i.film_id = fc.film_id
   JOIN category c ON fc.category_id = c.category_id
   JOIN film f ON i.film_id = f.film_id
   GROUP BY c.name, f.title
   ORDER BY total_revenue DESC;
   ```

3. Output the SQL query results to the **rental_report.csv** file:

   ```
   .output
   ```

By completing this project, you will gain experience in designing and executing advanced queries to generate rental data reports. These skills will enable you to analyze operational performance and make data-driven decisions.

Conclusion

In this chapter, you applied your SQL knowledge to practical, real-world projects, reinforcing key database concepts and skills. By designing and implementing databases for diverse scenarios such as CRM systems, sales data analysis, and blogging platforms, you demonstrated your ability to structure data, create relationships, and build functional applications. Additionally, you explored advanced techniques like automating data reports and integrating SQL with Python, highlighting the power of automation in streamlining workflows and improving efficiency.

Projects leveraging the Sakila sample database provided opportunities to design customer feedback and rating systems and generate detailed reports on rental trends. These exercises highlighted the value of SQL in analyzing data and delivering actionable insights. You practiced building queries, optimizing performance, and generating outputs tailored to specific use cases through these projects.

The hands-on nature of these projects allowed you to deepen your understanding of SQL and its applications in real-world scenarios. As you progress, the skills and experience gained in this chapter will enable you to confidently tackle complex database challenges and design efficient, scalable solutions tailored to various business needs.

The next chapter will focus on SQL best practices and tips to help you write clean, efficient, and maintainable code. You will learn techniques for debugging and troubleshooting queries, optimizing performance, and staying updated with the latest trends in SQL development. Integrating these best practices into your workflow will enhance your ability to build scalable and high-performing database solutions, ensuring long-term success in your SQL journey.

Join our Discord space

Join our Discord workspace for latest updates, offers, tech happenings around the world, new releases, and sessions with the authors:

https://discord.bpbonline.com

CHAPTER 15
SQL Best Practices and Tips

Introduction

In this chapter, you will explore essential best practices and tips to elevate your SQL skills and ensure optimal performance in database management. This chapter provides practical guidance for maintaining high-quality work, from writing clean and efficient SQL code to effectively debugging and troubleshooting complex queries. You will also explore techniques for performance tuning, enabling you to optimize query execution and enhance overall system efficiency. Additionally, this chapter emphasizes the importance of staying current with SQL trends and updates, empowering you to adapt to advancements in database technologies. By mastering these best practices, you will be well-prepared to tackle real-world SQL challenges with confidence and precision.

Structure

This chapter covers the following topics:

- Writing clean and efficient SQL code
- Debugging and troubleshooting SQL queries
- Performance tuning
- Keeping up with SQL trends and updates

Objectives

By the end of this chapter, you will understand the best practices for writing clean and efficient SQL code that is easy to read, maintain, and scale. You will gain the skills to debug and troubleshoot complex queries, identifying and resolving issues effectively to ensure accurate results. Additionally, you will learn performance-tuning techniques to optimize query execution and enhance database efficiency, even with large datasets. This chapter will also equip you with strategies to stay updated on SQL trends and advancements, ensuring your knowledge remains relevant in a rapidly evolving field. These objectives will empower you to deliver high-quality SQL solutions in diverse real-world scenarios consistently.

Writing clean and efficient SQL code

Writing clean and efficient SQL code is a critical skill for developers and database administrators, as it ensures readability, maintainability, and optimal performance. Clean code is easy to understand and modify, while efficient code minimizes resource usage, reduces query execution time, and enhances database performance. By adhering to best practices, you can produce high-quality SQL code that meets these criteria.

Use descriptive naming conventions

Descriptive names for tables, columns, and variables enhance the clarity and readability of SQL code. As you learned in *Chapter 3, Basic SQL Queries*, and in *Chapter 8, Managing Database Objects*, instead of generic or cryptic identifiers, use meaningful names that indicate the purpose of each object. For example, naming a table **customer_orders** instead of **tbl1** immediately communicates its purpose.

Similarly, use consistent naming conventions across the database schema. For instance:

- Use **snake_case** for table and column names: **order_details** or **customer_address**.
- If required, use a prefix for object types: **idx_** for indexes or **sp_** for stored procedures.

Descriptive and consistent naming helps new developers quickly understand the database structure, reducing the learning curve and minimizing errors.

Write modular and reusable code

Avoid redundancy by writing modular SQL code that can be reused across multiple queries or applications. As you learned in *Chapter 8, Managing Database Objects*, and *Chapter 11, Advanced SQL Techniques*, instead of duplicating complex logic in different queries, encapsulate it in views, **common table expressions** (CTEs), or stored procedures.

For example, instead of writing a complex join multiple times, create a view:

```
CREATE VIEW active_customers AS
SELECT c.customer_id, c.first_name, c.last_name
FROM customer c
WHERE c.active = 1;
```

Now, you can reference the active_customers view in queries without duplicating the logic:

```
SELECT * FROM active_customers WHERE last_name LIKE 'S%';
```

This approach ensures consistency, simplifies maintenance, and reduces the risk of errors when changes are required.

Follow indentation and formatting standards

As you learned in *Chapter 3, Basic SQL Queries,* proper indentation and formatting improve the readability of SQL code, making it easier to follow the logic and identify errors. Break long queries into multiple lines and align related elements for clarity.

For instance, let us look at a poorly formatted query:

```
SELECT c.first_name, c.last_name, o.order_date FROM customers c JOIN orders
o ON c.customer_id=o.customer_id WHERE o.order_date > '2024-01-01' ORDER BY
o.order_date;
```

The following code is formatted with proper indentation:

```
SELECT
    c.first_name,
    c.last_name,
    o.order_date
FROM
    customers c
JOIN
    orders o
ON
    c.customer_id = o.customer_id
WHERE
    o.order_date > '2024-01-01'
ORDER BY
    o.order_date;
```

This format enhances readability and makes debugging and peer reviews more efficient.

Optimize joins and filtering

Efficient use of joins and filtering conditions can significantly improve query performance. Always use the appropriate join type based on the relationship between tables. For instance, use **inner join** when only matching rows are needed or **left join** for scenarios where unmatched rows from the left table must also be included.

When applying filters, use indexed columns in the **WHERE** clause whenever possible to take advantage of indexing:

```
SELECT
    c.first_name,
    c.last_name
FROM
    customers c
WHERE
    c.last_name LIKE 'S%';
```

Avoid using functions on indexed columns in the **WHERE** clause, as this negates the index. For example, instead of:

```
SELECT * FROM orders WHERE YEAR(order_date) = 2024;
```

Rewrite the query to:

```
SELECT * FROM orders WHERE order_date >= '2024-01-01' AND order_date < '2025-01-01';
```

This ensures that indexes on **order_date** are used effectively.

Minimize use of SELECT

As you learned in *Chapter 3, Basic SQL Queries*, using **SELECT** * retrieves all columns from a table, which can increase query execution time and memory usage, especially with large datasets. Instead, explicitly specify the required columns:

```
SELECT first_name, last_name FROM customers WHERE active = 1;
```

This approach improves performance, reduces network overhead, and clarifies which columns are being accessed.

Leverage indexes wisely

Indexes can greatly enhance query performance by reducing the amount of data scanned during operations. However, too many indexes can impact write performance and increase storage requirements. Use indexes strategically by analyzing query patterns and focusing on columns frequently used in **WHERE**, **JOIN**, or **ORDER BY** clauses.

For example, adding an index to the email column in the customer's table improves the performance of this query:

```
SELECT * FROM customers WHERE email = 'example@example.com';
```

Monitor and maintain indexes regularly to remove unused or redundant ones, ensuring optimal performance.

Avoid hardcoding values

Hardcoding values in SQL queries reduces flexibility and reusability. Instead, use parameters or variables to make queries dynamic and adaptable to different scenarios. For instance, instead use the following code:

```
SELECT * FROM orders WHERE order_date > '2024-01-01';
```

Use a parameterized query:

```
PREPARE stmt FROM 'SELECT * FROM orders WHERE order_date > ?';

EXECUTE stmt USING '2024-01-01';
```

This approach improves security by preventing SQL injection and simplifies query modifications.

Document your code

Commenting and documenting SQL code ensures its purpose and logic are clear to other developers and your future self. Use comments to explain complex logic or decisions that are not immediately obvious:

Select active customers who placed orders in the last 30 days:

```
SELECT
    c.first_name,
    c.last_name
FROM
    customers c
JOIN
    orders o
ON
    c.customer_id = o.customer_id
WHERE
    o.order_date >= CURRENT_DATE - INTERVAL 30 DAY;
```

Avoid over-commenting by focusing on areas that require clarification rather than stating the obvious.

Use aggregate functions judiciously

Aggregate functions, such as **COUNT**, **SUM**, and **AVG**, are powerful tools for summarizing data but can be resource intensive. Optimize queries by using aggregate functions with proper filtering and grouping.

For example:

```
SELECT COUNT(*) AS total_orders FROM orders WHERE order_date > '2024-01-
01';
```

Combine aggregate functions with indexed columns to minimize computation overhead.

Test and refactor regularly

Test queries for performance and accuracy under different conditions. Use tools like **EXPLAIN** or **EXPLAIN ANALYZE** to understand how queries execute and identify bottlenecks:

```
EXPLAIN SELECT * FROM customers WHERE last_name = 'Smith';
```

Refactor inefficient queries to improve execution plans and adapt them to changing requirements.

By incorporating these practices into your workflow, you can write clean, efficient, and robust SQL code, which will improve database performance and maintainability.

Debugging and troubleshooting SQL queries

Debugging and troubleshooting SQL queries are essential skills for database developers and administrators. These processes help identify and resolve errors or inefficiencies in queries, ensuring accurate results and optimal performance. Effective debugging involves understanding the root cause of an issue and applying systematic techniques to address it.

Understanding common SQL query issues

SQL query issues often stem from syntax errors, logical flaws, or performance bottlenecks. Understanding these common problems is the first step in troubleshooting:

- **Syntax errors:** These occur when the query does not conform to the database's SQL syntax rules. For example:
  - o   Missing commas, parentheses, or semicolons.
  - o   Using incorrect SQL keywords or clauses.
  - o   Misspelled table or column names.
- **Logical errors:** These happen when a query runs without errors but produces incorrect results due to flawed logic. Examples include the following:
  - o   Joining tables incorrectly, resulting in duplicate or missing rows.

- o   Misplaced filtering conditions in the **WHERE** or **HAVING** clauses.
- o   Incorrect usage of aggregate functions or subqueries.

- **Performance issues:** These arise when queries take longer to execute than expected or consume excessive resources. Causes include the following:
  - o   Lack of appropriate indexes.
  - o   Scanning large datasets unnecessarily.
  - o   Using inefficient query constructs, such as nested subqueries.

Identifying which issue affects a query is crucial for selecting the appropriate debugging technique.

Techniques for debugging SQL queries

Debugging SQL queries involves a systematic approach to isolate and fix problems. Here are some effective techniques:

- **Review the query for syntax errors**: As you learned in *Chapter 3, Basic SQL Queries*, begin by carefully reading the query to check for syntax issues. Modern SQL editors and **integrated development environments** (IDEs) highlight syntax errors and provide suggestions for correction.

  Example: If a query returns an error like syntax error near **'FROM'**, verify the query structure:

  ```
  SELECT first_name last_name FROM customers; -- Missing a comma
  ```

  Correct the syntax:

  ```
  SELECT first_name, last_name FROM customers;
  ```

- **Break down complex queries**: As you learned in *Chapter 8, Managing Database Objects*, large and complex queries can be challenging to debug. Break them into smaller components and execute each part separately to identify the issue. For instance, isolate individual **JOIN** or **WHERE** clauses and test them independently:

  ```
  -- Original complex query
  SELECT c.first_name, c.last_name, o.order_date
  FROM customers c
  JOIN orders o ON c.customer_id = o.customer_id
  WHERE o.order_date > '2024-01-01';
  -- Isolate the join
  SELECT * FROM customers c JOIN orders o ON c.customer_id =
  o.customer_id;
  -- Isolate the filter
  SELECT * FROM orders WHERE order_date > '2024-01-01';
  ```

- **Use debugging tools**: As you learned in *Chapter 9, SQL Performance Optimization*, most database systems provide tools to analyze and debug queries:
  - **EXPLAIN or EXPLAIN ANALYZE**: These commands display the query execution plan, highlighting steps and resource usage. For example:

    ```
    EXPLAIN SELECT * FROM orders WHERE order_date > '2024-01-01';
    ```

    Analyze the output to identify bottlenecks, such as full table scans or unnecessary operations.
  - **Query profilers**: Tools like MySQL's **SHOW PROFILE** or PostgreSQL's **pg_stat_statements** provide detailed execution metrics.
- **Checking for data issues errors**: Data errors in data can affect query results. For example, NULL values or unexpected data types may cause queries to behave unexpectedly. Use checks such as:

  ```
  SELECT * FROM customers WHERE email IS NULL;
  SELECT COUNT(*) FROM orders WHERE order_date NOT BETWEEN '2024-01-01' AND '2024-12-31';
  ```

- **Review index usage queries**: Failing to use indexes often results in slow performance. Use **EXPLAIN** to verify index usage and create indexes on frequently queried columns:

  ```
  CREATE INDEX idx_order_date ON orders(order_date);
  ```

Troubleshooting logical errors

Logical errors require careful examination of query logic to ensure it aligns with the desired results. Consider these strategies:

- **Verify join conditions**: Incorrect join conditions can lead to missing or duplicated rows. For example:

  ```
  -- Incorrect join causing duplicates
  SELECT * FROM customers c JOIN orders o ON c.first_name = o.customer_id;
  ```

  Correct the condition to join on **customer_id:**

  ```
  SELECT * FROM customers c JOIN orders o ON c.customer_id = o.customer_id;
  ```

- **Validate filtering conditions**: Ensure that conditions in the **WHERE** clause accurately reflect the intended logic:

  ```
  -- Incorrect filter excluding some results
  SELECT * FROM orders WHERE order_date > '2024-01-01' AND order_date < '2024-01-01';
  ```

Correct the condition to include a valid range:

```
SELECT * FROM orders WHERE order_date BETWEEN '2024-01-01' AND
'2024-12-31';
```

- **Check aggregate functions**: Verify the placement of aggregate functions and grouping conditions:

```
-- Missing GROUP BY
SELECT customer_id, COUNT(*) FROM orders;
```

Add the required GROUP BY clause:

```
SELECT customer_id, COUNT(*) FROM orders GROUP BY customer_id;
```

- **Test subqueries**: Execute subqueries separately to confirm their correctness before integrating them into the main query:

```
SELECT * FROM orders WHERE customer_id IN (SELECT id FROM customers
WHERE active = 1);
```

Optimizing query performance

Performance optimization is a critical aspect of troubleshooting. Use the following tips to enhance query efficiency:

- **Reduce data scanning**: Retrieve only the necessary columns and rows:

```
SELECT first_name, last_name FROM customers WHERE active = 1;
```

- **Do not retrieve all data**: Avoid using **SELECT *** in production queries.

- **Optimize sorting and filtering**: Sorting large datasets can be resource intensive. Use indexed columns in **ORDER BY** clauses:

```
SELECT * FROM orders ORDER BY order_date;
```

- **Remove redundant calculations**: Perform calculations in the application layer or pre-compute values where possible:

```
SELECT price * quantity AS total FROM order_items; -- Reduce
repetitive calculations
```

- **Analyze query execution plans**: Use execution plans to identify costly operations and refine them:

```
EXPLAIN ANALYZE SELECT * FROM orders WHERE order_date > '2024-01-
01';
```

Best practices for debugging SQL queries

When faced with challenging SQL queries, applying proven debugging techniques can streamline the process and lead to quicker, more reliable solutions. The following are best practices for debugging SQL queries:

- **Start simple**: Simplify the query to identify the issue faster.

- **Document changes**: Keep a record of modifications made during troubleshooting for future reference.

- **Collaborate**: Seek input from team members to gain new perspectives on complex issues.

- **Use test data**: Work with smaller datasets or test environments to avoid affecting production systems.

- **Iterate**: Continuously refine queries based on findings from debugging tools and test results.

By adopting these techniques and strategies, you can efficiently debug and troubleshoot SQL queries, ensuring reliable and high-performing database operations.

Performance tuning

Performance tuning is vital to database management, ensuring that SQL queries execute efficiently, and systems handle workloads effectively. By optimizing query design, indexing strategies, and system configurations, you can reduce execution time, lower resource consumption, and improve overall responsiveness. Performance tuning requires a structured approach that includes analyzing execution plans, identifying bottlenecks, and implementing best practices.

Analyzing query execution plans

Query execution plans provide a detailed roadmap of how the database processes a query. As you learned in *Chapter 9, SQL Performance Optimization*, they help identify inefficiencies, such as unnecessary full table scans, poorly chosen indexes, or suboptimal join strategies. The following is a list of best practices for analyzing query execution plans.

- **Using EXPLAIN or EXPLAIN ANALYZE**: Most databases offer commands like **EXPLAIN** (MySQL, PostgreSQL) or **EXPLAIN PLAN** (Oracle) to visualize query execution paths. For example:

  ```
  EXPLAIN SELECT * FROM orders WHERE customer_id = 101;
  ```

  The output highlights table scans, index usage, and join methods.

- **Interpreting the results**: Key elements of an execution plan include:
    - **Cost**: Indicates the estimated time or resources required for each operation.
    - **Rows**: Shows the number of rows processed at each step.
    - **Filter**: Describes conditions applied to limit data retrieval.

- **Optimizing based on findings:** If the plan reveals a full table scan for a frequently queried column, create an index to reduce scan time.

Indexing strategies

Indexes are one of the most effective tools for improving query performance. They allow the database to locate rows more efficiently by creating a structured path to data. The following is a list of indexing strategies that can be used to improve query performance.

- **Using appropriate index types**:
    - **Single column indexes**: Best for queries filtering on a single column, such as:
      ```
      CREATE INDEX idx_customer_id ON orders(customer_id);
      ```
    - **Composite indexes**: Combine multiple columns into a single index for queries that filter or sort on more than one column:
      ```
      CREATE INDEX idx_customer_date ON orders(customer_id, order_date);
      ```
- **Avoiding over-indexing**: While indexes improve read performance, they can degrade write performance by adding overhead during **INSERT**, **UPDATE**, or **DELETE** operations. Use indexing judiciously based on query patterns.
- **Maintaining index health**: Regularly analyze and rebuild fragmented indexes using database tools such as:
    - **ANALYZE** or **VACUUM** in PostgreSQL.
    - **OPTIMIZE TABLE** in MySQL.
- **Covering indexes**: Design indexes that include all columns required by a query to eliminate the need to fetch additional data:
  ```
  CREATE INDEX idx_cover ON orders(customer_id, order_date, total_amount);
  ```

Optimizing join operations

Joins often account for significant resource usage in complex queries. As you learned in *Chapter 5, Advanced Data Retrieval*, optimizing join strategies is crucial for minimizing execution time. The following list provides tips on how to optimize join operations in your SQL queries:

- **Choose the right join type**:
    - **INNER JOIN**: Retrieves matching rows from both tables.
    - **LEFT JOIN**: Ensures unmatched rows from the left table are included.
    - **EXPLAIN**: To verify whether the chosen join type is efficient.
- **Order tables logically**: Place the smaller table first in the join operation, especially when working with nested loops.
- **Filter data early**: Apply filtering conditions before or within the join to reduce the number of rows processed:

```
SELECT c.first_name, o.order_date
FROM customers c
JOIN orders o ON c.customer_id = o.customer_id
WHERE o.order_date >= '2024-01-01';
```

- **Partitioned joins**: For large datasets, partition tables and perform joins on smaller chunks to improve performance.

Efficient use of aggregate functions

Aggregate functions like **SUM**, **COUNT**, **AVG**, and **MAX** can be resource-intensive, especially on large datasets. Optimize their usage by following these techniques:

- **Group data before aggregation**: Use **GROUP BY** to limit the number of rows processed:

```
SELECT customer_id, SUM(order_total)
FROM orders
GROUP BY customer_id;
```

- **Index grouping columns**: Create indexes on grouping columns to speed up aggregation:

```
CREATE INDEX idx_customer_id ON orders(customer_id);
```

- **Filter data first**: Apply **WHERE** conditions to reduce the dataset size before aggregation:

```
SELECT AVG(order_total)
FROM orders
WHERE order_date >= '2024-01-01';
```

- **Avoid redundant aggregations**: Store pre-aggregated values in summary tables when frequent aggregations are needed.

Minimizing data scanning

As you learned in *Chapter 3, Basic SQL Queries*, reducing the volume of data scanned by queries significantly enhances performance. Here are key strategies:

- **Retrieve only necessary columns**: Avoid using **SELECT *** and specify only the required columns:

```
SELECT first_name, last_name FROM customers;
```

- **Apply filters and limits**: Use **WHERE** clauses and **LIMIT** to restrict the number of rows processed:

```
SELECT * FROM orders WHERE customer_id = 101 LIMIT 10;
```

- **Partition tables**: Partitioning divides large tables into smaller, more manageable chunks based on a column, such as dates or regions. For example:

```
CREATE TABLE orders_2024 PARTITION OF orders FOR VALUES IN (2024);
```

- **Targeting partitions**: Queries targeting specific partitions reduce the data scanned.

Caching results

Caching can improve performance by storing frequently accessed query results in memory, reducing the need to re-execute complex queries. The following list contains caching tips to improve the performance of your queries:

- **Query caching**: Many databases, like MySQL, support query caching natively. For example:

```
[mysqld]
query_cache_type = 1
query_cache_size = 16M
```

- **Application-level caching**: Use tools like Redis or Memcached to cache results at the application layer.

- **Materialized views**: Precompute and store query results in materialized views for quick retrieval:

```
CREATE MATERIALIZED VIEW top_customers AS
SELECT customer_id, SUM(order_total) AS total_spent
FROM orders
GROUP BY customer_id
ORDER BY total_spent DESC;
```

Optimizing storage and resources

Efficient resource allocation and storage optimization improve query performance by reducing **Input/Output (I/O)** overhead. The following list outlines tips for optimizing storage and resources:

- **Normalize and de-normalize strategically**: Normalize data to eliminate redundancy but de-normalize for read-heavy queries to minimize joins.

- **Compress data**: Data compression reduces storage usage and improves I/O efficiency. For example:

  o Enable table compression in MySQL with `ROW_FORMAT=COMPRESSED`.

  o Use PostgreSQL's `pg_compress` feature.

- **Optimize resource allocation**: Allocate sufficient memory and CPU resources to database operations. Tune parameters like buffer pools and cache sizes.

- **Maintain statistics**: Regularly update table statistics to help the query optimizer make informed decisions:

```
ANALYZE customers;
```

Monitoring and refining queries

Performance tuning is an ongoing process that involves monitoring system behavior and refining queries over time. The following list outlines tips for monitoring and refining queries:

- **Track performance metrics**: Use monitoring tools to analyze query execution times, resource usage, and system bottlenecks. Examples include:
    - MySQL's Performance Schema.
    - PostgreSQL's pg_stat_activity.
- **Refactor inefficient queries**: Replace subqueries with joins or use **common table expressions** (**CTEs**) for better readability and performance.
- **Leverage query profiler tools**: Tools like SQL Profiler, SolarWinds, or pgAdmin provide in-depth analysis of query behavior.

By systematically implementing these performance-tuning strategies, you can ensure that your SQL queries are efficient and scalable, even as database workloads grow.

Keeping up with SQL trends and updates

Staying current with SQL trends and updates is vital for database professionals to remain effective in a rapidly evolving field. Database vendors such as MySQL, PostgreSQL, Microsoft SQL Server, and Oracle frequently release updates introducing new features, performance improvements, and security enhancements. Monitoring release notes and engaging with vendor-specific communities provide valuable insights into these advancements. By exploring new features in test environments, professionals can understand their applications before deploying them in production, ensuring systems stay optimized and secure.

Modern SQL has expanded significantly with features like window functions, JSON support, and advanced indexing techniques. For instance, window functions like **ROW_NUMBER** and **RANK** are now integral to analytical queries, while JSON integration allows SQL to handle semi-structured data seamlessly. New indexing techniques, such as partial and covering indexes, enable more precise performance tuning. These innovations simplify query writing and enhance database capabilities, making it essential to stay updated on their usage and implementation.

Automation and AI are transforming SQL workflows, enabling tools that automatically optimize queries and integrate machine learning capabilities into database systems. Platforms like AWS Performance Insights and Azure SQL Database Advisor suggest indexing strategies and adjustments, while managed services like Amazon RDS automate backups and scaling. Furthermore, serverless computing models like AWS Athena have introduced flexible, pay-as-you-go query execution. These technologies reduce the manual workload for administrators, allowing them to focus on strategic tasks.

The shift to cloud and hybrid architectures has redefined how databases are managed. Cloud-native solutions like Amazon Aurora and multi-cloud tools like Google BigQuery Omni offer unparalleled scalability and integration, allowing organizations to distribute workloads across different platforms seamlessly. Serverless SQL models and real-time analytics integrations further enhance flexibility, enabling rapid insights and agility in data management. Professionals must familiarize themselves with these trends to design resilient and scalable systems.

Engaging with the SQL community is another critical component of staying updated. Participating in conferences like SQLBits and PGConf or online platforms like Stack Overflow and Reddit provides opportunities to exchange knowledge and discover emerging technologies. Earning certifications and following thought leaders in the database field also helps professionals maintain expertise and adapt to new developments.

With growing concerns about data privacy and compliance, SQL practitioners must stay informed about trends in data governance. Data masking, encryption, and advanced audit logging are essential for meeting regulatory requirements such as GDPR and HIPAA. Additionally, the rise of real-time analytics and streaming integrations underscores the importance of SQL in handling live data for IoT metrics, stock analysis, and other time-sensitive applications.

To remain competitive, SQL professionals must commit to continuous learning and experimentation. Exploring advanced tools like procedural SQL extensions, experimenting with graph databases, and staying updated with SQL standards ensure that skills remain relevant. By embracing these practices, database professionals can leverage the latest innovations, optimize performance, and maintain robust, future-ready systems.

Conclusion

In this chapter, we explored essential best practices and techniques to refine your SQL skills and ensure the quality and performance of your database operations. We learned to write clean, efficient, functional, easy-to-maintain, scalable SQL code. The chapter also provided strategies for debugging and troubleshooting, enabling you to identify and resolve query issues effectively.

Additionally, we looked into performance-tuning techniques to optimize queries and database efficiency, equipping you to handle even the most complex datasets confidently. By emphasizing the importance of staying updated with SQL trends, the chapter prepares us to adapt to new advancements and maintain a competitive edge in data management.

Points to remember

Here are some key takeaways from this chapter:

- Use descriptive and consistent naming conventions to improve readability and maintainability.

- Write modular SQL code using views, stored procedures, and **common Table expressions** (**CTEs**) to avoid redundancy.

- Regularly test and debug queries using tools like EXPLAIN and execution plans to identify inefficiencies.

- Optimize performance by using appropriate indexes, minimizing data scans, and avoiding **SELECT** *.

- Stay updated on SQL trends, vendor updates, and emerging technologies through learning platforms and community engagement.

- Leverage automation tools and AI-driven solutions to streamline query optimization and database management.

- Continuously refine SQL practices through experimentation, certifications, and participation in the SQL community.

- Monitor query performance with tools like database profilers and refine indexing strategies for evolving workloads.

These points will help you write robust, efficient, and scalable SQL code while keeping pace with advancements in the field.

Join our Discord space

Join our Discord workspace for latest updates, offers, tech happenings around the world, new releases, and sessions with the authors:

https://discord.bpbonline.com

Index

A

access control and permissions
 access and permissions, auditing 249
 access control, integrating
  with application logic 250
 authentication 247
 authorization 247, 248
 best practices 249
 challenges 249
 dynamic access control 249
 principle of least privilege,
  implementing 248
 user identity, verifying 247
 user roles, defining 247, 248
ACID properties 7
Advanced Encryption Standard (AES) 250
aggregate functions 50, 51, 90, 91
 and GROUP BY 92, 93

AVG aggregate function 91, 92
COUNT aggregate function 91
COUNT DISTINCT aggregate function
 92
MIN and MAX aggregate functions 92
SUM aggregate function 91
aliases 82
 best practices 84, 85
 using, for columns 82, 83
 using, for tables 83
 using, in self-joins 83, 84
American National Standards
 Institute (ANSI) 5
American Standard Code for
 Information Interchange (ASCII) 60
auditing 257
 audit records, managing 259
 audit records, storing 259
 built-in database features 258, 259

compliance and reporting 260

database auditing 257

login and logout auditing 258

object auditing 258

privilege auditing 258

statement auditing 258

third-party and open-source tools 259

AWS CloudTrail 259

B

backup and recovery 260

backup integrity, testing 263

backups, automating 262

backup strategy, creating 262

backup types 260, 261

best practices 267

data archiving 267

database versioning 267

ransomware and disasters, handling 267

recovery models 263

BETWEEN operator 47

blog platform creation project 282

blog content, deleting 285

blog content, updating 285

blog data, querying 285

blog performance, analyzing 286

database, creating 283

database schema, designing 283, 284

database security 286

optimizations 286

sample data, inserting 284

SQLite 3, setting up 283

use case and scenario 282, 283

business intelligence (BI) tools 11

C

CHAR data type 58

CHARINDEX function 69

clean and efficient SQL code , writing 310

aggregate functions, using judiciously 314

code, documenting 313

descriptive naming conventions, using 310

hardcoding values, avoiding 313

indentation and formatting standards, following 311

indexes, leveraging wisely 312, 313

joins, optimizing 312

modular and reusable code, writing 310, 311

SELECT usage, minimizing 312

test and refactor regularly 314

column-family databases 22

columns 20

common performance pitfalls, avoiding 180, 181

aggregate functions optimization, failing 184

improper join usage 182

indexes, neglecting 181

nested subqueries, relying on 182, 183

query execution plans, ignoring 182

SELECT * overuse 181

temporary tables overuse 183

wildcards, using in LIKE clauses 183, 184

common table expressions (CTEs) 137, 177, 213, 310

benefits 213, 214

considerations 216

defining 213

for complex calculations 214, 215

in reporting 216, 217

limitations 216

multiple CTEs, chaining 215, 216

recursive CTE 214

using 213

comparison operators 45, 46

complex queries

simplifying, with views 151-155

SQL clauses, combining with 44

compliance and data protection 268

auditing and monitoring 269, 270

compliance requirements 268

data anonymization and
    pseudonymization 270

data protection policies, implementing
    269

encryption, for data protection 269

incident-free environment, maintaining
    271

incident response and breach
    management 270

regular assessments and audits 271

training and awareness 270, 271

composite indexes 171, 172

CONCAT() function 61, 74

CONCAT_WS function 68

constraints 31

check constraint 31, 32

default constraint 32

domain constraint 32

foreign key constraint 31

primary key constraint 31

unique constraint 31

covering index 172

indexing trade-offs, balancing 173

maintenance and monitoring 172, 173

CRM database 274

CRM database project

building 274

customer data, querying 276

data analyzing 277

database, securing 277, 278

database structure, creating 275

data summarizing 277

data update and management 276, 277

sample data insertion 275, 276

SQLite 3, setting up 275

use case and scenario 274

CROSS JOIN 50

customer feedback system creation project
    295

customer feedback, querying 296, 297

customer feedback table, designing 296

customer feedback table, populating 296

feedback data, securing 298

report generation 298

Sakila sample database, setting up 295

SQLite 3, setting up 295, 296

trends, analyzing 297

use case and scenario 295

customer rating system creation project
    299

customer rating table, designing 300

customer rating table, populating 300

ratings, analyzing 300, 301

ratings data, optimizing 302

ratings data, securing 302

ratings, querying 300, 301

result interpretation 302

Sakila sample database, setting up 299

SQLite 3, setting up 299

summary reports, generating 301

use case and scenario 299

customer relationship management (CRM) systems 22

D

data
  deleting, with DELETE 112-115
  insertion, with INSERT INTO 106-108
  updating, with UPDATE 109-112
database auditing 257
database key concepts 23
  columns 26
  entity relationship diagram (ERD) 24
  indexes 27
  rows 25
  tables 25
database management system (DBMS) 3, 168
database management tools 10
  Navicat 10
  pgAdmin 10
  phpMyAdmin 10
databases 17
  column-family databases 22
  document databases 22
  graph databases 22
  in-memory databases (IMDB) 23
  key-value databases 22
  NewSQL databases 23
  NoSQL databases 22
  object-oriented databases (OODBMS) 23
  relational databases 21, 22
  types 21
database security 244
  access control and permissions 247
  auditing 246
  core principles 245

integrating, into development lifecycle 246
  monitoring 246
  potential threats 245
  regulatory compliance and security 246
  security mindset, developing 247
  strong security foundation, building 245, 246
database selection, for project
  database management and maintenance 235
  ecosystem and compatibility 235
  future-proofing 236
  performance and scalability, evaluating 234
  project requirements, assessing 233, 234
  prototyping 236
  security and compliance 235
  testing 236
  use case scenarios 234
database structure 18
  columns 20
  index 20
  tables 18, 19
  views 20, 21
database tasks
  automating, with triggers 159-163
Data Control Language (DCL) 3
Data Definition Language (DDL) 3
Datadog 259
data encryption 250
  basics 250
  best practices 253
  compliance and regulatory requirements 252
  data at rest 250, 251
  data in transit 251, 252

key management 252
performance overhead 253
Data Manipulation Language (DML) 3
data reports automation project 291
database, populating 293
database schema, designing 292, 293
Python, setting up 292
report generation, automating with
Python 294, 295
SQLite 3, setting up 292
SQL queries, writing for reports 293, 294
use case and scenario 292
data retrieval 41
data type conversions 201
best practices 203, 204
combining, with other functions 204
common data type conversions 202
explicit conversions 202
implicit conversions 202
NULL values, dealing with 203
pitfalls 203
data visualization and BI tools 11
DBeaver 11
Power BI 11
Tableau 11
data visualization project 287
database, populating 288
database schema, designing 287, 288
data, exporting 289
data, querying 288, 289
Python and Matplotlib, using 289, 290
result interpretation 291
SQLite 3, setting up 287
use case and scenario 287
date and time functions 52
DBeaver 11

debugging and troubleshooting
SQL queries 314
best practices 317, 318
logical errors 316, 317
performance optimization 317
SQL query issues 314, 315
techniques 315, 316
default constraint 32
DELETE statement 112-115
denormalization 32, 35, 36
Digital Versatile Disc (DVD) 75
DISTINCT keyword
combining, with aggregate functions 86,
87
duplicate rows, eliminating with 85
limitations 87
performance considerations 86
practical use cases 88
using, with multiple column 85, 86
using, with single column 85
with JOIN operations 87
document databases 22
domain constraint 32
dynamic indexing strategies 173, 174

E

enterprise resource planning (ERP)
systems 22
entity relationship diagram (ERD) 24
EXCEPT operator 130-133
Extensible Markup Language (XML) 58

F

Flyway 12
foreign key constraint 31
foreign keys (FK) 6
FULL JOIN 49

G

Git 11
graph databases 22
GROUP BY clause
  data aggregating with 43
  data grouping with 88-90

H

HAVING clause
  grouped data, filtering with 43

I

indexes 20, 27, 148
  clustered index 29
  composite index 29
  full-text indexes 29
  non-clustered index 29
  primary index 28
  queries, improving with 148-151
  scenarios 29-31
  unique index 28
  using, in joins 173
  working 27, 28
indexing strategies 171
  basic concepts 171
  right columns, selecting to index 171
in-memory databases (IMDB) 23
INNER JOIN 48
IN operator 47
INSERT INTO statement 106-108
  transaction control 108
INSTR function 66
integrated development environment
  (IDE) 9
International Organization for
  Standardization (ISO) 5

Internet of Things (IoT) devices 234
Internet Protocol (IP) 75
INTERSECT operator 127-129
IS NULL operator 47

J

JavaScript Object Notation
  (JSON) 58
joins optimization 174
  Cartesian products, preventing 175, 176
  EXPLAIN, for analyzing performance
  176
  join columns, indexing 174, 175
  join types 174
  modern join techniques, using 176
  multi-table joins, optimizing 175
  number of rows processed, reducing 175
  temporary tables, for complex joins 176

K

key-value databases 22

L

LEFT function 69
LEFT JOIN 48
left pad (LPAD) function 67
LENGTH function 63
LIKE operator 47, 70
LIMIT clause
  results, restricting with 44
Liquibase 12
logical operators 46

M

many-to-many relationship 19
Microsoft SQL Server 229, 232
  features 232

monitoring 257
  built-in database features 258, 259
  database activities 258
  proactive strategies 260
  third-party and open-source tools 259
MySQL 228
  features 230, 231
MySQL Workbench 10

N

Navicat 10
nested queries 93-95
new relic 259
NewSQL databases 23
normalization 32, 33
  first normal form (1NF) 33
  second normal form (2NF) 33
  third normal form (3NF) 34
NoSQL databases 22
NULL values, in data modification
  best practices 117, 118
  handling 115
  handling, in conditional updates 116
  inserting 115
  records, deleting 117
  updating 116
NULL values, in queries
  aspects 96
  handling 96
  handling, with COALESCE 97, 98
  IS NOT NULL, using 96, 97
  IS NULL, using 96, 97
  using, in aggregate functions 98
  using, in joins 98, 99
  using, with comparison operators 97
numeric data handling 193

advanced numeric functions 196
aggregate functions, for
      summary calculations 194, 195
arithmetic operations, performing 193,
      194
best practices 197
decimal points, handling 195
division operations, handling 195, 196
NULL values, handling 195, 196
numeric data formatting 196
numeric functions, for combining
      for advanced use cases 197
precision, handling 195
numeric functions 52, 53

O

object-oriented databases (OODBMS) 23
one-to-many relationship 19
one-to-one relationship 19
online analytical processing (OLAP) tools
      5
Oracle database 230, 232
  features 232
Oracle SQL Developer 10
ORDER BY clause
  data sorting 42

P

parameterized queries 254
pattern matching 70
  with LIKE operator 70-73
performance tuning 318
  aggregate functions, using efficiently
      320
  caching results 321
  data scanning, minimizing 320, 321
  indexing strategies 319

join operations, optimizing 319, 320
  queries, monitoring and refining 322
  query execution plans, analyzing 318
  storage and resources, optimizing 321
pgAdmin 10
pgAudit 259
phpMyAdmin 10
PostgreSQL 229
  features 231
Power BI 11
primary key constraint 31
primary keys (PK) 6

Q

queries
  improving, with indexes 148-151
query execution plan 168
  accessing 168
  common performance issues, analyzing 169
  improving with indexes 170
  key elements 168, 169
  key metrics, interpreting 170
  optimizing 170

R

recovery models
  Microsoft SQL Server 263
  MySQL 264
  Oracle database 265
  point-in-time recovery 267
  PostgreSQL 264, 265
  SQLite 265, 266
recursive CTE 214
recursive queries 217, 218
  advanced applications 220
  cyclic data, working with 219

performance considerations 220
  practical use cases 218
  recursion depth, controlling 218, 219
relational database management systems (RDBMS) 228
relational databases
  foreign keys (FK) 6
  overview 6, 7
  primary keys (PK) 6
  tables 6
rental data reports creation project 303
  advanced reports, creating 306
  customer activity reports, generating 304, 305
  inventory performance report, generating 305, 306
  monthly rental trends, analyzing 305
  rental revenue, analyzing 304
  result interpretation 307
  Sakila sample database, setting up 303
  SQLite 3, setting up 303
  use case and scenario 303
REPLACE function 65, 70
RIGHT function 69
RIGHT JOIN 49
right pad (RPAD) function 67
Rivest-Shamir-Adleman (RSA) 250
role-based access control (RBAC) 245

S

Sakila Film Store 295
sales data analysis project 278
  basic sales data, querying 280
  database, creating 278
  database optimization 281
  database schema, designing 279
  database, securing 281

data visualization 282

sales trends, analyzing 280

sample data, inserting 279, 280

seasonal patterns, identifying 281

SQLite 3, setting up 278

use case and scenario 278

SET operators 121-124

combining, with subqueries 139, 140

multiple operations, combining 134

order and precedence 135, 136

parentheses, for complex operations 134, 135

practical applications 136, 137

usage 133

with ORDER BY clause 137-139

special operators 46

BETWEEN operator 47

IN operator 47

IS NULL operator 47

LIKE operator 47

SQL clauses 41

combining, for complex queries 44, 45

GROUP BY clause 43

HAVING clause 43

LIMIT clause 44

ORDER BY clause 42

WHERE clause 42

SQL conventions 13-15

SQL databases connection 236

basics 236, 237

best practices 240

Microsoft SQL Server, connecting to 239

MySQL, connecting to 237, 238

PostgreSQL, connecting to 238, 239

troubleshooting 240

SQL database systems 228

database-specific features and differences 230, 231-233

Microsoft SQL Server 229

MySQL 228

Oracle database 230

PostgreSQL 229

RDBMS 228

selecting 230

SQLite 229

SQL development, tools and software 9

SQL, with IDE 9

SQL environment

setting up 8

source code and database, downloading with Git 8

SQL functions 50, 157-159

aggregate functions 50, 51

date and time functions 52

multiple functions, using in query 53

numeric functions 52, 53

string functions 51

SQL injection attacks 253, 254

educating developers 256

input validation 255

least privilege principle 255

logging 256

measures, combining for security 257

monitoring 256

parameterized queries 254

special characters, escaping 255

stored procedures 254

vulnerabilities, testing for 256

Web Application Firewalls (WAFs), using 255, 256

SQLite 229, 231

features 231

SQLite 3

downloading 8, 9

SQL joins 47, 48
  CROSS JOIN 50
  FULL JOIN 49
  INNER JOIN 48
  LEFT JOIN 48
  RIGHT JOIN 49

SQL operators 45
  comparison operators 45, 46
  logical operators 46
  special operators 46

SQL query 12

SQL Server Management Studio (SSMS) 9

SQL syntax 13-15, 40

stored procedure 155-157, 254

string data
  generating dynamically 190
  manipulating 190
  regular expression, for
    advanced manipulation 192, 193
  replacing 192
  searching 192
  string case, transforming 191
  string functions, combining
    for advanced use cases 193
  strings, padding 191
  strings, trimming 191
  substrings, extracting 191

string data types 58
  CHAR data type 58
  considerations 60, 61
  TEXT data type 59, 60
  VARCHAR data type 59

string functions 51, 61
  CONCAT function 61
  CONCAT_WS function 68
  INSTR function 66

LENGTH function 63
LOWER function 64
LPAD function 67
REPLACE function 65
RPAD function 67
SUBSTRING function 62
TRIM function 63
UPPER function 64

strings
  extracting 68
  formatting 73-76
  modifying 68
  splitting 73-76

Structured English Query Language
  (SEQUEL) 4

Structured Query Language (SQL) 1-3
  data retrieving 41
  evolution 4, 5
  history 4
  importance, in data management 3, 4

subqueries 93-95

subqueries optimization 177
  columns, indexing 180
  correlated subqueries, using efficiently
    178
  CTEs, for complex subqueries 178
  EXPLAIN, for analyzing performance
    180
  nested subqueries, minimizing 179, 180
  role of subqueries 177
  SELECT *, avoiding 179
  subqueries, replacing with joins 177

SUBSTRING function 62, 68

T

Tableau 11

tables 18, 19

creating 144, 145

modifying 146, 147

temporal data

components, extracting from 198

date and time differences,
     calculating 199, 200

formatting 200

generating 197, 198

manipulating 199

temporal functions, combining
     for advanced queries 201

time zones, working 200

using, in conditional logic 201

TEXT data type 59, 60

transactions 221

ACID properties 221, 222

best practices 224

concurrency issues, resolving 222

deadlocks, resolving 223

locking mechanisms 223

optimistic concurrency control 223

partial rollbacks 224

pessimistic concurrency control 224

savepoints 224

Transparent Data Encryption (TDE) 232

trends and updates 322, 323

triggers 159

database tasks, automating with 159-163

TRIM function 63, 70

Triple Data Encryption Standard (3DES)
     250

U

UNION ALL operator 124-127

UNION operator 124-127

unique constraint 31

UPDATE statement 109-112

UPPER function 64

V

VARCHAR data type 59

version control and collaboration tools 11

Flyway 12

Git 11

Liquibase 12

views 20, 21, 151

complex queries, simplifying with 151-
     155

Virtual Private Database
     (VPD) 249

W

Web Application Firewalls
     (WAFs) 255

WHERE clause

data filtering, with 42

window functions 210

best practices 212

combining 212

LAG() function 212

LEAD() function 212

partitioning with 210

ranking functions, using 211

running totals and averages, calculating
     211